Greening the Corporation

Greening the Corporation

Management Strategy and the Environmental Challenge

Peter Thayer Robbins

Earthscan Publications Ltd
London • Sterling, VA

First published in the UK and USA in 2001
by Earthscan Publications Ltd

A catalogue record for this book is available from the British Library

ISBN: 1 85383 772 5 paperback
       1 85383 771 7 hardback

Typesetting by PCS Mapping & DTP, Newcastle upon Tyne
Printed and bound in the UK by Creative Print and Design, Ebbw Vale
Cover design by Declan Buckley
Index compiled by Indexing Specialists, Hove

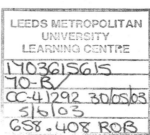

For a full list of publications please contact:

Earthscan Publications Ltd
120 Pentonville Road, London, N1 9JN, UK
tel: +44 (0)20 7278 0433
fax: +44 (0)20 7278 1142
email: earthinfo@earthscan.co.uk
http://www.earthscan.co.uk

22883 Quicksilver Drive, Sterling, VA 20166-2012, USA

Earthscan is an editorially independent subsidiary of Kogan Page Ltd and publishes
in association with WWF-UK and the International Institute for Environment and
Development

This book is printed on elemental-chlorine-free paper

Contents

List of Tables

Acronyms and Abbreviations

ACBE	Advisory Council on Business and the Environment
AEI	American Enterprise Institute
AIDS	acquired immune deficiency syndrome
AMOCO	Standard Oil Company of Indiana
ANWR	Arctic National Wildlife Refuge
APC	African, Pacific and Caribbean Countries
AQIP	ARCO Air Quality Improvement Programme
ARCO	Atlantic Richfield Corporation
B-M	Burson-Marsteller
BASF	*Badische Anilin Soda Fabrik*
BAT	British American Tobacco Corporation
BCSD	Business Council for Sustainable Development
BGH	bovine growth hormone
BHP	Broken Hill Proprietary
BP	BP Amoco (*formerly* British Petroleum)
BSR	Businesses for Social Responsibility
BST	bovine somatotropin
CBI	Confederation of British Industry
CEFIC	*Conseil Européen des Federations de l'Industrie Chimique*
CEO	chief executive officer
CEP	Council on Economic Priorities
CERES	Coalition for Environmentally Responsible Economies
CFC	chlorofluorocarbon
CH_4	methane
CIA	Chemical Industry Association
CO_2	carbon dioxide
COD	chemical oxygen demand
CSE	cultural survival enterprises
DBCP	dibromochloropropane
DESD	(United Nations) Department of Economic and Social Development

EH&S	environment, health and safety
EIA	environmental impact assessment
EMT	ecological modernization theory
EPA	(United States) Environmental Protection Agency
ESCAP	(United Nations) Economic and Social Commission for Asia and the Pacific
EU	European Union
EUROPIA	European Industry Association
FAO	Food and Agriculture Organization
FDA	(United States) Food and Drug Administration
FoE	Friends of the Earth
FREE	Foundation for Research on Economics and the Environment
GATT	General Agreement on Tariffs and Trade
GNP	gross national product
GOPAC	Grand Old (Republican) Party PAC
HAZOPS	hazard operability studies
HCFC	hydrochlorofluorocarbon
HFC	hydrofluorocarbon
IBM	International Business Machines Corporation
ICC	International Chamber of Commerce
ICI	Imperial Chemical Industries
IMF	International Monetary Fund
INBio	Costa Rica National Institute of Biodiversity
INFACT	*formerly known as* Infant Formula Action Coalition
IPCC	Intergovernmental Panel on Climate Change
IUCN	World Conservation Union (*formerly* International Union for Conservation of Nature and Natural Resources)
KAB	Keep America Beautiful
kW	kilowatt
LCA	life cycle assessment/analysis
LDC	London Dumping Convention
3M	Minnesota Mining and Manufacturing Company
M-form	multidivisional-form organizational structure
MGH	*Hupferexploration Sgessellschaft*
MIC	methyl-isocyanate
MOSOP	Movement for the Survival of the Ogoni People
MTBE	methyl tertiary butyl ether
NC	new consumer
NEPA	(United States) National Environmental Policy Act 1969
NGO	non-governmental organization
NO_x	nitrogen oxides

NWF	National Wildlife Federation
O_3	ozone
OSHA	(United States) Occupational Safety and Health Administration
3P	pollution prevention pays
PAC	(United States) Political Action Committee
PCB	polychlorinated biphenyl
pH	a measure of a solution's acidity or alkalinity
PNG	Papua New Guinea
PO	propylene oxide
ppm	parts per million
PR	public relations
PSE	Royal Dutch/Shell Corporation Product Safety and Environmental Conservation Committee
R&D	research and development
RAN	Rainforest Action Network
RJR	R J Reynolds
SEA	strategic environmental assessment
SHE	safety, health and environment
SMART	save money and reduce toxics
SO_2	sulphur dioxide
SPOLD	Society for the Promotion of LCA Development
TBA	tertiary butyl alcohol
TCMD	Transnational Corporations and Management Division
TFAP	Tropical Forestry Action Plan
TNC	transnational corporation
TOC	total oxygen content
TQM	total quality management
UA	units of account
U-form	unitary-form organizational structure
UK	United Kingdom (of Great Britain and Northern Ireland)
UN	United Nations
UNCED	United Nations Conference on Environment and Development
UNCTC	United Nations Centre on Transnational Corporations
UNDP	United Nations Development Programme
UNEP	United Nations Environment Programme
UNEPIE	United Nations Environment Programme, Industry and Environment Office
UNPO	Unrepresented Nations and Peoples Organization
VOC	volatile organic compound
WBCSD	World Business Council for Sustainable Development
WCC	World Council of Churches

WCED	World Commission on Environment and Development
WHO	World Health Organization
WICE	World Industry Council for the Environment
WMI	Waste Management Incorporated
WMP	ARCO Waste Minimization Programme
WMX	Waste Management Incorporated
WWF	*formerly known as* World Wildlife Fund *and* World Wide Fund For Nature

Acknowledgements

No one completes a research project alone. I owe a debt of gratitude to many people for their direct or indirect contribution to this project. I am grateful to Jonathan Sinclair Wilson and Pascale Mettam at Earthscan for undertaking the publication of this book and for useful editorial suggestions. Leslie Sklair provided exemplary guidance as my mentor and supervisor. Throughout the research, many people assisted me with the collection of data, the clarification of ideas and additional contacts, in particular, Michael Hansen, Paul Dushevsky and Amy Frankel at the UNCTC were very helpful. My thesis examiners, Yvonne Rydin at LSE and Chris Rootes at Kent, raised a number of very helpful points that are reflected in the analysis. I am also grateful to the students whom I have taught at LSE, Richmond University, the University of Reading and Cranfield University; their enthusiasm, questions and debates often stimulated me in my own work.

My family was instrumental in the completion of this project. My parents provided much needed financial and moral support. Special thanks goes to my wife, Vaneeta-marie D'Andrea who combined loving support, encouragement and academic criticism. Lastly, although I am grateful to those whom I have mentioned as well as others who prefer to remain anonymous, none should be held responsible for what is written in this book.

Peter Thayer Robbins
June 2001

Preface

The idea for this book began to evolve in the late 1980s and early 1990s when public debates were ongoing about business and the environment. The 1970s had been characterized by an adversarial relationship between corporations and environmental groups. During the 1980s this relationship began to change as politicians, economists, executives and some environmentalists began developing proposals for the integration of economic and environmental objectives. Some businesses began to view the environment as a business opportunity and proactively pursued a 'green market'. Others placed themselves at the forefront of 'a new form of capitalism' that considers environmental and social concerns when conducting business. Collectively, this phenomenon began to be referred to as 'greening the corporations'.

Greening or 'going green' have their origins in Reich's (1970) book *The Greening of America*, a work that encapsulates this 'new' environmental awareness in the following passage:

> 'The extraordinary thing about this new consciousness is that it has emerged out of the wasteland of the corporate state, like flowers pushing up through the concrete pavement... For one who thought the world was irretrievably encased in metal and plastic and sterile stone, it seems a veritable greening of America' (pp394–395).

Since then, the term has had much more widespread use and is now employed to describe the growth of environmental awareness related to a wide variety of entities, including groups, places and organizations.

At the time when I began this research, few sociological analyses had been conducted that systematically considered corporate greening. From my perspective, because corporate responses to environmental problems are located in what could be termed a social change process, the question that was most compelling and which guides this book is: How can corporate responses to environmental crises be understood sociologically?

This analysis grew out of my PhD research at the London School of Economics working under Leslie Sklair. In examining the guiding question, I was interested in getting an insight into the cultural and organizational factors that engendered good environmental practice. It could be expected that corporations would address environmental challenges through management systems that include unique structures, styles and cultures, and these are examined in the course of the book.

In order to explore the development of green corporate management systems, I conducted in-depth case studies of four corporations. These were: Atlantic Richfield Corporation Chemical Company-Europe (ARCO), Ben & Jerry's Homemade, Inc, an ice cream and frozen yoghurt manufacturer, The Body Shop International, plc, a health products company and the Royal Dutch/Shell Group of Companies (Shell). The four cases I compare are divided between those with what I have called a 'traditional' corporate culture and those with a 'social-environmental' corporate culture. A corporation with a 'traditional' corporate culture is one that is focused primarily on generating wealth for its shareholders through a corporate cultural ethic such as: 'continuous improvement', 'safety first', or 'total quality management'. In a social-environmental corporate culture, the focus is on generating wealth for shareholders while being socially–environmentally active. This is often guided by a corporate cultural ethic such as: 'linked prosperity', 'profits and principles' or 'caring capitalism'. ARCO and Shell represented traditional corporate culture, and Ben & Jerry's and The Body Shop the social-environmental corporate culture.

The four corporations also differ on a range of factors. They are based in the United States and the United Kingdom, from the extractive and retail/agricultural sectors, large, old and small, young corporations. This allows for an analysis of corporate responses to environmental crises based on a range of potential determining factors including country of legal domicile, industrial sector, corporate age and size, as well as corporate culture.

Greening is an extremely sensitive issue for corporations, and conducting research for this project was not without its challenges. An example of this is the study conducted by a team at Tufts University, USA, in which a survey on environmental management practices was mailed to 4500 corporations and only 98 responded (Flaherty and Rappaport, 1991)! Another hurdle is posed by what have been called corporate greenwashing campaigns (Athanasiou, 1996). Such campaigns are designed to present corporations with environmentally challenged records as 'green' to the public, spearheaded by major public relations firms on behalf of corporations. The Business Council on Sustainable Development (see Schmidheiny, 1992), for example, although seeming completely legitimate, was said to have been conceived and shaped by the Madison Avenue firm J Walter Thompson so that major corporations, some with especially environmentally problematic records, could share their 'environmental successes' and present themselves as 'green' (Deal, 1993). This does not mean that the corporations involved were not greening, but it does raise questions with regard to why it was especially important that these challenged corporations appear particularly environmentally benevolent. It also suggests that certain corporations with constructed environmental reputations may need to protect them effectively. Finally, it says something about how important environmental issues have become to the public that corporations need to guard their reputations so carefully.

In fact, corporate executives from even the most socially and environmentally active businesses take a risk when they talk to researchers. For example, within Ben & Jerry's, there is a well-known story of an academic researcher who was given carte blanche to investigate the activities of the company. This openness was subject to a mutual agreement about certain information being proprietary. After an uneventful tenure at the company in which the researcher was 'given free reign' to examine green practices, she went back to her academic institution to write up the research. Ben & Jerry's executives later found that information was being published by the researcher about the company, which portrayed it in a 'one-sided' and negative light, as well as revealing information that was regarded as being confidential. The experience left people at Ben & Jerry's feeling 'burned'. The result was that there remained 'an extremely bad taste' among executives towards outside researchers, and resistance to subsequent investigators conducting research projects. These risks, it was argued, prevented the company from sharing information beyond what was portrayed in official corporate reports submitted to investors and governmental bodies, which were all part of the public record. Although a review of the academic literature did not reveal any research by the author the company was worried about, the story says something about the importance of maintaining a good image. Notably, Ben & Jerry's portrays itself as open, with social and environmental audits, and advocates within its documentation the importance of dialogue with outsiders.

Interviews allow for the discovery of information that some are willing to share on a personal or private level but not publicly. In all, the book is based on 55 interviews with a range of those involved in the greening process. These include:

- corporate executives in environmental departments;
- corporate business association personnel;
- corporate environmental consultants;
- staff at consumer organizations which monitor the activities of corporations;
- officers at intergovernmental organizations;
- governmental employees in the US Environmental Protection Agency and the UK's Department of the Environment – Advisory Council on Business and the Environment (ACBE);
- environmental organizations; and
- relevant academics.

The interview material was compared with documentary evidence including: corporate annual reports, environmental evaluations of corporations, environmental organization reviews of corporations, as well as a comprehensive analysis of the documents held by the United Nations Centre on Transnational Corporations (UNCTC). These were systematically examined to provide confirming or disconfirming data as well as the 'official' corporate view on greening and environmental action.

The key UNCTC document I analysed is entitled *Environmental Management in Transnational Corporations: Report of the Benchmark Corporate Environmental Survey* (1993) (referred to hereafter as the *UN Survey*), a study of the corporate environmental management practices of 210 large corporations with annual sales over US$1 billion. The Transnational Corporations and Management Division of the Department of Economic and Social Development (TCMD/DESD), formerly known as the United Nations Centre on Transnational Corporations, conducted research for this UN study.[1] The *UN Survey* was completed as part of the United Nations Conference on Environment and Development (UNCED) held in Rio de Janeiro in 1992. It is the most comprehensive survey of corporate management responses to environmental crises to date.[2]

Chapter 1 introduces some major environmental challenges faced by corporations and explores responses to them. Chapter 2 looks at overarching sociological theories and concepts that can help us to understand corporate greening. Chapter 3 examines structural variables in environmental management and introduces a typology of environmental management styles. This model is used to analyse the cases that are presented in Chapters 4 and 5. Finally, Chapter 6 presents conclusions on the model of management styles developed in Chapter 3 and considers the analysis within the wider theoretical literature as well as presenting avenues for future research.

1

Environmental Challenges and Corporate Responses

INTRODUCTION

In order to begin to explore corporate greening, the first issue that needs to be investigated is the specific environmental challenges faced by corporations, the second is the ways in which corporations can respond to such challenges. This chapter begins by summarizing seven key environmental challenges to the activities of corporations: atmosphere, toxic chemicals and waste, freshwater, land, oceans, biotechnology and biodiversity. It then addresses ways in which corporations can take action. This can be delineated into four areas of change: innovation, technology, organization and strategy. Understanding environmental challenges and responses introduces the main physical and organizational dilemmas connected with corporate greening.

The environmental challenges facing most corporations are air, toxics and freshwater. They also have historically received the most public and regulatory attention. Land issues are closely linked to toxics in that much of the legislation in this area deals with toxic waste disposal or hazardous waste production facilities. Oceans are important for some of the largest corporations and those in extractive industries since products must be transported by sea. Finally, biotechnology and biodiversity are most applicable to large agricultural and pharmaceutical corporations that exert a great deal of control over emerging patents and technologies.

ATMOSPHERE

Compared with other environmental issues, the atmosphere is an area on which most corporations focus their attention. This can be explained by a number of factors:

- Air quality and atmospheric protection are regulated intensely. The Clean Air Act (1970) in the US is perhaps the most expensive and wide-ranging set of environmental regulations in the world.[1]
- The international deliberations on ozone depletion and climate change indicate that more regulatory changes in this area will be ongoing (Susskind, 1994).
- Public awareness of atmospheric issues is high (Rowlands, 1995).
- All governments that have developed environmental regulations have tended to consider air pollution more than other environmental problems.
- Ozone issues have become an important part of the corporate agenda. This is possibly because of international agreements, but more likely because of consumer pressure combined with competition around the emerging markets in chlorofluorocarbon (CFC) alternatives (Porter and Brown, 1991).

From the start of the global environmental change debate, air pollution issues have become particularly important for corporations. This is because about half of all global greenhouse gases[2] are, at some level, related to the activities of corporations (see Table 1.1) (UNCTC, 1992). These include half of all carbon dioxide (CO_2) emissions, 10–20 per cent of methane (CH_4) emissions, 60–70 per cent of CFC emissions and 50 per cent of other potentially damaging gases including nitrogen oxides and tropospheric ozone.[3]

Carbon dioxide is produced in large quantities because of the burning of fossil fuels. CFCs can be linked to more than 15 per cent of global warming. This is due to the fact that the impact of each molecule of CFC can be several hundred to 20,000 times greater than the impact of carbon dioxide, depending on the type of CFC. Additionally, the lifetime of CFCs is more than 100 years. Other greenhouse gases include nitrogen oxides (NO_x), sulphur dioxide (SO_2),[4] methane (CH_4) and tropospheric ozone (O_3), which cause acid rain and city smog and are also produced by burning fossil fuels.

Around 50 per cent of all emissions of greenhouse gases can be traced in one way or another to the operations of corporations. This would include half of oil production, practically all of the production of road vehicles in developed countries, most of the CFC production

Table 1.1 *Estimated involvement of corporations in the generation of human-produced greenhouse gases*

Gas	Amount of gas generated by corporations (approximate percentage of total amount)	Significant sources of greenhouse gases generated
CO_2	50%	Emissions from automobiles; most of the oil and gas use in developed countries; half of coal use in developed countries; half of fossil fuel use in developing countries
CH_4	10–20%	Half from oil and gas production and use; half from emissions from coal mines
CFCs	60–70%	Use of aerosol sprays, car air conditioners, solvents, foam products and refrigerators in developed countries
Other (eg NO_x and O_3)	50%	Emissions from automobiles; three quarters of oil and gas use in developed countries; half of coal use in developed countries; half of fossil fuel use in developing countries

Source: Adapted from UNCTC, 1992, p15

and a large proportion of electricity production and use. Corporations are also greatly involved in the production and use of toxic materials which include asbestos, dioxins, polychlorinated biphenyls (PCBs) and volatile organic compounds (VOCs) which, when dispersed into the air, land or water, can cause serious health problems (UNCTC, 1992).

Corporations are active in transboundary atmospheric issues[5] that have a history of being regulated, like sulphur dioxide and carbon dioxide. At present, the reduction of greenhouse gas emissions, carbon dioxide in particular, is not a priority for corporations. In the words of an American Enterprise Institute (AEI) report, a scholarly think tank contracted by many of the largest corporations such as Exxon and General Electric, reduction of some of these emissions have been shown to be 'cost-ineffective' (Hawken, 1994, p112). As indicated above, corporations have policies that deal with air quality but not with greenhouse gases per se. This could be because greenhouse gas issues are relatively recent and politicians have not developed regulatory effectiveness of greenhouse gas issues to the extent of air quality policies; also, few countries at present have regulations specifically geared to these concerns.[6]

Corporations have addressed issues of air quality through the elimination of CFCs and other ozone depleting substances (*UN Survey*, 1993). Activity in the area of ozone substance reduction was motivated by the decision of some of the largest chemical corporations to pursue CFC substitutes, which created a new market. Many corporate responses specifically followed the Montreal Protocol, which had also been influenced by some of the largest corporations. Large chemical corporations strongly supported an international agreement on CFCs because they perceived it as being weaker than domestic regulations on CFCs in the US where many of the largest chemical corporations are based (Porter and Brown, 1990). Ozone depleting substances and carbon dioxide emissions have also been important issues on the national, regional and international political agenda (Susskind, 1994; Rowlands, 1995). These have influenced corporate responses as well.

TOXIC CHEMICALS AND HAZARDOUS WASTE

Since 1900, around 10 million chemicals have been created in laboratories around the world. Most are 'base'[7] or 'intermediate'[8] chemicals that are used to manufacture millions of end products, many of which are toxic. Toxic chemicals are discharged into the environment, in some cases directly such as fertilizers, pesticides and some solvents. In other cases, they are discharged indirectly into waste streams, such as mining, industry and fuel burning. Hazardous chemicals can be released either in solid, liquid or gaseous form into the air, water and land.

Every chemical is toxic to some extent. The degree to which a chemical is harmful is a combination of its toxicity and the degree to which a living thing has been exposed to the chemical and experienced harmful effects. People can be affected immediately after being exposed to only a few parts per billion of a very toxic chemical or via extended contact with high doses of a less toxic chemical over a long period. Recent scientific efforts in this area have evaluated the impact of chemicals on chronic health problems.

The degree to which anything is carcinogenic is difficult to assess. This is because some chemicals are not carcinogenic but are transformed into cancer-causing substances in living organisms. Others promote the growth of cancerous tumours. Sometimes a problem in determining the extent to which a substance causes cancer is the time between exposure to the substance and the appearance of symptoms. In addition, some carcinogens only produce effects in the offspring of the people exposed.

Because the environment is currently so polluted, it is often hard to determine what has caused a tumour since every day most people are exposed to many known or suspected carcinogens. Some substances are harmful at levels so minuscule that they become difficult to measure, others, like dioxin, cost a great deal to measure.

Pesticides and herbicides kill between 10,000 and 40,000 people in developing countries every year. A number of these chemicals are substances banned in developed countries. Interestingly, the banana industry in Costa Rica imports 25–30 per cent of all pesticides used. Most pesticides are reformulated in Costa Rica creating applications that are twice as strong as those used in developed countries. Many of the pesticides used in this industry are banned in the US including heptachlor, chlordane, lindane, ethyl parathion and methyl parathion. The pesticides are then applied to land owned by North American based corporations, and then exported back to the US on produce grown there. Pesticide runoff from these plantations has destroyed the coral reef off the Caribbean coastline of Costa Rica. The soil fertility in Costa Rica has also been decimated by the use of pesticides. Over 80,000 hectares of banana plantations have been abandoned along the Caribbean coast since 1979 (Lewis, 1992, pp289–90).

Pesticides are arguably the only toxic chemicals 'deliberately' introduced into the environment. They cause water pollution, soil degradation, insect resistance and resurgence, the destruction of native flora and fauna, and some deplete the ozone layer as well. The persistent use of pesticides leads to resistant strains of pest: crop losses from some pesticide resistant strains have risen to 30 per cent, the amount of crop losses seen before the 'chemical age' (Ekins, 1992, p180). Organic methods of farming can be as or more effective than farming using chemicals; however, currently they are neither as lucrative nor as widely employed as chemical-based farming (Badiane, 1994).

Pesticides are big business. Sales of the top 25 companies involved in this industry amounted to nearly US$23.5 billion in 1990 and US$24 billion in 1991. This market is dominated by a small number of corporations; the top ten companies, based in the US and Europe, account for almost 73 per cent of the market. In 1991, Latin America and Asia combined accounted for 21 per cent of the market and Africa almost 6 per cent. Corporations in developing countries market pesticides on the rationale that pesticides will increase agricultural production and thus increase access to food and reduce hunger. Increased production will boost exports and foreign exchange and benefit the country's gross national product (GNP). In most developing countries, the agricultural sector uses the most pesticides (NC/CEP, 1993, pp65–6). It is becoming increasingly clear that in the long term, their harmfulness outweigh any (short-term) benefits that their use might bring about (NC/CEP, 1993, p64). Fertilizers can be similarly problematic. World fertilizer use went from 14 million metric tons in 1950 to 143 million metric tons in 1989. The use of fertilizers is rapidly increasing in developing countries as well. However, the 'benefits' they provide are declining. It has been found that each metric ton of fertilizer applied to US corn or Indonesian rice paddies now enhances crop yields by half as much as in the 1970s (NC/CEP, 1993, p64).

Hazardous wastes include those that contain metallic compounds, halogenated organic solvents, organo-halogen compounds, acids, asbestos, organo-phosphorus compounds, organic cyanide, phenols or ethers. Most of these wastes are produced by industry. In 1987, industry in the US alone produced 275 million tonnes of hazardous waste (Cutter, 1993). In the US, most of this waste comprises chemicals like plastics, paints and solvents. In Europe, most hazardous wastes comprise solvents, waste paint, heavy metals, acids and oily wastes.

Recently there have been some important international agreements on transboundary movements of toxic chemicals and hazardous wastes. The Code of Conduct on the Distribution and Use of Pesticides, and the London Guidelines for the Exchange on Information on Chemicals in International Trade both oversee pesticide use and information exchange on chemicals, and have been strengthened in recent years (DESD/TCMD, 1993). In developing countries the 1991 Bamako Convention on the Ban of the Import into Africa and the Control of Transboundary Movement and Management of Hazardous Wastes within Africa was signed in order to stem the tide of hazardous wastes flowing into Africa. The Bamako Convention was created in response to the Basel Convention on the Control of Transboundary Movement of Hazardous Wastes, which many developing countries maintain does not address the export of hazardous waste to poorer countries. The Basel Convention also does not deal with the issue of radioactive waste export. Another important treaty is the Lome IV Convention between the European Union and African, Pacific and Caribbean (APC) countries, which bans toxic waste exports from EU to APC countries (DESD/TCMD, 1993).[9]

The issue of corporations and toxic wastes and hazardous substances is one of the most 'important' environmental issues related to corporations. The unscrupulous dumping of waste by some corporations is well documented (see Allen, 1992; Cutter, 1993). In 1992 alone, Pepsi Cola Bottling Corporation exported over 7000 tons of plastic waste from California to Madras and Bombay, India (Leonard, 1993, p23).

The management of toxic materials is an area that most corporations are now putting near the top of their corporate agenda. However, some companies take advantage of less stringent environmental codes in developing countries, since it is cheaper to relocate environmentally challenging operations to such countries than to invest in cleaner technologies in developed countries. A 1992 Greenpeace report states that 'the growing trend to transfer lead smelting operations to developing countries appears to be one of economics based largely on the difficulties of achieving strict pollution control standards [in developed countries] ' (Greenpeace, cited in Leonard, 1993, p23).

While responses to atmospheric issues have mostly been driven by regulatory changes and international agreements, corporate responses to toxic chemicals and hazardous waste have been brought about as a result of highly publicized accidents in chemical factories. Responses include the development of policies and programmes not only related to accidents but also to other environmental issues. For example, the chemical industry has had to be cognizant of most environmental matters related to their business to reassure the public that they are ensuring the safety of their operations.[10]

FRESHWATER

In the past 300 years it is likely that withdrawals from worldwide freshwater sources have grown more than 35-fold. A number of countries are facing water shortages, and if the human population reaches 10 billion by 2050 as has been predicted, the current patterns of freshwater use are unsustainable (IUCN/UNEP/WWF, 1991, p137).

This is an important issue for corporations in agribusiness and other sectors. In the majority of countries, agriculture is the main consumer of freshwater, and globally it accounts for around 70 per cent of freshwater use. In developed countries, industry is the largest consumer of freshwater, accounting for 50–80 per cent of the total demand, while in developing countries industry's consumption is only 10–30 per cent of total demand (Shiklomanov, cited in *UN Survey*, 1993).

Some of the ways in which industries use water are for cooling, processing, cleaning and removing industrial wastes. When industries use the water it is returned for the most part to the water cycle, often heavily polluted with chemicals and heavy metals. The production of wastewater[11] amounts to 87 per cent of industry's total freshwater use.

The main sectors that pollute freshwater are the pulp and paper, chemicals, petrochemicals and refining, metalworking, food processing and textiles industries. These industries use huge amounts of water. For example, making one kilogram of paper can consume up to 700 kilograms of water, and producing one ton of steel can use up 280 tons of water (Postel, 1993, p32). The polluted water from these industries, mostly consisting of heavy metals or synthetic organic compounds, can enter freshwater through direct discharge or waste site leakage.

In developed countries, industrial waste discharges are tightly regulated. However, the pollution of freshwater from wastes discharged into the environment over the last century has continued. In developing countries, the discharges of industry into the water cycle are, for the most part, uncontrolled, which greatly affects water quality. Where industrial plants are concentrated, water contamination is a severe problem. The Rhine after the Basel, Switzerland, Sandoz plant fire, the Rio Grande because of the *maquiladora* industries along the US–Mexican border (Sklair, 1994b), and rivers and lakes in the former Eastern Europe, are all examples of industrial contamination of freshwater. Agenda 21[12] argues for international cooperation to establish water quality and enforceable standards for industrial discharges.

According to Postel (1993):

> 'Most of the world's wealthier countries now require industries to meet specific water quality standards before releasing wastewater to the environment. As it turns out, the most effective and economical way to comply with these requirements is often to treat and recycle water thereby discharging less. Pollution control laws have therefore not only helped clean up rivers, lakes and streams, they have promoted conservation and more efficient water use' (p33).

That is, according to Postel, pollution control laws have been effective in creating an incentive for corporate responses to water challenges.

Corporations are involved in water conservation mainly due to the success of pollution control laws. In developed countries, water quality standards mean that the most effective and economical way for companies to comply with these laws is to treat and recycle water, discharging less water borne pollutants (Postel, 1993). A number of corporations maintain that they have reduced their water consumption by upwards of 90 per cent through water conservation programmes. While this does point to a great deal of corporate water wastage, it also indicates that such programmes are important in minimizing the corporations' discharges.[13]

The corporate responses to land hazards have been more mixed.

LAND

Land resources are extremely important to society. These include minerals, fuels, agriculture and forestry. Raw materials gleaned from the land are also central to most corporate products and processes. Dependence on land resources has brought about many environmental problems that include desertification, soil loss, deforestation and land degradation.

The loss of forests has become an important issue in this area. Forests support a variety of plant and animal species; and provide a carbon sink that could help to counteract global warming. About half of the world's mature tropical forests are still standing. Forests once covered 75 per cent of the globe's land area, today this figure is less than 30 per cent. Tropical forests once covered 14 per cent of the land, and now cover 7 per cent (NC/CEP, 1993, p68). In 1990 around 17 million hectares of tropical forest were eliminated worldwide. In the same year, corporations cut down 1.7 billion cubic metres of wood (Worldwatch, 1991).

In developing countries, forests are also used locally, but damage caused through local use is often not as extensive as when corporations 'use' forests. It has been said that: 'Seldom does the gathering of wood for fuel result in the destruction of rich primary forests. [Corporate harvesting] on the other hand, is a major cause of primary forest destruction in both temperate and tropical nations' (Worldwatch, 1991, p76). The global market for forest products has increased by 50 per cent since 1965, and its total trade is now $85 billion. Yet, it may be impossible to sustain this level of forest harvesting (Worldwatch, 1991, p76).

Land exploitation has wide-ranging consequences. The natural carbon sink[14] provided by forests can be lost through deforestation; it is estimated that tropical deforestation has accounted for anywhere between 10 and 30 per cent of the net annual increase in atmospheric carbon emissions (Worldwatch, 1991, p80). Of course, the larger issue would be the industrialized countries' production of the lion's share of the carbon rather than the developing country issue of cutting down the tropical forests, but it is also important to note the effect that tropical deforestation could also have on the global environment. Losing primary forests also affects biodiversity,[15] through the impact on plant and animal species that live in the forests. Forest plantations often consist of a single genetic species of tree that maximizes timber output.

Corporations are also an important factor in global agricultural production. Family farms are being replaced by agribusiness. For example, in the US, 29 companies own more than 21 per cent of the total cropland. Large companies control most of the food production in the US: 51 per cent of fresh vegetable production, 85 per cent of the citrus crop, 97 per cent of broiler chickens and 40 per cent of egg production (Rifkin, 1989, p154).

Methods of farming based on monoculture[16] have meant short-term profits at the expense of long-term production. Loss of nutrients and the pollution of land and water resources from pesticides and herbicides are becoming more widespread. Soil degradation and desertification are also caused by monocultural practices and overgrazing (*UN Survey*, 1993, p122).

The main site for the disposal of hazardous wastes and other toxic materials including PCBs, heavy metals and dioxin is on land. These wastes can leach into drinking water supplies. When these wastes have been disposed of illegally near communities, people have become ill.[17] Even when these wastes have been disposed of legally, a growing body of sociological research in the US demonstrates that environmental racism is responsible for these dumps being sited near poor or ethnic minority communities (see Bullard, 1993; Hofrichter, 1993; Cutter, 1995; Bryant, 1995). Major corporations have often been seen as central antagonists in environmental racism cases in the US, with dumps and hazardous processes sited in poor or minority areas.

Land resource issues have prompted national and international actions to deal with some of the above problems. The World Bank developed the Tropical Forestry Action Plan (TFAP), which promotes sustainable use of tropical forests. The International Tropical Timber Organization is attempting to establish sustainable practices for the international tropical timber trade. The Food and Agriculture Organization (FAO) Code of Conduct on the Distribution and Use of Pesticides has attempted to deal with the preservation of agricultural resources and human health. As in similar agreements, corporate executives must support the agreements noted above in order for them to be effective. In this, as in other cases, sustainable use of land resources can benefit the long-term interests of business (*UN Survey*, 1993, p123).

Overall, there tends to be a mixed corporate response to land challenges. About two-thirds of companies have not established comprehensive land management policies. It is surprising that agricultural and forestry-based corporations trail behind other sectors in some areas like land policy and pest management programmes.[18] Corporate environmental policies or programmes tend not to focus explicitly on desertification and soil degradation. In addition, it is notable that only a few corporations have safety zones[19] around manufacturing plants, especially in developing nations. In so far as safety zones provide an additional security cushion if there were to be an accident at a plant, and prevent the contamination of nearby communities, they might be expected to be commonplace (*UN Survey*, 1993).

Of all potential land issues to respond to, afforestation programmes are being established in many corporations.[20] This may be because it is a relatively easy policy to undertake. For example, corporations with almost no involvement in the paper or pulp industries are as likely to have afforestation programmes as those in other sectors that are more likely to affect land resources. The other sectors are engaged in these programmes to about the same extent as the agricultural sector, and this includes the service sector. Tree planting programmes are obvious indicators of corporate 'concern' for the environment. More comprehensive land policies and programmes tend to be undertaken by the largest corporations. Smaller companies are not as likely to be involved in this area. North American based companies are also more likely to have land policies. This is due in large part to the impact of the Superfund's Title III[21] regarding land hazard reporting.

OCEANS

Marine resources in many parts of the world are being rapidly degraded because of human activities on land and at sea. The degradation is caused by the release of pollutants into rivers and the atmosphere that finds its way into the oceans, or is directly dispersed into the oceans. Ocean protection is a relatively unregulated area, including pollution caused by land runoff. Most ocean pollution originates on land and ends up in the sea; 40 per cent of this pollution enters the sea from rivers, and 30 per cent from the atmosphere. The last 30 per cent is a result of shipping, dumping, offshore mining and oil production.

The main contaminants of the oceans have been prioritized by the Group of Experts on the Scientific Aspects of Marine Pollution, and include in descending order: nutrients from urban sewage and urban runoff, microbial contamination from sewage, plastics from land and sea dumping, synthetic organic compounds (eg pesticides and industrial chemicals), and oil from transportation and spills. Plastics and pesticides harm marine mammals even in remote areas of the oceans. Corporations are not the major polluters of the oceans but their actions contribute most of the arsenic, mercury, chlorinated hydrocarbons and other toxic substances (WRI/UNEP/UNDP, 1990, p182).

Around 600,000 tonnes of oil is dispersed into the oceans each year, and petroleum contamination is the central polluter of the oceans (*UN Survey*, 1993, p131). Even though oil spills are the cause of much public concern, less than 25 per cent of marine contamination is due to this type of dispersal. Most ocean pollution comes from day-to-day shipping including transportation at 45 per cent, municipal and industrial waste and runoff at 36 per cent, the atmosphere at 9 per cent, leakage and erosion at 8 per cent, and offshore oil production at 1 per cent (WRI/UNEP/UNDP, 1990, p186).

Oceans are also polluted through sea dumping of sewage and industrial wastes. Corporations that are active in mining and metal and chemical processing as well as oil production produce much of this waste. Sea dumping is banned in many areas, and the North Sea and Atlantic Ocean have become the major dumping areas. The London Dumping Convention[22] banned heavy metal and carcinogenic sea dumping, but tonnes of these materials are still dumped legally due to the allowance of trace amounts of these substances in wastes (Goldsmith and Hildyard, 1988, p191). The main impacts of corporations on oceans are in the areas of oil exploration, dumping, hazardous substance transport and effluent discharge.

Some of the largest petroleum corporations have lobbied against tougher international agreements on ocean resources since the 1950s (Porter and Brown, 1990). There is little regulation, and environmental issues related to the oceans are not high on the corporate agenda now. There are corporate efforts to minimize oil spills and chemical and oil companies' attempts to prevent oil and chemical spillage. However, outside the extractive-based sector, there tend to be few efforts to protect the oceans. On the other hand, policies in other areas such as wastewater and freshwater may, inadvertently, have a positive effect on the oceans, even if minimal.

BIOTECHNOLOGY AND BIOLOGICAL DIVERSITY

Biotechnology[23] is a relatively recent area of scientific research, around 20 years old, which covers everything from fermentation processes to DNA and tissue culture technologies. Genetically engineered products are also an emerging area. The genetic engineering market is estimated at US$50 billion. Most research in this area is undertaken by small private companies, funded and controlled by large corporations with exclusive patent rights to the technologies. Once the technologies are developed, the companies are often taken over by the corporations (NC/CEP, 1993, p69).

There are three main areas of biotechnological products:

- high value genetically engineered medical products;
- amino and organic acids used in foods and animal feeds; and
- low value products that result from old fermentation processes.

There is also the possibility for a devastating environmental effect from biotechnologies. Many of the largest pesticide corporations are attempting to develop pesticide tolerant plants. Most of the major seed companies are trying to do this as well. This could bring about greater chemical dispersal into the environment and thus added degradation. This has important implications for developing countries. Almost all of the major crops in developed countries are not native, and therefore do not have wild relatives in the countries in which they are grown. However, in Asia and South America, the wild relatives of developed countries crops exist as weeds. Scientists suggest that herbicide tolerant crops could cross-pollinate with weeds and create herbicide tolerant weeds that would be problematic in developing countries (see Kloppenberg, 1990).

Some genetically engineered organisms have been found to be useful, for example, in combating environmental pollution from oil spills. Waste managing organisms can be directly applied at the source to reduce pollution. Biotechnology can also be used by the chemical industry to replace food additives, nitrate fertilizers and pesticides with organisms rather than chemicals. Some organisms have been used to recover metals from ore and others could be developed to recover oil trapped in rock formations. Thus, there are benefits and drawbacks to the use of biotechnology.

The diversity of biological species is important to sustaining life on Earth. While 30 million species exist, scientists have only identified around 1 million. Some elements of economic development can result in the further loss of species, through for example the clearing of tropical rainforests for cattle production. Species are being lost at a rate 400 times faster than in any other recent geological time period (Goldsmith and Hildyard, 1988, p153). Twenty-five per cent of species are expected to be extinct or in serious danger by 2050 (IUCN/UNEP/WWF, 1991). Seed houses, such as Cargill, now control about one-quarter of seed sales in developed countries, and 5–10 per cent of seed sales in developing countries (NC/CEP, 1993, p69; see also Kneen, 1995).

Species are important to future technologies and products. The genetic variety in the natural world is the main source for new crops, medicines, fibres and foods and therefore should be important to corporations. Globally, drugs that are derived from plants constitute a market of US$40 billion (UNEP, 1992, p56). Only 1 per cent of the globe's 250,000 flowering plant species have been examined for pharmaceutical uses. An example of the potential is the rosy periwinkle, a rainforest plant that became an important medicine for childhood leukaemia (Wallace, 1991, p37). Samples of the rosy periwinkle were removed from Madagascar and later used for cancer-fighting drugs like vincristine and vinblastine. These drugs generate annual sales around the world of US$100 million, none of which Madagascar receives (Will, 1995, p5). Until 1995, developing countries had never received royalties on drugs developed from specimens collected by corporate employees.[24]

The degradation of the rainforest, however, has occurred mainly through national and global demand for tropical hardwoods, crops and clearing of forests for grazing to satisfy demands for meat. McDonald's Corporation was alleged to have purchased beef from rainforest land cleared for cattle grazing in the 1970s. This led the company to discontinue its practice of importing Brazilian beef in 1983. The fast-food industry has been widely criticized for its role in the destruction of tropical rainforests (Carey, 1996, p13).

Agriculture is increasingly dependent on genetic (and hence 'biological') diversity to maintain disease resistance in commercial crops. For example, wild strains of plants have fortified domestic plant relatives potentially at risk from pest devastation. A strain of wild wheat from Turkey provided resistance to wheat varieties that amounted to US$50 billion annually to the US alone (UNEP, 1992, p56). Other plant species are important for ensuring the genetic diversity of crops as well. Problems arise because most agricultural methods involve single genetic species in order to increase crop yields.

Development occurs at the expense of biological diversity. Forest clear-cutting, oil and gas drilling, mining and road building eliminate habitats and animal and plant species. Corporations are faced with conflicting necessities to fulfil short-term demands for higher profits and long-term financial–environmental obligations.

Biotechnology is still a relatively 'new' area and can be seen as potentially beneficial and potentially problematic to the environment. Most biotechnology firms are large US-based corporations that have lobbied against agreements that benefit developing countries. A problematic issue is corporate use of biotechnology in developing countries where no regulations or weak regulations exist.[25] Many corporate executives do not understand the term 'biodiversity' (*UN Survey*, 1993). One first step towards comprehensive environmental stewardship would be if every company assessed its environmental impact on the lives of plants and animals. Some companies, in all sectors and sales sizes, have found biodiversity action to be beneficial to public relations. It can also demonstrate a 'commitment' to environmental issues.

CORPORATE RESPONSE TO SPECIFIC ENVIRONMENTAL CHALLENGES

This section examines the ways in which corporations have responded to specific environmental challenges. As is suggested by the review of challenges above, corporations address specific environmental issues that have a history of regulation. These include air, water and some land issues. Other issues tend not to be addressed. For example, the Superfund legislation in the US has led many US companies to focus on land issues. Regarding specific 'sustainable development' environmental issues, corporations respond to CFC elimination more than to global warming. Developing country issues tend to be ignored by many corporations based in developed countries. Corporations seem to respond to issues which are concrete and easily quantifiable and where there is pressure for them to change from powerful governments or groups (*UN Survey*, 1993). In cases where there is confusion about what constitutes an 'environmental problem' (Yearley, 1996), and where there is a lack of regulation or enforcement, corporations seem to be environmentally inactive and even destructive. Table 1.2 summarizes public, regulatory and corporate responses to specific environmental challenges. Those cases where corporations have developed specific and holistic responses to environmental challenges through the 'greening' of their management practices are examined in the next section.

Management responses

This section addresses corporate management responses to the environmental challenges that affect corporate operations. In addition, it examines how environmental aspects of corporate activity can be understood, innovatively, technologically, organizationally and strategically.

Table 1.2 *Public, regulatory and corporate responses to specific environmental challenges*

Challenge	Response			
	Public awareness	National regulation	International agreements	Corporate lobbying
Atmosphere	✔	✔	✔	✔
Toxic waste	✔	✔	✔	
Water	✔	✔	✔	
Land	✔	✔	✔	
Oceans			✔	✔
Biotechnology	✔		✔	✔
Biodiversity			✔	✔

Corporate response to environmental challenges tends to be linked to companies' desire to increase their competitiveness. For example, Gouldson and Murphy (1998, p23) have identified a variety of ways that companies can become more competitive by making environmental changes to their operations. These include:

- improved product quality;
- increased staff commitment;
- improved safety performance;
- reduced risk exposure;
- lower insurance premiums and finance costs;
- improved public relations record;
- assured present and future compliance;
- reduced waste management costs;
- better utilization of by-products;
- reduced downtime;
- improved materials and energy efficiency; and
- enhanced yields.

Whether companies choose to exploit these advantages is determined by their own internal cost-benefit analyses,[26] including an estimation of the great uncertainty and risk that is presently associated with environmental improvements and investments for corporations.

How corporate managers weigh these decisions can be understood by exploring the ways in which firms deal with uncertainty in the context of corporate environmental management. Ashford (1993) identifies four organizational barriers that exist, even where this may lead to increased wealth creation. These include problems with uncertainty, as well as with managerial and financial obstacles:

- lack of information on the costs and benefits of environmental management;
- lack of confidence in the performance of new technologies and techniques;
- lack of managerial capacity and financial capital to deal with transition costs associated with reorganizing the production process; and
- lack of awareness of the long-term benefits of environmental management resulting in low priority being assigned to environmental issues (Gouldson and Murphy, 1998, p24).

One way to reduce the problems associated with ambiguity is to spread the risk connected with it across the firm or across a number of cooperating firms. Consistent with this process of diversification, corporations often enter into strategic alliances for the development of new products, processes or markets where there is a great deal of risk or uncertainty. Some motivations for firms entering into strategic alliances are:

- exploit economies of scale;
- low cost entry into new markets;
- low cost entry into new industry segments and new industries;
- learning from competition;
- managing strategic uncertainty;
- managing costs and sharing risks; and
- to facilitate tacit collusion (Kogut, 1988; Hennart, 1988).[27]

Once the decision is made to make a corporate response to environmental challenges, ways of bringing about shifts can be understood through an analysis of environmental: innovation, technology, organization and strategy.[28]

Environmental innovation

Because incorporating environmentally relevant products and processes for most companies involves entering into new areas of economic activity, it is important to understand the concept of management innovation[29] when considering corporate management responses to environmental challenges. The notion of innovation is concerned with engaging in new economic activity and can refer to all stages of this process from initial invention through product development and introduction to the market. In other words, environmental innovation can be thought of as corporate change, or the process of making environmental improvements as part of a response to environmental challenges. Innovations can occur rapidly, involving new technologies or techniques, or they can occur slowly with small incremental steps to new technologies or techniques. In the past, management writers have placed greater emphasis on radical innovations since they are seen as opening up new areas of economic possibilities and providing for greater economic growth. Incremental innovations such as continuous improvement[30] have recently also been seen as having importance. Most environmental adjustments to corporate products and processes are associated with technologies or techniques. Some authors have suggested that incremental innovations are central to understanding the sorts of changes that occur when corporations deal with environmental challenges.[31]

Neither radical nor incremental environmental innovations are mutually exclusive, nor does either necessarily guarantee environmental 'success'. Radical environmental innovations, for example, are supported by small successes, incremental environmental innovations will eventually encounter economic and technical limits created by aspects of the system that remain unchanged which ultimately affect profit margins. Periods of radical change are therefore needed in an overall path of incremental environmental innovation in order for the firm to grow effectively. Whatever path of environmental innovation a corporation may decide to follow, one of the first aspects its directors will need to evaluate is the role of existing and potential technologies used or produced by the corporation (Gouldson and Murphy, 1998).

Environmental technology

All technologies, including materials and equipment, have actual and potential environmental impacts. At the same time, it is possible to identify a range of technologies that can be called 'environmental technologies'.[32] Environmental technologies can be categorized as either control or clean technologies, each of which has different economic and environmental characteristics. Control technologies are sometimes known as 'end of pipe' technologies, for example a scrubber retrofitted to a smokestack. Control technologies tend to be easy and inexpensive to incorporate into existing systems and have a straightforward benefit to companies in terms of complying with environmental regulations. Clean technologies are 'general processes or products which fulfil a non environmental objective as their primary purpose but which integrate environmental considerations into their design and/or application in order to anticipate and avoid or reduce their impact on the environment' (Gouldson and Murphy, 1998, p30). Clean technologies tend to be more expensive and more difficult to retrofit to existing technologies. Thus, the technology cannot generally be added on, it must be 'designed in'.[33] In the process of making products and processes more environmentally responsible it may make sense for some companies in the short run to adopt control technologies, while aiming for the medium- and long-term solution of clean technologies which have higher initial cost but greater economic and environmental efficiency in the longer term. The implementation of environmental technologies can have important implications for the analysis of a corporation's responses to environmental challenges. This implementation cannot take place without an organizational structure that can effectively incorporate responses to environmental challenges.

Environmental organization

The basic shift from control to clean technologies has a corresponding organizational shift of environmental considerations into mainstream business decision making. Managerial systems that respond to environmental challenges can, in some cases, assist or obviate the need for technological changes. Management systems can integrate and systematize disparate elements of a corporation's response to environmental challenges. They assign responsibilities, coordinate activities and facilitate flows of information throughout an organization. This allows corporations to translate objectives into departmental working practices. Through monitoring, environmental management systems can allow corporations to be more flexible and continue to improve environmental performance.[34] They can also provide the means for making a shift from control to clean technologies.

Guidelines and principles for good environmental management have been established and promoted by many national and international organizations: the International Chamber of Commerce (ICC), the Business Council for Sustainable Development (BCSD), the Confederation of British Industry (CBI), the Coalition for Environmentally Responsible Economies (CERES), the Chemical Industry Association (CIA) and the European Industry Association (EUROPIA). The guidelines include various common elements:

- a policy statement that indicates the organization's overall commitment to the improvement of environmental performance, including conservation and protection of natural resources, waste minimization, pollution control and continual improvement;
- a set of plans and programmes to implement the policy throughout the organization, including the advancement of the programme through suppliers and customers;

- the integration of the environmental plans into the day-to-day operation of the organization, developing innovative techniques and technologies to minimize the impact of the organization on the environment;
- the measurement of the environment management performance of the organization against the plans and programmes, auditing and reviewing progress towards achieving policy; and
- the provision of information, education and training to improve understanding of environmental issues, publicizing aspects of the environmental performance of the organization (Gilbert, 1993, pp7–8; cf Winter, 1995).

Management systems in corporations currently are put into place for areas such as sales, purchasing, expenses, tax law, personnel, product design and performance. This includes defining requirements and putting into place a system to meet them. Product requirements, set by the customer, can be addressed by a quality system. This system has management procedures in place to establish priorities, set targets, deploy resources, educate and train staff, monitor performance, audit the system, review and make changes to continue to make progress towards the goals that have been set.

Managers could also use ecological accounting,[35] environmental impact assessment[36] and ecological weakness analysis.[37] Ecological accounting is an advanced method of eco-controlling. Environmentally relevant activities of the company are recorded as physical units, such as kilograms, cubic metres or joules. 'Environmentally relevant' means all the inputs of materials and energy from the natural environment required by the company. Inputs and waste materials are given equivalence coefficients (or eco factors) depending on the extent to which they are a burden on the natural environmental. For example, the depletion of natural resources or pollution of the environment could be highlighted. This provides an index, expressed in units of account (UA), for wasted heat, consumption of non-renewable raw materials and production of waste.

The UA total indicates the overall environmental pollution produced by the company. The equivalence coefficients take account of two different concepts such as 'capacity certainty' (limited capacity of the atmosphere to absorb pollution) and 'cumulative scarcity' (the depletion of non-renewable resources). Provided the same equivalence coefficients are used, this system also allows a company to compare its impact on the environment with that of another company in the same industry or region. However, its main purpose is to help companies to make decisions and channel the available resources into those areas where the benefit to the environment will be greatest. It is useful in that it shows to management the environmental impact of its entire range of products or individual products and production methods. It identifies the ecological weaknesses of a company and focuses management attention on problem areas. It enables management to increase the company's real net output without increasing ecological problems, but rather to decrease them; a qualitative growth strategy. It can operate as an effective shadow accounting system alongside financial accounting without mixing monetary values and real values. It can provide a tangible base for cooperation with authorities in the area as well as valuable information about the measures taken by the company to protect the environment. It can also improve the credibility of public relations work and help to provide an objective basis for advertising (Winter, 1995, p221).

Environmental strategy

Environmental strategy concerns shifting the overall direction of the firm towards the response to environmental challenges. This goes beyond merely striving for change through environmental innovation, deciding on how to institute environmental technologies and systematizing the response to environmental challenges through environmental management systems. Environmental innovation, as noted above, is concerned with the search for new ways of doing things, new markets, new processes and new profits. The reasons why companies do or do not explore new areas were suggested to be related to problems largely related to information, confidence and managerial capacity as well as financial capital. Firms see high risks associated with radical environmental innovations. Sharp and Pavitt (1993) suggest that senior management of organizations can approach strategic decisions in myopic or dynamic ways, which have direct relevance to understanding how they view environmental strategy. Myopic approaches deal with traditional cost-benefit analyses focusing on the direct and tangible economic impacts of an investment. Therefore, they are less likely to advocate radical change where high risks and uncertainty are evident, as in many environmental investments. Dynamic approaches are different in that they recognize indirect and intangible impacts of an investment related to, for example, technological, organizational and market learning, which could be more amenable to engendering useful corporate responses to environmental challenges.

CONCLUSION

The main aim of those seeking to engender environmentally benign practice in firms is to find ways of retaining corporate competitiveness, that is, through the maintenance of an environmental 'level playing field' where no one firm or group of firms has an 'unfair' economic advantage over another or others. Spurred by regulations and market incentives, firms can become 'leaner' and 'greener'. It is true that many large corporations are highly visible, they are held accountable for their actions and can often afford to make environmentally beneficial changes to their production processes. While corporate greening can be explained partially by referring to such economic and organizational changes, it also reflects a wider social change process. Understanding this social process allows us to better comprehend obstacles as well as opportunities afforded to corporations by the environmental challenge. The models that allow us to do this are examined in the next chapter.

2

Theories of Corporate Greening

INTRODUCTION

This chapter outlines some ideas that are used throughout the rest of the book and can help to inform an understanding of the sociological aspects of corporate greening. I will look at three sets of ideas in particular: ecological modernization, the sociology of management and green economics and business. The overarching framework used in the rest of the book is ecological modernization, which tries to understand the ways in which institutions, like business, integrate environmental and economic objectives as part of an overall process of social change (Spaargaren and Mol, 1992; Mol, 1995; Hajer, 1995, 1996; Gouldson and Murphy, 1998). The sociology of management helps to show the ways in which businesses as organizations tend to respond to changes like greening, and green economics and business provide the basis of an analysis of how the process of corporate greening can take place.

ECOLOGICAL MODERNIZATION

The discourse of ecological modernization

Hajer (1995) argues that the discourse of ecological modernization emerged with the 1984 World Commission on Environment and Development (WCED). At the meetings of the commission, sustainable development was defined as development that 'meets the needs of the present without compromising the ability of future generations to meet their own needs' (WCED, 1987, p8). This definition broke with earlier conceptions of society–nature relationships held by critics of development which saw poverty and environmental degradation as being created by those institutions which claimed to be alleviating it; such as: structural adjustment programmes of the World Bank, and foreign direct investment in poorer countries by corporations based in wealthier countries. Ecological modernization implicitly endorsed such development, albeit environmentally amended, as a path out of economic and environmental disadvantage.

Sustainable development is paradigmatic of ecological modernization. This notion grew out of the political climate of the time which was characterized by the idea that there were limits to economic growth which if not acknowledged could lead to environmental collapse (Meadows et al, 1972). The environmental political project of the 1970s included both direct actions and the creation of alternative paradigms for relationships between society and nature. The time was also characterized by practical legal–administrative responses to pollution and environmental degradation, which included the creation of various 'Departments of the Environment' in industrialized countries. The latter focused on guaranteeing a certain environmental quality.

Ecological modernization discourse stresses the structural character of environmental problems, while advocating that change can come through a more 'benign', more environmental development process. It acknowledges in certain respects that the previous character of socio-economic growth was flawed. It maintains that ecological problems can only be remedied through further economic development, through further ecologically inclusive modernization. Society, including corporations, governments and consumers among others, can therefore modernize itself out of the ecological crisis.

Ecological modernization theory

Ecological modernization theory was developed from a critical reflection on the work of Huber who suggested that industrial society develops through three stages:

1   the industrial breakthrough;
2   the construction of industrial society; and
3   the ecological shift of the industrial system through the process of what he calls 'superindustrialization' linked to the development of new technologies.

It is his view that ecological modernization is a historical phase of modern society (Huber cited in Hannigan, 1995).

Ecological modernization draws from the reflexive modernization school and specifically the risk society (Beck, 1992; Beck et al, 1994).

The risk society model sees contemporary 'post scarcity' society as increasingly defined by distributions of environmental risks rather than wealth. The emphasis of this model is the unknowability of risks and the potentially devastating consequences from living with the effects of unforeseen environmental consequences. From the ecological modernization viewpoint the risk society model focuses on 'high consequence' risks, such as nuclear power, which are extrapolated to a whole range of environmental issues. While ecological modernization theorists accept that contemporary global risks have become disembedded from time and space, and that scientists can no longer ensure certainties related to environmental risks, they reject the reflexive modernization approach as too pessimistic.

Ecological modernization theory also perceives an ecological shift in the industrialization process that takes into account the maintenance of existing societal wants. This optimistic view is similar to that articulated in the definition of sustainable development (WCED, 1987). Theorists of ecological modernization have the 'conviction that the only possible way out of the ecological crisis is by going further *into* the process of modernization' (italics in original, Mol, 1995, p42). They argue that ecological crises can be dealt with in a rational manner incorporating economists, natural scientists, corporate executives, politicians, civil servants and others. Economists can be called on to develop plans for the green economy; natural scientists can determine pollution limits for the environment; corporate executives can incorporate clean technologies and management practices which strive for environmental efficiency; and politicians can combine command and control regulation with market incentives for cleaner production.

To summarize, ecological modernization theorizes the ways in which environmental and economic contradictions (characteristic of many debates in the 1960s and 1970s) have been decoupled, integrated and converged to create a plan for the continued development of modern industrialized societies that includes both growth and environmental responsibility (characteristic of the 1980s, 1990s and beyond).

Three key aspects of ecological modernization

The theory of ecological modernization can be viewed from a number of different perspectives:

- institutional learning;
- technocratic project; and
- cultural politics.

These are explored below to elucidate an understanding of the theory's potential usefulness for clarifying and establishing a wider social analysis of corporate responses to environmental challenges.[1]

Ecological modernization as institutional learning

The central assumption of ecological modernization as institutional learning is that institutions can learn and that their learning can produce meaningful change. In this context the ecological crisis comes to be seen as a primarily conceptual problem (Spaargaren and Mol, 1992; Mol, 1995; Gouldson and Murphy, 1998). Environmental degradation is seen as an 'externality'[2] problem and 'integration'[3] is the conceptual solution. It is argued by adherents of ecological modernization as institutional learning that economists have too long seen the environment as a free good;[4] politicians have not paid enough attention to the effects of collective action and have failed to devise the political arrangements that could deal with 'the global environmental crisis'. Adherents of ecological modernization as institutional learning argue that scientists have for too long sought to understand nature in a reductionist way; what is needed now is an integrated perspective of nature and society.

Ecological modernization as institutional learning starts with the assertion that the radical environmental agenda has been institutionalized in ways similar to other movements before it, such as the labour movement. By adopting notions of ecological modernization, environmental activists now speak an 'acceptable' language and have been integrated into business advisory boards. The relationship of these groups and business had in the past been mostly characterized by conflict and environmental group direct action. This demonstrates to theorists of ecological modernization as institutional learning that modern industrial societies can design or 'learn' new institutional forms to come to terms with environmental problems.

What is required for theorists of ecological modernization as institutional learning is a specific set of social, economic and scientific concepts that make environmental issues calculable and facilitate rational decision making. Hence, the natural sciences are called on to determine the amount of pollution nature can absorb, and should suggest the degree to which nature can be used. Engineering sciences can devise technological equipment that achieves ecological quality standards defined by governmental regulations.

The view of ecological modernization as institutional learning assumes that the existing political institutions can internalize ecological concerns or can at least influence new types of transnational management that can deal with relevant issues. For example, it is a sign of the strength and scope of ecological modernization that the World Bank has integrated environmental concerns. Adherents of ecological modernization as institutional learning argue that national governments can rethink their policies and that the network of corporatist interest groups can be altered in such a way that it becomes sensitive to ecological matters. Those who support ecological modernization as institutional learning therefore are hopeful about the prospects for an ecologically integrated modernization process, and think that it is possible to integrate ecological and economic aims, given a rational and systematic approach supported by appropriate governmental policies and regulations.

Ecological modernization as technocratic project

The idea of ecological modernization, as technocratic project,[5] is that technology, not nature, is out of control. Ecological modernization in this sense is put forward by an elite of policy makers, experts and scientists that imposes definitions of problems and solutions on the debate (Redclift, 1984, 1994; Buttel and Taylor, 1994; Foster, 1994). For example, support for sustainable development can only be generated by going along with the main institutional interests of national and international elites as expressed by nation-states, intergovernmental and financial organizations like the World Bank or the International Monetary Fund (IMF), and the various industrial interests associated with them.

Ecological modernization as technocratic project can be seen as a critical interpretation that extends Habermas's (1981) argument of modernization as the 'colonization of the lifeworld'. Further, in line with Habermas, it could also be seen as a call to redesign modern rationality into something that would allow for human emancipation, since it suggests that social change sparked by new social movements is necessary to redress the current state of affairs. If ecological modernization as institutional learning represents ecological modernization's hopeful interpretation, and ecological modernization as technocratic project represents its bleak interpretation, then ecological modernization as cultural politics attempts to steer a path clear of such polarities and suggests what meaning ecological modernization can have for giving human beings options.

Ecological modernization as cultural politics

Ecological modernization as cultural politics focuses more directly on ways in which ecological modernization can provide humanity with choices regarding how to conceptualize society, technology and nature (Hajer, 1996). It focuses on asking the question: why are certain aspects of reality now socially constructed as 'our common problem', such as 'global environmental change'? Ecological modernization in this sense is seen as the establishment of a 'new set of story lines' that provides the conceptual plans and possibilities for social action. Thus, the investigation of ecological modernization in this sense is similar to an analysis of the social construction of the environment (Hannigan, 1995). Proponents of ecological modernization as cultural politics consider the role of discourses and the social construction of reality as central. Metaphors, categorizations or definitions of solutions 'always structure reality making certain framings of reality seem plausible and closing off certain possible future scenarios while making other scenarios "thinkable"' (Hajer, 1996, p260).

Like other versions of ecological modernization theory, ecological modernization as cultural politics incorporates the reflexive modernization argument of Beck (1994) and others. However, it suggests that technology should not be seen as inherently problematic. The discourse of ecological modernization has the potential to reconstitute the relationships between nature, technology and society. This could occur if the debate is focused on societal choices rather than ideologies. That is to say, it seeks to deconstruct the ecological debate, to analyse it as consisting of a certain set of story lines about society, technology and nature, and by doing so facilitate human emancipation. For such an analysis, a critical understanding of the rhetorical quality of the environmental debate is central (Myerson and Rydin, 1996), and having this understanding allows people to make more informed choices. Thus, ecological modernization as cultural politics is based on a social constructionist perspective. This view advocates democratic pluralistic processes to achieve greater human freedom through an enhanced society–nature relationship.

Ecological modernization and its various interpretations is very relevant to this book because it directly addresses many of the issues examined and theorizes that economic and environmental aims are being integrated by all institutions in society, including corporations. In effect, this study provides an empirical investigation of how the theory works in practice via an analysis of corporate responses to environmental crises. As there are different interpretations of ecological modernization, there are also different interpretations of corporate responses to environmental crises. The three interpretations of ecological modernization correspond to different sets of empirical evidence that can be provided to explain ways in which corporations have responded to environmental crises; this is examined in the course of the book and summarized in the concluding chapter.

Ecological modernization as institutional learning suggests that corporate management responses are based on a type of incremental shift associated with overall societal processes of 'greening'. Ecological modernization as technocratic project maintains that corporate management responses are inappropriate responses to socio-environmental crises because they support productive and consumptive relations that create and recreate environmental crises. Ecological modernization as cultural politics argues that corporate responses to environmental crises can transform the relationship between society and the environment, through the debate about the future construction of society.

THE SOCIOLOGY OF MANAGEMENT

Ecological modernization provides an understanding of the relevance of the greening of corporations in terms of a process of social change. Adding specific socio-economic variables can further understanding of how corporations respond specifically to changes engendered by environmental crises. Scholars of the sociology of management typically consider issues such as: changes in organizational structures (Reed, 1992), the characteristics of social relationships in management hierarchies (Hill, 1981) and managers as an elite (Goldthorpe, 1980). They also explore models of managerial decision making. The purpose of this section of the literature review is to examine models within the sociology of management that can help to inform a sociological analysis of corporate responses to environmental crises. These include rational choice theory and models from organizational sociology dealing with bureaucracy, organizational change and corporate culture.

Rational choice theory

Rational choice theory tries to analyse how corporate managers make decisions about areas of uncertainty including environmental crises (Coleman et al, 1992). In rational choice theory, social actors are seen as maximising their personal preference satisfaction, that is, they maximize benefits to themselves and minimize costs. Thus, if profit maximization is central to a corporation, then rational choice analysis would hold that the corporate managers would maximize benefits and minimize costs. Rational choice analysis when applied to environmental issues might suggest that environmental regulations could be seen as an obstacle to profit maximization by corporate executives who would then use their collective influence to ensure that any regulatory changes would be minimal so as to promote wealth creation.

Rational choice theory, similar to other theoretical approaches, can sometimes present a general model of social interaction that does not always apply in the 'real world'. For example, the sub-concept of bounded rationality suggests that, while intending to act rationally, executives were prevented from doing so because they often do not have all of the information needed to make a truly informed, hence rational, decision (March and Simon, 1958). Gathering information becomes important to overcome bounded rationality. It can follow that in the politics of environmental policy what is often evident is both the process of deciding on the nature of environmental problems and deciding between competing interests involved in a problem (Weale, 1992). Because decisions are taken with incomplete information, individuals and groups will aim to 'satisfice' (sic), or achieve certain goals that they consider attainable, rather than have an overall 'maximizing objective'. In other words, decision makers attempt to attain something they know that they can achieve rather than their preferred goal that they may consider unachievable (Simon, 1957). The way corporate managers set about achieving environmental goals, for example, is often through an organizational response. This response is based on a rational choice, taking into account corporate cost-benefit analyses, and constrained by bounded rationality to the extent that some factors may be characterized by uncertainty including markets, regulations and environmental impacts. Rational choice analysis is examined in depth in Chapter 3 where the corporate management responses to environmental challenges are investigated.

Organizational Theory

Corporate responses to environmental crises also occur within corporate structures that need to be understood as well. This area of analysis is referred to as the sociology of organizations. Classic sociological theory regarding bureaucratic structures is the foundation for this school of thought and Weber's work is viewed as central to any discussion of bureaucracy.

Weber developed an 'ideal type' of bureaucracy; this was his notion of a pure form of organization. He identified a number of characteristics of bureaucracy, including: a defined hierarchy, written rules, full-time salaried officials, and the separation of work and home life, among others. Within the hierarchical set-up, which looks like a pyramid, power and autonomy are concentrated at the top of the organization. A clear chain of command is established whereby officials at each level control and monitor those in the level below.

Organizational rules are well defined but tend to be more flexible at the top of the hierarchy, and more rigid at the bottom. Weber saw the ideal type comprising officials who spent their career in the organization and worked their way up the organizational hierarchy over the years through a combination of capability and seniority. He also conceptualized a clear separation of work and home life, with official duties and activities distinct from those outside the workplace (Weber, 1979).

Organizational sociologists, using bureaucratic analysis as an analytical tool, observed a variety of managerial styles and institutional forms. Burns and Stalker, in *The Management of Innovation* (1961), identified two in particular and utilized conceptual categories originally defined by Durkheim in 1893 to distinguish them (Durkheim, 1960). The first is a mechanistic system, similar to Weber's ideal type, characterized as bureaucratic, suitable for stable conditions, uncompetitive markets and unchanging technology. The second is an organic form which maximizes personal discretion, decentralizes decision making and minimizes rule-bound behaviour whenever possible. They saw the latter as ideal for changing conditions.[6] Environmental management systems that have been successful have often been based on organic forms of organization that allow for the incremental improvements necessitated by many environmental crises (Burns and Stalker, 1961).

Organizational researchers have identified two types of organizational power relations: the unitary or U-form and the multidivisional or M-form. In U-form organizations all power is maintained at the top of the organizational hierarchy through the tight command and control structure, rather than being diversified to individuals, departments and suppliers. This form is consistent with Weber's ideal type of bureaucracy and Burns and Stalker's mechanistic form. Organic management can also occur within corporations through the development of structures that are more decentralized and flexible. In the M-form various subsidiary units are grouped into divisions and each division is run as a semi-autonomous business (Williamson, 1985). This way risks can be diversified throughout many individual or departmental 'profit centres' and to outside suppliers. Nevertheless the chief power and decision-making centre of the corporation remains with the board of directors.

Corporations that approximate Weber's ideal type are able to exert a great deal of control over the way work is organized and carried out. In corporations that are decentralizing, there is a greater potential of loss of control. Thus, top management sees 'corporate culture' as becoming more important since it creates normative control where there is no structural control (Peters and Waterman, 1982). Many Japanese and large corporations which are economically successful are characterized by decentralization, flexible specialization, managerial teams that operate across departments, flexible roles which are not rigidly defined, minimal rules and regulations, bottom up decision making as well as a 'strong corporate culture' (Ouchi, 1982).

Corporate culture

Organizational sociologists and management writers use the term 'corporate culture' to refer to a set of norms found in organizations or to a pervasive way of life. These norms might revolve around the exercise of authority and power, expectations about formality in the workplace, working hours and even appropriate dress for the job. An analysis of corporate cultures also suggests that while there may be one 'dominant' culture within organizations, other 'sub-cultures' may exist within different departments. For example, corporate research and development departments may be characterized by more flexibility and less rule-bound behaviour than other departments within a large corporation (Schein, 1985; Meek, 1992). Three common types of corporate cultures include:

1   role;
2   task;
3   power.

Role culture

A role culture is commonly thought of as approximating Weber's ideal type of bureaucracy. In this culture 'the role, or job description, is often more important than the individual who fills it. Individuals are selected for satisfactory performance of a role, and the role is usually described so that a range of individuals could fill it' (Handy, 1985, p190).[7]

Role culture is also characteristic of mechanistic organizational structures and is found in corporations that exist in stable non-competitive markets. Organizations that tend to have role cultures are the civil service (since it is a type of monopoly), the automobile and oil industries (they have long product life cycles and oligopolistic situations which can exist with large mature corporations), life insurance companies and retail banking (long product life cycles). Role cultures would tend to respond slowly to change, for example to changes in environmental regulations or public expectations.

Task culture

The task culture is job or product oriented. It is also a team culture, where the outcome, the result, the product of the team's work tends to be the goals that organize the group. The task culture is seen as extremely adaptable. Groups and project teams can be formed for a specific purpose and then reformed or abandoned as needed. Power is generally linked to knowledge rather than hierarchical status within the organization, and individuals generally have good working relationships based on mutual respect and a great deal of autonomy in the job (Souder, 1987).

Task cultures are most appropriate where flexibility and sensitivity to changes in the market are needed. They are found where the market is competitive, the product life is short and where creativity and quick responses are important. However, economies of scale or depth of expertise cannot be produced. For example, large factories are seen as being unable to be organized as flexible groups, because they can be organized more effectively on the basis of many specialized workers rather than a few multi-talented and creative individuals. Task cultures are common in product groups of marketing departments, general management consultancies, and merger, takeover and new venture sections of merchant banks. Task cultures are therefore most associated with innovation, although they may not always be seen as the most effective culture for certain conditions noted above.[8]

Power culture

A power culture is found typically in small, founder led, entrepreneurial organizations. The power culture depends on a central 'power source', usually the organization's founder or founders, which extends to the rest of the organization like a spider's web. The organization tends to depend on trust and empathy for its effectiveness and on 'telepathy and personal conversation' for communication. The aim of the people at the centre is to choose the right people who think similarly to themselves and leave them to get on with their jobs. Typically, there are few rules and procedures, little bureaucracy. Control is exercised through the centre largely through the selection of key people. 'It is a political organization in that decisions are taken very largely on the outcome of a balance of influence rather than on procedural or purely logical grounds' (Handy, 1985, p189).

If corporate cultures are defined by top corporate managers, the power culture, and the structures and organizations based on it, are seen to be especially strong. This contrasts with role cultures where decisions are slowed because they are often associated with bureaucracies; task cultures are also more flexible than role cultures, but more unstable than power cultures. Since those who define the power culture tend to exert so much influence over the organization, the organization's success is dependent on the abilities of those managers who control it to make the organization succeed. Size is the central issue for organizations that have power cultures. As the organizations with power cultures grow it is often difficult to maintain power at the centre. Power cultures emphasize the contributions of individuals rather than committees, and tend to judge results rather than the ways by which people in the organization achieve them. Power cultures tend not to be able to survive over the very long term since they require a powerful group of well-qualified and experienced people that can be difficult to maintain over time.

The sociology of management school of thought provides an insight into some of the organizational and economic models for understanding how corporations respond to environmental crises. Rational choice facilitates an investigation of reasons why corporate managers choose to make environmental investments or not, while organizational theory helps to explain how firms respond to change and the ways in which their structures and cultures can produce management styles in response to environmental crises. However, this literature does not provide an understanding of the social change driving the corporate greening process. The literature to be examined below provides additional insight into corporate greening because it addresses areas unexplored in the preceding literatures.

GREEN ECONOMICS AND BUSINESS

The literature on green economics and business, which contributes to a wider social analysis of corporate management and environmental crises, has at least three strands, which cover economics, business and ethics. As an overview of these three strands, this section provides illustrations of some of the ideas most relevant to understanding corporate responses to environmental crises, which informs the analysis of the evidence examined in later chapters. Many aspects of these literatures, covered briefly here, will be examined in greater detail later in the book.

Environmental economics

Environmental economics includes models where free market or neoclassical paradigms have been reshaped or revised to take account of environmental threats (Block, 1990; Pearce et al, 1990; Daly, 1991;

Daly and Goodland, 1992; Daly and Cobb, 1994). The area is not new; there has been an established literature in environmental economics for over 20 years. One of the more interesting elaborations of environmental economics is the steady-state school. The idea of a steady-state economy is one in which all variables grow or contract at a constant rate. For example, population could grow at 3 per cent a year, national income at 4 per cent and capital stock at 5 per cent. Where these rates are maintained indefinitely, steady-state growth exists. This is distinct from balanced growth in which all variables grow at the *same* constant rate. Theories of economic growth have considered the extent to which steady-state growth is likely to be achieved. According to steady-state theorists, a steady-state economy is necessary and desirable through major changes in values, and radical institutional reforms. While acknowledging that even a steady-state economy cannot be sustained forever, it is argued that the need for economic growth must be replaced by a focus on the satisfaction of basic needs. Once this shift has taken place then the establishment of a steady-state becomes easier. 'But unless the underlying growth paradigm and its supporting values are altered, all the technical prowess and manipulative cleverness in the world will not solve our problems and, in fact, will make them worse' (Daly, 1991, p1). The steady-state school theorizes new socio-economic relationships that are based on the shift from 'more is better' to 'enough is best' and therefore presupposes some radical institutional changes. It does not concentrate on using existing market conditions to bring about change.

The market oriented intervention school tries to use existing market conditions to bring about change and emphasizes valuing the Earth in terms of its natural capital. It defines sustainability as 'a rule that required each generation to pass on to the next one a stock of natural environmental assets ("natural capital") no less than the stock of assets already in existence' (Pearce, 1992, p391). Because it can help to explain ways in which firms react to environmental crises, the free market environmental economists' work on market-based environmental policy is most useful in understanding how environmental problems, which affect corporations, can be conceptualized.

The economic analysis of the way environmental change targets can be achieved is especially apt. From this standpoint, there are three ways in which such targets can be achieved: command and control, pollution taxes and tradable permits. Command and control measures are defined by government and do not involve market mechanisms. However, pollution taxes and tradable permits are market based in that they use the market to ensure a certain standard of environmental quality. Pollution taxes are based on taxing polluting industries or consumers who consume a polluting commodity. Tradable permits are based on allowing polluters to switch between sources of pollution as long as they remain within agreed maximum levels of pollution (Pearce, 1992).

Most environmental policy is presently based on command and control. Regulation involves setting pollution targets for polluters; this represents 'command'. Monitoring, inspection and the allocation of penalties represents 'control'. Command and control only works where the penalties for exceeding pollution limits are greater than the profit earned from exceeding the limits. Corporations and other polluters tend to prefer command and control because there is less uncertainty; pollution limits tend to be long established and fines for exceeding limits are clearly delineated. There also tends to be room for negotiation with regulators over special problems faced by industry. Command and control is seen as not being as economically efficient as other systems of pollution control because: (1) it requires that the regulator acquires information from the polluter, and (2) the system is inflexible for the polluter. That is, if a pollution standard is set, it must be followed by two hypothetical polluters equally, even if pollution reduction is considerably cheaper for one polluting industry than for another (see tradable rights to pollute, below). The market oriented intervention school sees economic efficiency in pollution control as likely to be increasingly important as the costs of environmental protection rise, a legacy of having failed to respond to environmental crises more effectively in the last 20 years (Pearce, 1992).

Taxation solutions are based on taxing polluters for emissions. For example, if carbon dioxide emissions need to be controlled, then polluters can be taxed on the amount of carbon dioxide they emit. If coal burning were taxed at a higher rate than oil, and oil at a higher rate than natural gas, the effect would be threefold. First would be the substitution of lower carbon fuels for higher carbon ones, second, the substitution of non-carbon fuels, for example, nuclear power and renewable fuels, for carbon energy and, third, energy conservation. Less polluting behaviour would be brought about through the desire of polluters to avoid the tax. Taxation solutions, in contrast to command and control strategies, generate revenue. Pollution taxes can also represent a continuing incentive to develop new, more environmentally efficient technologies, as a way for polluters to avoid the tax. This contrasts with command and control, which is based on the idea of the 'best available technology' for pollution control; therefore, it does not provide as great an incentive for developing new technologies (Pearce, 1992).

Tradable rights to pollute are seen as more advantageous, through their greater flexibility and cost-effectiveness, than the other two measures. The concept is based on government defining an acceptable level of pollution for a given environmental crisis, for example lead in petrol, CFCs and chemical production. First, a unit of pollution must be defined, which would vary depending on the substance and the acceptable limits of its emission into the environment as defined by scientists and regulators. If, for example, 100 units of pollution is the limit defined for any given polluting substance, then 100 permits, each with a value of one unit of emission could be issued. Once polluters are allocated pollution permits, then they are free to trade them; this is seen as the key benefit of the system since it is less costly for polluters and regulators than the previous two approaches. A given corporation that finds it relatively inexpensive to reduce its pollution of a given substance will profit from selling its permits to a corporation that finds it more costly to reduce pollution. The 'inexpensive' polluter corporation (the seller) therefore earns a higher profit by selling its permits to an 'expensive' polluter corporation (the buyer) than the cost of reducing pollution with fewer permits. The 'expensive' polluter corporation (the buyer) will find it more profitable to buy pollution permits and pollute more than, for example, to install technologies which would lessen its own emissions. By trading, the control of pollution will be concentrated among those polluters who find it 'cheap' to pollute, and permit holders will be concentrated among those who find it expensive to pollute. At the same time, environmental quality is maintained because the amount of permits, and thus the acceptable level of pollution, has remained the same. Furthermore, trade can occur between firms, as well as within subsidiaries of the same firm (Pearce, 1992). Thus, tradable rights to pollute are seen as the most flexible system of pollution control and are effective when supported by the other two methods.

The greening of business

Literature on the greening of business can also be relevant to an understanding of corporate responses to environmental crises (Elkington and Hailes, 1988; David, 1991; Plant and Plant, 1991; Smith, 1993).[9] The greening of business can inform an understanding of the ways in which business executives create management systems that respond to environmental issues; this can exemplify processes of social change related to modernization and the environment. Schools of thought in this literature are based on those advanced by business and management writers from a business perspective (Smith, 1993), and those written from a perspective that is critical of business (Plant and Plant, 1991). Works written from the business perspective are geared towards audiences of businesspeople and business educators and students. They can cover: accounting, business economics, legal issues, marketing, risk assessment and corporate responsibility. Authors organize ideas around the perception of a shift in societal and corporate values related to the environmental aspects of business, and the ways in which managers should respond to this shift, including corporate actions and plans for environmental improvements. For example, responding to industry's 'dirty' image through public relations and pollution abatement practices, as well as through specific economic, legal, accounting and marketing shifts. The aim of this literature is to explore the issue that:

> *'corporate bodies need to anticipate and prevent future societal concerns about their operations; in other words they will need to adopt a more strategic view of the problem. Such a paradigm shift in the culture of business will be difficult to achieve without the wholesale cooperation of managers, shareholders and business educators. A failure to incorporate a new set of environmental values at the heart of the corporate culture will result in a process of simply "bolting on" a false consciousness in the form of a green tinge'* (Smith, 1993, p9).

By undertaking efforts in this area, writers within the practical school attempt to raise environmental issues to the business community. The environment is presented as a relatively new challenge to business, to which business must find ways of responding culturally, organizationally and technologically. Reasons why business should respond to environmental crises are given both in terms of future wealth creation as well as the ethical dimensions of responding to legitimate crises facing societies.

Other perspectives within the 'greening of business' literature are more critical of the notion that business can respond to environmental crises effectively (Plant and Plant, 1991). The school that is critical of business focuses on the difficulties faced by businesses trying to pursue 'legitimate' greening within the competitive market, and corporate attempts to appear 'green' while maximizing wealth creation. Relevant areas for such authors are the critique of green consumerism, an exploration of the way corporations market the environment, and the involvement of environmental groups with businesses. Solutions that the critical school provides to the problem areas it defines can be based on bioregional economics, community supported agriculture and alternative forms of critical consumption. It can be said that both practical and critical perspectives of the greening of business are useful to understanding corporate responses to environmental crises. The practical perspective is useful because it provides a model of ways in which business can slowly shift towards environmentally benign practices, similar to ecological modernization as institutional learning. The critical perspective is helpful as it provides a corrective to the notion that business and the competitive market can necessarily respond to environmental crises, similar to ecological modernization as technocratic project. One literature essentially offers what the other lacks. The practical perspective provides market-based plans for environmentally responsible behaviour, and the critical perspective, which is sceptical of business, provides an analysis of the benefits corporations can receive from engaging in polluting practices.

Business ethics and the environment

Business ethics and the environment is another area that can inform an analysis of corporate responses to environmental crises (Engel and Engel, 1990; Hoffman et al, 1990). Sustainable development can be pursued as a moral question 'the elemental moral question of what way of life human beings ought to pursue' (Engel, 1990, p1). The ethics of sustainable development school argue that in order for societies to embrace sustainable development a new ethic is required which incorporates concern for all living things as well as the development of environmentally useful technologies. Morality can spur social change as much as changes brought about by the use of self-interest for a greater good, as in market-based proposals for dealing with environmental crises. While some authors consider many ethical and philosophical issues around the unfolding of sustainable development, others have a more practical view of the relationship between business, ethics and the environment.

The ethics of business and environment school is unique in that it is geared towards businesspeople and business academics but is not primarily concerned with the monetary cost-benefit of environmental protection. The main concern is with the ethical obligations that corporations have for protecting the environment. Specifically, corporations can pollute the environment. The pollution can cause illness, and responsible officials are morally compelled to help people who become ill. An analysis of the ethical aspects of business and the environment relies on a 'harm-benefit' analysis, rather than a traditional 'cost-benefit' analysis. For example, industrial accidents occur, factories shut down and pollutants are released into the atmosphere, but by and large the main benefits of economic activity offset the environmental harm business causes. If it is shown that a certain business activity caused harm, then the business involved is morally required to prevent or ameliorate that harm. However, it must be done in a way that takes into account two further issues. First, businesses should not be put at a competitive disadvantage which can cause further harm to employees and prevent the alleviation of the harm caused to the public. Second, businesses may be morally required to lobby the government for legislation that reduces environmental harm caused by business practices. In this view, it is morally unacceptable for businesses to lobby government against regulations that prevent or minimize corporate pollution.

This literature deals with philosophical issues related to business and the environment, such as suggesting the ethical challenges presented by the sustainable development debate. It can also focus on certain ethical environmental dilemmas faced by business with the hope that by clarifying the moral obligations that businesspeople have to the environments in which they operate, a redefinition of basic values can occur. Similar to other outcomes suggested within the business ethics literature,

> *'the place to begin this investigation is with the values we hold – the things we hope our actions will preserve, promote or protect. It is here, if anywhere, that we can truly begin to deal with the environmental dilemmas we face'* (Frederick, 1990, pxxiii).

While all three strands are helpful starting points, they do not provide a specific social focus on the 'greening' of corporations and its impact on environmental problems. A sociological investigation into the ways in which corporations are affected by environmental challenges is therefore a particularly fruitful area of research. This is seen in the fact that, to date, the majority of work published in this area has been in the form of research guides and agendas (Toth et al, 1989; Buttel and Taylor, 1994; Sklair, 1994a). Yearley's work, which analyses the ways in which environmental issues are constructed, mediated and redefined, begins to explore the understanding of the sociological implications (Yearley, 1996; cf Redclift and Benton, 1994). A similar line of enquiry is Hannigan's (1995) analysis of the role of interest groups in the social construction of environmental knowledge.

The environmental justice school tries to incorporate an analysis of corporate power more directly in terms of an environmental social justice framework. This body of work has been developed by sociologists (and geographers: Cutter, 1993, 1995) mostly based in the US (Brown and Mikkelsen, 1990; Bullard, 1990; Bryant and Mohai, 1992; Hofrichter, 1993; Szasz, 1994). Specifically, the environmental justice school has focused on the role of bureaucratic and corporate power in creating unequal exposure to environmental pollution. For example, it argues that decisions to place toxic waste facilities and environmentally hazardous production processes in poorer communities will result in gender, class and racial inequalities of exposure. The social justice school provides a background to the socially problematic aspects of corporate responses to environmental crises, but its focus is on the communities affected and not on the overall process of social change linking the environment and modernization of which corporations are a part. Therefore, it informs but does not provide a comprehensive model of corporate responses to environmental crises.

CONCLUSION

Ecological modernization develops a theory of social change of which corporate responses to environmental crises are a central part. Ecological modernization as institutional learning suggests that corporations can learn to respond more effectively and efficiently to environmental crises. The technocratic perspective sees corporations as relatively unchanged by environmental crises. The cultural politics perspective emphasizes democratic pluralism in order that the environmental debate surpasses disagreements about the role of technology and begins to reconceptualize society–nature relationships. The sociology of management provides an important part of the sociological explanation for corporate responses to environmental crises, without connecting these changes to larger processes of social change.

Other literatures deal with the problem more directly and help to explain some aspects of it, but are also not adequate in themselves since they cannot explain greening as a social change process. For example, environmental economics, business and ethics considers corporate responses to environmental crises in terms of markets, businesses or moral choices without addressing the social relationships which create or ameliorate environmental problems. This book considers the ways in which one of the dominant institutions of society, the corporation, transforms or is transformed by a fundamental crisis to its operations. It would seem that the ecological modernization model is most appropriate to understand this issue. Is an analysis of corporate greening as part of the process of ecological modernization amenable to being understood in terms of institutional learning, technocratic project, cultural politics, or another evaluation altogether? Chapter 3 begins this exploration by examining the evidence of management structures and management styles consistent with corporate 'greening'.

3

Corporate Management of Environmental Challenges

INTRODUCTION

This chapter explores whether there are management structures and management styles consistent with corporate 'greening'. The structures of corporate 'greening' include corporate policies[1] and corporate programmes.[2] These form the corporate management response to environmental challenges. If environmental challenges are managed well, they can represent financial rewards for the corporation. If environmental challenges are mismanaged, they can represent high costs and liabilities to the corporation. In order to make sense of the evidence in terms of specific corporate responses to environmental challenges, data are considered in light of organizational and management concepts and theories relevant to an understanding of corporate responses to challenges, in particular ecological modernization. An analysis of these data, informed by discussions in Chapters 1 and 2, generates a fourfold model of corporate management styles in response to environmental challenges. This model is introduced in the second half of the chapter. In Chapters 4 and 5, the model is applied to help to evaluate the four case studies, then it is extended to explain the relationship between environmental management structures, management styles and corporate cultures.

CORPORATE ENVIRONMENTAL MANAGEMENT STRUCTURES: POLICIES

Corporate environmental policies indicate organizations' overall commitment to the improvement of environmental performance. This can include conservation and protection of natural resources, waste minimization, pollution control and continuous improvement. Environmental policies are often all encompassing, while programmes are usually issue specific. An environmental policy is an important aspect of a corporation's 'commitment' to environmental action; it provides a public statement from management to workers, investors, politicians, regulators, environmental groups and other companies about what can be expected from the corporation.

Most environmental policies are not especially concrete, and the language employed is repeated across statements. Common phrases include 'environmental excellence', 'environmental stewardship', 'environmental leadership', 'long-term environmental commitment', 'environmental challenges', 'success', 'innovative', 'first' and 'pioneering'. Stakeholders can potentially hold a corporation accountable to these commitments. Imprecise corporate sentiments of greening stated in terms of corporate costs and benefits include terms which come up again and again in the corporate literature, such as: the aim to 'get it right', the pitfalls and prices to pay 'if we get it wrong', the qualities of 'being a good neighbour', 'being a good corporate citizen' and, occasionally, 'cleaning up our (or others') mess' (Willums and Goluke, 1992). In interviews for this study, corporate personnel repeated similar statements about wanting to 'get it right' (interview with Shell Environment staff member, London, 9 February 1994). The 'it' refers to environmental investments, innovations, technologies and strategies.[3]

Regarding the content of policies, the details vary. A review of the UN data suggests that there is a difference between larger and smaller firms. Large, complex companies produce general policies such as 'will operate in an environmentally friendly manner' or 'will pursue best practice'. Smaller, less complex companies are more likely to produce more concrete, specific policies regarding what targets will be achieved by whom and when.[4] The policies generally encompass the following areas: a definition of environmental protection, research and development, production and product issues, health, production and environmental protection technologies, methods for control and environmental information gathering, role of workers, environmental management, environmental protection aims, emergency plans, public information and customer relations.

They also include the environmental aims of the corporation. The following are common sentiments in the policies:

• compliance with existing regulations and laws;
• highest standard;

- best contemporary practice;
- environmentally responsible manner;
- a high degree;
- reduce adverse effects to a practicable minimum;
- without unacceptable effects to the environment;
- minimize environmental consequences;
- ensure activities continue on a sound basis environmentally;
- technically feasible, financially possible and ecologically justifiable;
- highest practicality achievable standards;
- have the least possible long-term impact on the environment;
- ecologically motivated, technically possible and economically reasonable;
- be a good citizen within the local community in which it operates; and
- best environmental practice (*UN Survey*, 1993, pp11–12).

These policies tend to focus on environmental action within the production process and the final product through technologies. Organizational or personnel issues are second to these issues, although personnel responsible for the production and product aspects are sometimes mentioned. There is also a set of programmes and other plans to implement the policy throughout the organization, ideally through suppliers and customers as well. These are discussed in the section below on management programmes.

In 1991, at the time of the *UN Survey*, 43 per cent of the corporate respondents had a published international environmental policy.[5] It was also found that 70 per cent of North American companies had a formal published environmental policy.[6] Comparisons of these findings with a survey completed in 1974 of 516 US corporations, found that 40 per cent of the sample had completed environmental policies (Lund, 1974). There is an increase of around 30 per cent in the number of firms that have been preparing such a policy over the last 20 years.

The *UN Survey* also found that the largest corporations are about twice as likely to have an environmental policy as the smallest: 58 per cent versus 30 per cent; and the extractive sector is also much more likely to have an environmental policy than the finished goods, agricultural or service sectors: 60 per cent of extractive corporations have an environmental policy. Therefore, corporations with operations that affect the environment greatly and those that have extensive capital and managerial resources tend to respond more comprehensively to environmental challenges than those companies without these attributes.

SUMMARY OF CORPORATE POLICIES

Corporate policies indicate that the response to the environmental challenge has been fragmented. While some companies have given environment, health and safety matters a great deal of thought, others have not. For example, some policies indicate that the corporation will comply with all applicable laws. Other corporations have attempted to integrate environmental matters with financial matters, and more seriously consider the impact of their operations on those outside the company. A corporate policy is a document for which the company can be held responsible by the public, and can therefore be seen as more than simply company propaganda.

Using ecological modernization to explain corporate policies suggests that corporations that merely comply with environmental laws can be seen as those for which the traditional relationship between environmental action and economic wealth creation is maintained (representing contradiction), whereas for corporations that integrate environmental and financial matters, this negative relationship is decoupled (representing convergence). The corporations that have integrated economic and environmental aims successfully may be seen by some as benefiting from institutional learning.

CORPORATE ENVIRONMENTAL MANAGEMENT STRUCTURES: PROGRAMMES

The *UN Survey* focused on 22 specific programmes, going beyond national regulations, which companies might apply throughout their operations (noted in Table 3.3). These programmes concern issues such as air, water, soil pollution, health, safety, disposal of wastes and sustainable development. It was found that 75 per cent of the corporations have programmes; 20 per cent of the companies have over 15 programmes; and the average corporation has programmes that apply throughout the corporation (see Tables 3.1 and 3.2).[7]

A regional analysis of Tables 3.1 and 3.2 suggests that North American and Asian corporations, as well as companies in the extractive and finished goods sectors, and the largest corporations, are most likely to have environmental programmes. European corporations and companies that process raw agricultural materials are least likely to have any of the 23 programmes in place.

The highest programme priorities are those that relate to energy programmes. One of the reasons for this may be the 1970s energy

Table 3.1 Corporate programme priorities: Corporate activities on EH&S and sustainable development – energy and health and safety activities

Activity	R&D for energy efficient production (%)	Programmes for conserving energy supplies (%)	Company-wide worker health and safety programmes (%)	Company-wide accident prevention programmes (%)	Company-wide emergency preparedness programmes (%)	Standardized hazard assessment procedures (%)	Programmes for conserving non-renewable resources (%)	International conservation of energy supplies (%)
Total	71	68	68	60	58	57	54	54
Home country region:								
Asia	78	62	78	65	66	69	49	47
Europe	60	56	52	43	40	35	44	48
North America	75	86	72	74	67	65	71	67
Sector:								
Agricultural	67	66	42	42	38	41	50	62
Extractive	80	68	79	73	71	67	66	59
Finished goods	71	71	74	62	61	64	52	51
Services	50	57	71	79	53	39	36	33
Sales size:								
Top third	89	83	84	76	74	67	74	71
Second third	71	71	60	53	53	59	50	45
Bottom third	53	49	60	53	48	44	40	45

Source: UN Survey, 1993, Annex D1, p22

Table 3.2 Corporate programme priorities: Corporate activities on EH&S and sustainable development – traditional environmental activities

Activity	Recycling (%)	Standardized waste handling procedures (%)	Company-wide waste disposal programmes (%)	Company-wide waste reduction technologies (%)	Company-wide water quality/ pollution programmes (%)	Company-wide air quality/ pollution programmes (%)	Company-wide noise pollution programmes (%)	Standardized soil quality/ pollution programmes (%)
Total	85	56	52	49	48	47	41	31
Home country region:								
Asia	83	84	61	55	69	66	63	32
Europe	76	36	30	28	24	29	19	19
North America	96	59	65	65	51	47	41	44
Sector:								
Agricultural	88	38	37	32	29	28	32	21
Extractive	88	62	60	60	58	60	44	48
Finished goods	86	67	59	54	59	56	50	27
Services	57	43	33	33	20	20	20	20
Sales size:								
Top third	94	65	69	66	61	65	58	45
Second third	83	58	53	47	50	46	41	32
Bottom third	77	46	34	34	34	32	25	17

Source: UN Survey, 1993, Annex D1, p228

crises and the financial benefits of energy savings. Again, the North American corporations are more involved in energy saving than the other regions. Many corporations link environment, health and safety (EH&S). The reason for this is that health and safety in the workplace can directly affect the likelihood that the corporation can create or avoid an environmental disaster. For example, lax health and safety practices at Union Carbide's plant at Bhopal, India,[8] led to the release of toxic gas that resulted in thousands of fatalities.[9] Human error is linked to most accidents which create environmental challenges; preserving worker health, through a safer and more efficient manufacturing process which minimizes worker injuries or the threat of injury, makes for a safer and more environmentally stable operation. ARCO Chemical, similar to other corporations within the chemical industry, has endeavoured to create a corporate culture based on 'safety'; the company sees this as its first environmental priority. Similarly, Gouldson and Murphy argue that companies can become more competitive by making environmental changes to their operations. Among these related to EH&S are increased staff commitment, improved safety performance, reduced risks exposure, lower insurance premiums and finance costs, and improved public relations record (Gouldson and Murphy, 1998, p23).

The general finding from Tables 3.1 and 3.2 is that health and safety programmes are more evident than those regarding the environment generally. The reason for this is that health and safety has been more highly regulated than environmental issues. Bjorn Stigson, the chair of AB Slakt and BCSD member, notes the historical difference between treating workers and the environment as 'externalities': 'We treat nature like we treated workers a hundred years ago. We included them at no cost for the health and social security of workers in our calculations, and today we include no cost for the health and security of nature' (Cairncross, 1990, p3). The other reason for the concentration on worker health and safety is that it has a direct link to output, and accidents tend to be linked to worker error. Also, the largest companies are more likely to engage in accident prevention and health and safety than the smallest (60–80 per cent versus 35–55 per cent). The reason for this is that the big companies have 'more extensive operations, face greater legal consequences, and possess the needed managerial and financial resources to undertake such programmes' (*UN Survey*, 1993, p25). This is supported by Ashford's (1993) research on large organizations and environmental innovation. The service sector, which usually is behind the others in environmental consideration, is one of the leaders in accident prevention programmes and worker health and safety.[10]

Sustainable development issues

The WCED's 1987 report (commonly referred to as the Brundtland Report) defined sustainable development as meeting the needs of the present without compromising the ability of future generations to meet their needs. Earlier, it was noted that this notion of integrating economic well-being with environmental preservation as delineated in the Brundtland Report marked the beginning of what has been called ecomodernist discourse, the discourse of ecological modernization. In order to respond to the challenge of sustainable international development, corporations' responses to environmental challenges would have to include dealing with global environmental issues, such as ozone depletion, carbon dioxide production and protection of ocean resources as well as those with specific reference to their developing country operations, which can be linked with global issues, for example, challenges involving rainforests. If corporations do not respond to environmental challenges representative of ecological modernization, an analysis of these non-responses can inform our understanding of the process and meaning of ecological modernization.

In terms of the activities of corporations, some of the policy implications of the sustainable development debate which corporations have chosen to target are developing country and global concerns, like rainforests and ocean challenges, the environmental problems of developing countries, and carbon and CFC emissions (compare Lower priority and Higher priority areas of Table 3.3). It should be noted that less than half, and in a number of cases only a handful, of the corporations surveyed were involved in 'lower priority' types of sustainable development activities.

Afforestation programmes were one of the more popular of the 'lower priority' sustainable development activities of the respondents to the *UN Survey*, sometimes linked to greenhouse gas reduction programmes. In Japan, Toyota[11] aims to offset global carbon dioxide emissions with South American tree planting projects. Mitsubishi Paper Mills[12] and Daio Paper also have afforestation projects in Latin America. Oji Paper[13] and Honshu Paper have similar projects in Southeast Asia including an 11,000 hectare project in Honshu, Papua New Guinea. Because nearly all of these companies have been involved in the tropical timber trade in Southeast Asia,[14] they have faced international criticism over tropical deforestation. It is perhaps not coincidental that many Japanese corporations have subsequently developed 'afforestation programmes'.

In the area of responses to global environmental change, less than 20 per cent of the companies have programmes aimed at the global commons, such as research and development for renewable energy,

Table 3.3 *Corporate programme priorities on EH&S and sustainable development*

Higher priority areas	Percentage of respondents
Energy related activities	
R&D for energy efficient production	71
Programmes for securing energy supplies	68
Programmes for conserving non-renewable resources	54
Energy conservation	54
Health and safety activities	
Worker health and safety	68
Accident prevention	60
Emergency preparedness	58
Hazard assessment procedures	57
Traditional environment activities	
Water quality/pollution	48
Air quality/pollution	47
Noise pollution	41
Soil quality/pollution	31
Waste/disposal related activities	
Recycling	85
Waste handling procedures	56
Waste disposal programmes	52
Waste reduction technologies	49
Lower priority areas	
Genuine sustainable development activities	
Afforestation programmes	40
R&D for greenhouse gas generation reduction	39
Renewable energy sources	22
Preservation of endangered species	16
Conservation of biodiversity	10
Programmes for protection of wetlands/rainforests in LDCs	9

Source: Adapted from *UN Survey*, 1993, p26

and rainforest or biodiversity protection programmes (see Table 3.3). In the corporate policies reviewed, little attention is paid to sustainable development issues. The exceptions to this are one-third of the corporations that are active in the areas of greenhouse gas reduction and around 40 per cent that have afforestation programmes. This would indicate that there has been some response to global environmental change although it tends to be in high publicity or cost saving areas.

Table 3.4 *Developing country issues on specific aspects of the UNCED themes*

Higher priority aspects	Percentage of respondents
Has provisions for infrastructure etc for workforce	49
Monitors disposal of generated hazardous wastes	48
Has toxic education programme for workforce and community	41
Monitors its stacks for air emission components	37
Uses CFCs or related products in plants	27
Lower priority aspects	
Has plants near drinking water supplies	16
Releases effluents into oceans off developing countries	14
Holds land for safety zones	14
Has wetland and rainforest protection programmes	9
Surveys on biological species on undeveloped land	9
Has product hazards to drinking water supplies	3
Markets any genetically engineered products	3
Practises mono-cropping or clear cutting	2

Source: Adapted from *UN Survey*, 1993, p28

As in the other *UN Survey* findings, the largest corporations, the extractive corporations and North American companies are more likely to be engaged in global environmental change issues than their counterparts. Exceptions to this are the finished goods sector (all regions) and European corporations, which are leading in research and development for greenhouse gas reduction.

With regard to developing country issues (see Table 3.4), a number of companies are involved in at least some environmental activities in developing countries. Over 50 per cent of the companies respond that they engage in one or more of the 13 developing country activities mentioned in the *UN Survey* questionnaire. While about 60 per cent of Asian (Japanese) and North American companies are active in developing country environmental issues, less than 40 per cent of the European corporations are involved. About 60 per cent of the extractive-based and finished goods corporations have developing country environmental activities. Additionally, 70 per cent of the largest corporations are engaged in such activities while only 40 per cent of the smallest companies are. The largest corporations are more likely to be active in developing countries, and therefore they would need to take account of such issues, more so than smaller companies. The most common environmental developing country activities are those regarding pollution monitoring, local infrastructure support and education on how people can protect themselves from the toxic substances used or produced by the corporations.

An interesting finding in the *UN Survey* is that between 20 and 30 per cent of the corporations reported that data were insufficient at headquarters to answer specific questions about their developing country activities. This might suggest that communication links between developing country operations and company headquarters are poor. This was confirmed in a study by the consulting firm McKinsey which found that most chief executive officers (CEOs) outside developing countries are uncertain whether the 'level of knowledge in their industry is adequate to deal with the relevant developing countries' environmental issues effectively' (McKinsey & Company, 1991, p14).[15]

Corporate headquarters often claim that they do not know about the environmental performance of developing country operations, due to 'decentralized structures', 'lack of communications with affiliates', 'bureaucratic problems' and 'language problems'. This would be supported by the general move in the 1980s toward a decentralized 'M-form' or multidivisional organizational structure. This allows corporations to spread business risks, thereby creating many individual 'profit centres'. Still, within an 'M-form' organizational structure the chief power centre of the corporation remains, and can define worldwide standards of practice on environmental issues. This is why the 'M-form' organizational structure explains part of the issue but not all of it. If the business issue at hand is seen as an important one by the corporation, executives in the corporate headquarters should be aware of its status in all parts of the corporation.

Union Carbide, since the Bhopal disaster, claims to have developed many programmes in which the company aims to be equal to or better than its competition. Programmes incorporate anticipating emergencies and providing hazard and emergency response information to surrounding communities, all of which were problems that contributed to the Bhopal tragedy (Gladwin, 1987). This also includes independent contractors at Union Carbide plants, who are asked to carry out their work in compliance with EH&S requirements. There are also programmes for independent offsite contractors to ensure that processing and storage also comply with EH&S requirements.

Other programmes address worker information and training, visitor safety, communications, internal reporting and follow up. These programmes aim to provide assurance that potential problems are identified, avoided and considered in making business decisions. Programmes must also deal with all parts of operational life from conceptualization, design and construction, to operation and decommissioning. There are also a myriad of programmes related to employees regarding safety issues, from proximity to safety equipment, to protection of the fetus,[16] and protection from noise, and physical, chemical and biological agents. There are also programmes on groundwater, air and waste minimization.[17] The execution of all of these programmes should have the effect of strengthening Union Carbide economically. The programmes indicate that the corporation is active in every aspect of Gouldson and Murphy's list of corporate responses to environmental challenges from which companies can become more competitive (Gouldson and Murphy, 1998).

SUMMARY OF CORPORATE ENVIRONMENTAL MANAGEMENT STRUCTURES

Most companies, especially North American and Asian corporations, have set in place environmental programmes. While some corporations cover many issues, others do not have any company-wide programmes. Corporations focus on issues with high costs and liabilities. This explains the high proportion of corporations with programmes in accident prevention, waste reduction and energy conservation. It also explains the North American corporations' response to their regulatory climate at home. Furthermore, the companies deal with 'traditional environmental areas' like air, water and soil degradation, while sustainable development programmes are given little attention. Around 50 per cent of the companies are active in any of the 13 developing country areas, and a small number of these have developing country programmes. Thus, it can be said that corporate action in developing country issues is minimal. Even with the great publicity around global environmental change issues, few corporations have developed programmes to tackle this area.

In developing useful solutions to environmentally degrading processes of corporations, it is important to remember that only a handful of corporations have begun integrating environmental and economic aims in a meaningful way. The majority of corporations still respond only to environmental regulations, and a number of corporations break environmental codes repeatedly. Although some corporate 'greening' of corporate management structures does seem to be taking place, it can be a slow process.

Redclift would see the process by which corporations define and implement managerial responses to environmental challenges as illustrative of the way 'capitalist development makes use of the environment' (1994, p126). This argument is also along the lines of ecological modernization as a technocratic project. According to Redclift, viewing the environment as a 'problem' to be solved is doomed to failure for five major reasons:

- corporations consider the environment *after* the 'development' objectives have been set (it is prescriptive and reactive);
- environmental consequences are separated from social and economic imperatives when ecological objectives usually imply social ones;
- environmental management can be an important means of social control, that is *who* is to 'manage' the environment?;
- corporations take as a given social and environmental inequality produced as part of capitalist development and 'compensates' damage as needed; and
- environmental managerialism can deflect attention away from the social causes of environmental degradation; Blaikie (1984) argues that the environmental context and not disadvantaged people are the starting point in environmental managerialism (italics in original, Redclift, 1994, pp133–134).

It has been shown that corporate structures that respond to environmental challenges tend to be based on a 'problem solving' approach rather than on an understanding of the structural and social causes of environmental degradation.[18] This becomes a particular concern when there is a great deal of uncertainty about what constitutes environmental problems. That is, they can be seen as social constructs (Cutter, 1993; Yearley, 1996). Even if 'environmental impact studies' are conducted, they may be invalid because the impact is unknown. As Avery and others argue:

> *'the practice of "science" can be subject to the influence of social and political factors. Techniques such as risk assessment are heavily laden with value judgements: there are no internationally agreed criteria for assessing the relative importance of risks or benefits relating to the environment, public health, workers' rights and animal welfare'* (Avery et al, 1993, p111).[19]

As suggested above, Redclift's analysis illustrates ecological modernization as a technocratic project in that he stresses the problems of managerialism in the way in which corporations 'make use' of the environment. However, ecological modernization is more complex than this; the research suggests that the process of ecological modernization is an uneven one. Some corporations are geared towards compliance with the law, while others are geared towards preventing pollution. The most progressive corporate environmental management practices cannot be explained very well by ecological modernization as a technocratic project. This is where the concepts of institutional learning and cultural politics can be useful. The next section presents a fourfold typology of corporate management styles in response to environmental challenges, and attempts to understand the unevenness of such corporate management responses.

CORPORATE ENVIRONMENTAL MANAGEMENT STYLES

Guided by the *UN Survey* data and organizational and management literature, the research reported in this book thus far suggests that at present, four different corporate environmental management styles are evident in corporations. In this section, a typology of management styles is created based on an examination of their environmental management structures. Each type is also considered in terms of a 'green spectrum analysis', which rates the styles on the degree of their environmental progressiveness (see also Robbins, 1996). The 'green spectrum' ranges from 'brown' to 'light green' to 'green' to 'dark green' styles. The 'compliance style' is placed at the least environmental ('brown') end of the spectrum, followed by 'preventive style' ('light green'), 'strategic style' ('green') and 'sustainable' ('dark green') style.[20] This typology begins to elucidate the different environmental management strategies which exist in corporations and which can have important implications for public discourse on the role of corporations in the 'sustainability' debate.

Table 3.5 outlines the major corporate management styles, activities, reasons for responding to environmental challenges and green spectrum ratings. The analysis of the management styles, including the rationale for why each style responds to environmental issues, and the green spectrum rating, should be seen as suggestive rather than prescriptive. Ultimately, they serve as good models to compare with future cases and those examined in the following two chapters.

Compliance oriented management

The first management style, compliance oriented, is the least progressive of the four and represents the ways in which corporations have traditionally responded to environmental challenges. The reason for responding to environmental challenges in this case is primarily to comply with environmental legislation and litigation. I have labelled

Table 3.5 *Corporate EH&S management styles and response to environmental challenges*[21]

Management style	Corporate activities	Reason for response to environmental challenges
I. Compliance	End of pipe, abatement, compliance, response	Comply with legislation and litigation [brown]
II. Preventive	Audits, prevention, minimization, information, conservation, accounting	Maintain and protect markets [light green]
III. Strategic	Dialogue, audits, disclosure, planning, cradle to grave, R&D, targets	Anticipate or pursue green markets [green]
IV. 'Sustainable Development'	Developing country, ethical sales, climate change, afforestation, global policies and auditing	Create a 'sustainable corporation?' [dark green]

Source: Adapted from *UN Survey*, 1993, p155

this style 'brown', in terms of a green spectrum analysis, as it represents business merely reacting to environmental law.

Two examples of this style are food corporations. Borden Inc, a US based food and chemical company, exemplifies a compliance style. Their policy suggests that corporate activities are geared towards: 'Complying with applicable environmental laws and regulations while generating internal initiatives, programmes and procedures that address the letter and spirit of those laws and regulations' (cited in *UN Survey*, 1993, p20).[22] Unilever plc,[23] a food corporation based in the UK, also represents a compliance orientation in its policy that includes the following:

- develop products and packaging that are environmentally acceptable;
- operate their factories in an environmentally responsible manner to ensure the health and safety of their employees and those people living within the vicinity of their operations;
- design, operate and maintain processes and plants so that they satisfy, at the minimum, all national and local environmental legislation;
- establish and maintain procedures for the environmental auditing, monitoring and control of their operations;
- establish and maintain close working relationships with all relevant government and local authority environmental agencies and third parties;

- together with central Unilever advisory services, continuously reassess operating processes with respect to their environmental effects; and
- ensure that all employees at every level and function are aware of their environmental responsibilities and that they are appropriately trained, motivated and involved (*UN Survey*, 1993, pp20–21).

The content of the two policies is geared primarily towards fulfilling legislative demands. Any innovative practices are geared to better compliance with environmental laws.

Preventive management

The second style goes beyond regulation compliance towards pollution prevention and reduction of the use of resources. This can be labelled a preventive management style. Companies that have this style react to growing waste disposal costs, raw materials or insurance costs. There are great capital savings to be had when they develop programmes to reduce liabilities and costs through pollution prevention. Corporations with a preventive management style also respond, in a preventive and protective fashion, to green trends such as potential shifts in environmental legislation and green consumerism. In this case, the reason for responding to environmental challenges is to maintain and protect markets. This management style is 'light green' because it goes beyond merely responding and complying with environmental legislation and treats the green challenge with a preventive strategy.

Some corporations with a preventive style highlight 'product stewardship'. Waste Management International is an interesting example. Its policy focuses on the prevention of pollution and updating practices with changes in environmental science. Waste Management maintains that all companies have a responsibility to conduct business in an environmentally responsible manner, and that they should not compromise the environment for future generations. Of course, its abysmal environmental record contradicts these policies.[24] Another, less contentious, example of a preventive style is that of ARCO Chemical, examined in the next chapter. Its overall strategy is based on the prevention of industrial accidents and pollution.

The majority of companies that responded to the *UN Survey* were characteristic of the preventive management style. These companies anticipate and prevent costs and liabilities through EH&S management styles or innovative production processes and products. Between 60 and 80 per cent of these corporations have EH&S programmes which deal with issues such as waste reduction, energy conservation and accident prevention, costs saving areas. An example of this is Chevron's SMART programme which stands for 'Save Money and Reduce Toxics', which has reduced hazardous waste by 60 per cent and saved the firm over US$10 million in waste disposal costs over a three year period.[25] Toyota, commonly seen as pursuing a 'sustainable' management style, also established a wastewater minimization programme that reclaims more than 98 per cent of the water used in its manufacturing processes (cited in *UN Survey*, 1993).[26]

Within the preventive management style, managers are kept informed of EH&S issues with the aim of preventing accidents and liabilities. The processes which ensure this include auditing and assessment of risks and hazards. Around two-thirds of the corporations in the *UN Survey* have hazards assessment procedures in place or carry out environment and safety audits. Some companies have developed sophisticated methods for auditing EH&S issues. New informational technologies also can measure and quantify environmental impacts. Environmental accounting is used as an important method for calculating abatement and clean-up costs of a given product. About one-third of the survey respondents claimed that they had environmental accounting procedures in place (*UN Survey*, 1993).

Strategic environmental management

The third style incorporates EH&S aims into the overall economic strategy of the corporation and seeks to exploit the growing green market. This can be termed a strategic environmental management style. It goes beyond environmental audits and accounting, and moves towards cradle to grave analyses, environmental research and development and other environmental aims and objectives. The management style responds to environmental challenges for strategic reasons by anticipating or pursuing potential green markets. This style is 'green' because it responds to environmental challenges in a more proactive fashion than the previous two styles, and because it is strategic but not at the level of corporate environmental leadership evidenced in the policies of the 'dark green' group.

Many of the Japanese respondents are characterized as having strategic environmental management strategies (interview with UNCTC Environmental Lawyer, New York, 9 March 1993; interview with UNCTC Environmental Officer, 9 March 1993). The highest placed managers within a corporation coordinate this type of environmental management strategy. The corporate areas of top management, strategic planning and market research are active in Japanese corporations in creating environmental programmes.

Japanese corporations are also more likely to have environmental research and development than other regions. Environmental research and development in products and processes is an example of companies attempting to proactively pursue green markets. Furthermore, the decentralized, flexible, task-based organizational set-up of many Japanese firms helps them to respond to the environmental challenge proactively.

An additional component of a strategic style is a 'cradle to grave' ethos in which environmental and resource issues are part of all stages of a product's life cycle. In many cases this can be part of a total quality management (TQM) strategy which most of the companies already have in place. Some major corporations, such as Xerox and Volvo, have put into place cradle to grave or life cycle policies (Shrivastava, 1996).

Companies which have a strategic EH&S management style actively employ public relations to buttress their public image, to engage with consumers, investors and politicians who are sensitive to the environmental activities of corporations. Environmental disasters can lead to problems with regulators and consumer protest, and can damage the morale of the workforce as well as affect recruitment. A successful environmental public relations strategy can establish the company within a 'green' market niche.[27]

The pioneer of the strategic targeting of environmental concerns was the Minnesota Mining and Manufacturing (3M) company, which developed the corporate philosophy 'pollution prevention pays' (3P) (Hajer, 1995).[28] Amoco Corporation, the US based oil and chemical corporation, states that 'environmental leadership produces business leadership'. This is a clear expression of the integration of economic and environmental concerns. The Canadian construction corporation, Noranda, argues that 'a change in corporate culture would be necessary to face the environmental challenge of the 1990s and the 21st century' (*UN Survey*, 1993, p14). Pennzoil, the US based energy corporation, also uses an integrated approach when it publicly commits to considering financial and environmental criteria equally when assessing managers' performance. Furthermore, the company also pledges to set aside resources to meet environmental objectives.

Many companies are also beginning to see the environment as an economic opportunity. Imperial Chemical Industries (ICI) maintains that:

> '*by stepping up environmental protection and minimizing environmental consequences of operations, a company also stands to gain a* significant comparative edge ... *We*

> *must recognize the fact that our work is also judged on the basis of its impact on Nature ... A satisfactory environmental performance is* fundamental *to a successful business strategy'* (emphasis added, *UN Survey*, 1993, p15).[29]

Chevron Corporation, a US based energy corporation, is also considering the environmental challenge proactively. They:

> *'seek opportunities to participate in the formulation of safety, fire, health and environmental legislation, regulation or policy issues that may significantly impact our business. Work actively with the appropriate government agencies to ensure timely, reasonable and cost effective solutions for issues whenever possible'* (*UN Survey*, 1993, p15).

However, for Chevron, as suggested in the ICI case above and in the endnotes, these opportunities may be pursued in developed countries but not in developing countries.[30]

Strategic management goes beyond more efficient production and liability minimization to include targeting the environment specifically.[31] Such firms seek to enter the market for environmental services and equipment, and see the environment as an opportunity. Notably, Amoco, ICI and Noranda have all indicated in their policies the benefits of linking environmental and economic considerations.[32]

Sustainable development management

The most proactive management style is 'sustainable development' management. Only a few corporations may be at this stage and have established developing country programmes and global commons programmes. I put 'sustainable development' in quotes because it is unlikely that any corporation could be truly 'sustainable'. However, I use 'sustainable development' in the sense that the United Nations uses it, that is environmental activities which are usually geared towards global environmental issues or developing country issues, even though some might argue that they are only 'technical fixes'. This management style is also represented by some of the social-environmental corporations examined in Chapter 5, as well as more progressive companies like Toyota, Volvo and Shell. These corporations have developing country policies, 'ethical' sales policies, a commitment to environmental disclosure, and climate change and afforestation policies. In addition, they have a global vision of policies and auditing practices, which is rare among corporations now. The reason for responding to environmental challenges in this case can be seen as the possible desire to create a sustainable corporation. This management style is 'dark green', because this group of corporations is treating environmental challenges in the most proactive fashion of all corporations.

Corporations with a sustainable development management style indicate corporate aims to take a 'leadership role' in the response to environmental challenges. Corporations with this style are notable both in their efforts to be leaders in their industries regarding responses to environmental challenges, and also in their objective to implement global programmes and practices, which, as the results of the *UN Survey* suggest, are carried out by only a handful of corporations.

Two examples are Toyota and Volvo. Interestingly, these corporations reflect the data presented thus far that some corporations in the most environmentally challenged industries tend to be more active in progressive environmental management practices. Both of these corporations are vehicle manufacturers, involved in possibly the most environmentally degrading industry if road building, air, land and sea emissions, resource exploitation, refining, vehicle manufacturing and disposal are included in its environmental impact. Both Toyota and Volvo are well known for their innovative environmental practices, detailed in the endnotes.

Toyota Motor Corporation, based in Japan, has an approach that reflects the idea of continuous improvement associated with incremental environmental innovations. The aim of becoming an environmental leader, thus having the ultimate goal of radical environmental innovation, must be supported by small successes (or *kaizen*, 'small steps'). Toyota's policy exemplifies this and maintains that:

> 'although we are at the forefront in environmental activities, we are not satisfied with the present state of affairs. We will continue to search for new ways to take the protection of the environment to ever higher levels... Our basic principle in environmental management is to emit no pollutants...[and] ...create plants that are environmentally sound, with due regard for the greater good of the community' (UN Survey, 1993, p15).[33]

Volvo AB, the Swedish automotive corporation, in its 'Group Environmental Policy', also illustrates the aim to become a 'corporate leader' through a management plan based on TQM, a similar management plan to continuous improvement noted above:

- develop products and market products with superior environmental properties that will meet highest efficiency requirements;
- opt for manufacturing processes that have the least possible impact on the environment;
- participate actively in, and conduct our own research in the environment field;
- select environmentally compatible and recyclable material in connection with the development and manufacture of our products and when we purchase components from our suppliers;
- apply a total view regarding the adverse impact of our products on the environment; and
- strive to attain a uniform, worldwide environmental standard for processes and products (*UN Survey*, 1993, p16).[34]

Volvo's policy is notable for its closer link to the recommended environmental management system. Specifically, it suggests an attempt to implement the policy throughout the organization, including adopting worldwide standards, and extending its policy to its relationships with its suppliers.

Both these policies indicate that the corporations see themselves as not merely being proactive in environmental issues, but actually being leaders in the area. In particular, the policy of Toyota to emit no pollutants is notable given the managerial systems of many corporations which are at less developed stages of environmental management. Furthermore, Volvo's attempt to standardize environmental aspects of its operations worldwide seems that much more progressive given that many respondents to the *UN Survey* indicated that corporate headquarters are not always aware of the environmental aspects of operations in their developing country subsidiaries.

A further example of a corporation with aspects of sustainable development management is Shell.[35] In 1990, the corporation began to develop responses to the sustainable development challenge when Shell Canada put forward its 'Sustainable Development Policy' in place of the previous 'Environmental Policy' which had been established in 1969. In 1997, Shell revised its existing policy to include aspects of social justice along with sustainable development (Cowe, 1997). The company claims that the new policy advocates the integration of environmental and economic decision making. Specifically, the CEO has indicated that while there is scientific uncertainty about climate change, there is enough data to suggest that precautionary measures are warranted. This suggests a move towards the precautionary principle[36] in the sense of aiming for 'thoughtful action in advance of scientific proof'.[37]

Many corporations with sustainable development management styles would aim to be particularly proactive in environmental aspects of developing country operations. Agenda 21, the policy document which came out of the 1992 UN Conference on Environment and Development (UNCED), was the subject of intense lobbying by corporations. Many large corporations were involved in UNCED; many of the corporations already mentioned were especially influential (*UN Survey*, 1993). Corporations were advised to adopt global standards, take into account the challenges of developing countries and develop policies to tackle the unique problems faced by people in poorer countries. This would include developing special worker and management training programmes for developing country operations, company standards in countries which lack sufficient or enforced regulations, facilitating the transfer of useful technology, and taking into account local communities and cultures. These are some of the things corporations with a sustainable management style can attempt to carry out.

SUMMARY OF CORPORATE ENVIRONMENTAL MANAGEMENT STYLES

It is important to note that this is an analysis of present corporate environmental management styles. Greener corporate management styles are being conceptualized (see Welford, 1994; cf Toffler, 1980, Chapter 18). Another survey of corporate environmental reporting which uses a five stage model of corporate greening (from least environmentally active to most environmentally active) indicated that 39 per cent of companies are at Stages 1 or 2, 25 per cent are at Stage 3, 11 per cent are 'making the transition' to Stage 4, and only 5 per cent are actually at Stage 4. Stage 5, the most environmentally active stage, 'remains largely unexplored territory' (see UNEPIE and SustainAbility, 1994). An emerging trend for corporations is to have mission statements that attempt to integrate some form of ethical and/or environmental action in their operations. Regardless of some of the contradictions inherent in corporations and environmental action, the typology is useful as a way of understanding where corporations are in terms of their engagement with environmental challenges, and where it may be possible for some of them to go. It also illustrates the extent to which some management styles illustrate a convergence of economic and environmental aims.

Economic and environmental aims may be successfully integrated in many ways; however, shareholder value can supersede environmental stewardship. Until more effective government controls exist which can integrate environmental and economic objectives with market instruments, such as tradable rights to pollute, alongside more basic command and control policies, which operate across national borders, there may be examples of corporate environmental management contradictions. In any balanced analysis of corporate greening, neither the failures nor the successes of corporate responses to environmental challenges can be ignored. This argument is taken up in more detail in Chapter 6.

CONCLUSION

The preliminary conclusion from an examination of corporate management structures in response to environmental challenges is that corporations generally focus their attentions on areas that most directly affect the growth of the corporation. The data support the notion that the largest corporations are the most environmentally active due to their superior managerial resources and financial capital (Ashford, 1993). The most environmentally intensive industries have most to gain from making environmental improvements, first from the standpoint of making their operations more environmentally, hence economically, efficient. Second, public perceptions of such industries warrant joint ventures and other forms of cooperation (reducing strategic uncertainty) around developing more environmentally sound alternatives; the chemical industry's Responsible Care is an example of this. Very large corporations can also pool their resources to develop new environmental management practices, which benefits them by creating a 'level playing field' that reduces 'unfair advantages' in competition. The data also lend some support to the success of the North American command and control style of regulation. While this strategy has produced some antipathy between regulators and business that does not exist in most European settings, command and control has developed a more systematic approach to corporate pollution. This includes the development of environmental impact assessment models and corporate policies and programmes designed to incorporate them into corporate activities.

Management structures in response to environmental challenges are therefore designed, in the majority of cases, to ensure compliance with environmental regulations in areas where it is likely that corporations could face massive fines if they are caught polluting. From the perspective of ecological modernization as a technocratic project, corporate management responses to environmental challenges are consistent with the environmental managerialist paradigm that is 'problem focused', heavily prescriptive and reactive, and tends to deal with the environment as a problem to be solved after financial and other issues have been addressed. Addressing environmental problems through environmental management structures, such as 'impact studies', does not necessarily mean that environmental problems are alleviated because the impact of a number of industrial activities is still unknown. Furthermore, management structures such as impact studies can be based on an ideal type 'environment' that does not take into account the fact that it has already been managed (Redclift, 1987, 1994).

In international operations, corporations tend to have elaborate structures for dealing with environmental issues in areas where they are highly regulated. In developing countries, where environmental frameworks are either non-existent or not enforced, corporations tend not to direct their attention towards developing 'environmentally sound' activities. This is not to say that all corporations do not actively exploit developing country 'pollution havens' (there are many cases in which this occurs).[38] It appears to be more a case of the absence of controls on corporations which can lead them to neglect developing country environmental issues. This is enhanced by a decentralized, 'M-form' organizational structure in which risks and therefore responsibilities are diversified, with ultimate responsibility held by the board of directors (Reed, 1992).

Although the aforementioned is true of many corporations, not all corporations are the same. Four management styles can be distinguished, based on: compliance, prevention, strategy and 'sustainability'. The largest corporations have the financial and managerial resources to be at the forefront of many aspects of environmental management. It is evident in these cases that some institutional learning around environmental issues has taken place, even if it is mainly in the richer countries of the world. Some of the more advanced corporations in terms of environmental management help to reframe debates about environment and development, in line with some arguments about the value of ecological modernization as cultural politics.

An analysis of corporate culture, whether traditional or 'social-environmental' is also valuable in understanding corporate greening. Chapters 4 and 5 consider the fourfold typology generated in this chapter in relation to four case studies of corporations: ARCO, Ben & Jerry's, The Body Shop and Shell, to understand their particular corporate environmental management strategies and to see whether understanding their different corporate cultures is useful in assessing corporate management responses to environmental challenges.

An Analysis of Two Corporations with a Traditional Corporate Culture

INTRODUCTION

This chapter examines two corporations with a traditional corporate culture, Atlantic Richfield Corporation Chemical Company (ARCO) and the Royal Dutch/Shell Group of Companies (Shell), and their responses to environmental crises. For the purposes of this book, corporations with traditional cultures are mainly concerned with the traditional business activities of providing a return to their shareholders, maximizing profits, and some 'corporate philanthropy', which directs typically around 1 per cent of pre-tax profits towards charitable ventures. To maximize returns, traditional corporations prevent pollution as a way to save money and to avoid costly fines. Large traditional corporations also develop environmental technologies, which are increasingly lucrative. In other words, the environment becomes another level of 'traditional' business management. ARCO and Shell have a dominant role culture, which is defined by their attributes as being large mature corporations within the extractive industrial sector.

ARCO CHEMICAL COMPANY

The first example of a traditional corporation is ARCO Chemical Company. Its parent company is a petroleum corporation based in Los Angeles, California. In 1994, it was ranked 16th in petroleum, 214th in the Global 500, and number 53 in the US. The company had US$17.2 billion in annual sales. In 1995, the company had slipped in its US rank to number 54 with US$16.7 billion in annual sales. By 2000, its global rank was 373 (136 in the US), having achieved US$13.1 billion annual sales in 1999. ARCO Chemical Company is one of the main divisions of the corporation, with its headquarters in Newton Square, Pennsylvania. ARCO Chemical operates regionally, in the Americas, Europe and Asia Pacific, and is the largest producer in the world of propylene oxide (PO). Two main by-products of the process that synthesizes PO, are tertiary butyl alcohol (TBA), which is a high octane fuel component, and styrene monomer, which is a basic component of the rubber and plastics industry. The styrene monomer has widespread household and automotive applications, including furniture cushions, car bumpers, cosmetics, paints and engine coolants.

ARCO Chemical Company Europe is based in Maidenhead outside London; it manufactures PO/TBA at Botlek in the Netherlands and Fos-sur-Mer on the Mediterranean coast of France. It also manufactures polyols at Rieme, Belgium, as well as at Fos-sur-Mer. The company has a European Technical Centre at Villers St Paul, outside Paris, which executes applications research and is responsible for customer technical services and plant operations support.

In this case, I shall argue that ARCO's corporate culture, in response to environmental crises, is based on safety, which prevents accidents. An initial example of the culture of safety at ARCO is that unlike other corporations that have departments of 'environment, health and safety', its department is called 'safety, health and the environment' (SHE). Thus, by focusing on safety, this preserves health, and minimizes environmental problems.

A public relations staff member at ARCO Chemical Europe articulated the reason for this in an interview on 20 December 1994.[1] The chemical industry, he conceded, in recent years has begun to suffer from terrible public relations. In the 1960s, public support of the chemical industry was anywhere between 70 and 80 per cent. This support fell substantially, until, in the 1990s, polls indicated that only 20–30 per cent of the public 'trusted' the chemical industry. This, it was argued, is in large part due to well-publicized disasters such as those at Seveso,[2] Basel[3] and Bhopal.[4] Chemicals can be dangerous, cause health problems and pollute the environment.

One of the ways in which the chemical industry has responded to its image problem is through the Chemical Industries' Responsible Care Programme, to which ARCO Chemical belongs. Responsible Care aims to 'restore the image of the industry through fostering communication and "best practice" amongst its members' (interview with ARCO Chemical-Europe public relations staff member, 20

December 1994). Thus, Responsible Care has the benefits of a strategic alliance in sharing information that could result in a state of reduced competition, that is, 'creating a level playing field', learning from the competition, managing strategic uncertainty and sharing risks (Kogut, 1988; Hennart, 1988). Members of Responsible Care ascribe to the Programme's Guiding Principles, notably commitments among members to the safe manufacture, transport, use and disposal of chemicals. In addition, they are committed to educate and inform the community, employees, officials, customers and the public about the hazards of their products, and their safety measures.

To most large chemical companies, accidents are events that they cannot afford; this is why corporate managers endeavour to develop a culture of safety. Their business depends on government, consumers and the public having confidence in them. As the ARCO Chemical representative said: 'The chemical industry views itself as earning the respect of the public; nothing is for sure'. Moreover, the chemical industry perceives that the steel industry is much more environmentally damaging than the chemical industry; however, it has a much more benign public image. Companies like ARCO Chemical rarely have serious accidents, but when they do, they are usually explosive, and workers can get hurt and even killed. In 1991, ARCO Chemical experienced a serious plant explosion at its factory in Channelview, Texas, and as a result, the company had to pay around US$4 million in fines and penalties in the US (ARCO, 1996, p22). The executive from ARCO Chemical independently mentioned this event and indicated that it had a significant effect on the SHE concerns of the company. He said that the event had concerned the company because of the huge amount of media attention it had drawn. He argued that the accident, like many accidents at chemical companies, was the result of human error at operating levels.

The obsession with safety was related in a reference to Du Pont, seen within the chemical industry as the standard bearer of best environmental practice. The lengths to which Du Pont go in order to ensure 'safety' include that 'all employees, management and workers must hold the handrail going up and down staircases at company headquarters, otherwise they can be disciplined' and 'if a supervisor sees you jaywalking outside of work, you can be disciplined' (interview with ARCO Chemical-Europe public relations staff member, 20 December 1994). Thus, the aims of environmental health and safety management systems are to 'reduce the risk of human error and the risk of mechanical failure'. Furthermore, all employees' understanding of safety should be both conscious and unconscious to the extent that Du Pont expects this safety standard to be practised both on and off the job. This diverges from Weber's ideal type that includes a separation of work and home life.

The key management ethos in ARCO Chemical Europe, which drives environmental action and corporate improvement in all areas of business, is flexible and based on the ethic of continuous improvement. Its incarnation at ARCO is called Achieving Excellence, defined as 'a process of continuous improvement in all aspects of our business'. The rationale for Achieving Excellence is that 'we believe these steps will lead to continued superior returns for our stockholders' (ARCO Chemical Europe, 1994b, p5). Thus, Achieving Excellence is the path towards greater shareholder value. Achieving excellence in all aspects of business includes the areas of product quality, customer service, entering new markets such as China[5] and the Russian Federation, product development, technology, manufacturing, and environmental health and safety issues, with the aim of 'building value for shareholders, customers, employees and the public' (ARCO Chemical Europe, 1994b, p6). Under the Manufacturing Excellence programme, at ARCO Chemical Europe recordable injuries were down 55 per cent between 1991 and the end of 1993.

Environmental policy[6]

ARCO Chemical Company's SHE policy is as follows:

> *ARCO Chemical Company's policy is to manage worldwide operations in a manner that protects the environment and health and safety of employees, customers, contractors and the public. To accomplish this, we:*
>
> - *comply with laws and regulations pertaining to safety, health, and environmental issues in all Company activities as a minimum standard;*
> - *emphasize the priority of safety, health and environmental factors where there is competition with other business issues;*
> - *define the responsibility of each employee and hold each accountable for safety, health and environmental performance;*
> - *audit and measure managers and supervisors for safety, health and environmental performance; evaluate and report total company performance;*
> - *design facilities and manage operations to minimize environmental, human health, physical risks and impacts to workers and neighbouring communities;*

- *provide professional staff to support and continuously improve safety, health and environmental programmes;*
- *educate employees and neighbouring communities in safety, health and environmental requirements and potential hazards;*
- *participate in programmes designed to enhance knowledge and improve technology, laws and regulations (ARCO Chemical Europe, 1994, Appendix 2).*

The first point of the environmental policy is a 'compliance and safety' statement as characterized by the compliance management style delineated in the last chapter. The whole eight part policy also has features of more advanced management styles especially in their notion of technology as being important to responses to environmental crises. This suggests a move from control to clean technologies in the fifth and eighth point. Additionally, the focus on incremental innovation through continuous improvement (see point six) also suggests a more advanced management style, such as the strategic management style, as well as the importance of all employees' responsibilities to safety and environmental issues, and the company's commitment to reporting and dialogue. The policy does not go as far as to suggest that the company is strategically targeting safety and environmental issues. It is most geared towards a 'prevention' management style, in that the key feature is safety in order to prevent accidents and minimize human error. In fact, most points of the environmental policy suggest a 'prevention' management style in their focus on continuous improvement in order to prevent accidents. Including the development of technologies and the inclusion of all employees is the sign of more advanced environmental practice, but at this point is geared mostly to the prevention of accidents.

ARCO Chemical Europe's head of SHE, as well as the company's SHE managers, are responsible for monitoring changes to legislation, and to ensure compliance with environmental regulations. The company meets with regulators through the national chemical industry association in each country in which it manufactures and sells products. Within the European Union, CEFIC (*Conseil Européen des Federations de l'Industrie Chimique*) represents the chemical industry. CEFIC is based in Brussels and includes the 15 national chemical federations within Europe, as well as the largest chemical companies, like ARCO Chemical Europe. CEFIC is responsible for representing an industry that employs 2 million and constitutes 30 per cent of global chemical production.

The company, as evidenced in its policy, aims to 'go far beyond compliance with the law'; the aim of this is to anticipate regulatory changes rather than an interest in being environmentally strategic. ARCO Chemical sets standards in anticipation of more stringent regulations, it continuously brings in outside consultants who audit the firm's operations and make recommendations for changes. Based on these audits the company aims to remain well ahead of changing regulations.

The prevention of pollution is implied in its environmental reports, suggesting that the corporation is geared towards waste reduction. Since 1981, it has reduced its generation of hazardous wastes by 70 per cent around the world, ahead of the industry average of 20 per cent. Waste minimization is an important part of this process. The company also anticipates additional waste handling and disposal costs; 'the freedom to move waste across national borders is rapidly being curtailed' (ARCO Chemical Europe, 1994b, p8). The company has also generated a waste neutral policy, which means that 'any new facilities we install should not add to the total waste generated at that location' (ARCO Chemical Europe, 1994b, p11). The other relevant policy geared towards the move from control to clean technologies is 'designing out waste' which aims to make plants more efficient, including reuse and recycling of materials. Corporate programmes to reduce waste have been successful at the company's Rieme plant in Belgium because of the continuous improvement in reducing waste programme; the waste to production ratio fell by 48 per cent in two years. Between 1986 and 1990, energy use per ton also was reduced by 9 per cent. Waste reduction at the company is carried out through two related programmes: the Air Quality Improvement Programme (AQIP) and the Waste Minimization Programme (WMP). Because of these programmes, air emissions fell by 85 per cent from 1986 to 1991, and liquid and solid waste were reduced by 40 per cent (ARCO Chemical Europe, 1994a).

Air emissions can be classified as either point source or fugitive. Point source emissions occur with the manufacturing process and are therefore easier to control; fugitive emissions occur as the results of leaks. Clean technologies have been pursued through the improvement of the design of ARCO Chemical's European plants, which recompress and route emissions to heat generators. This has resulted in the reduction of point source emissions at European plants of over 95 per cent between 1986 and 1991.[7]

Fugitive emissions are more difficult to control. The Fos plant in France has more than 20,000 possible leakage points through, for example, valves and pipe connections or through pump or compressor shafts. The process of dealing with such leaks is to identify leak points, then establish a systematic method of inspecting, measuring and monitoring the area.

Some of the liquid and solid wastes from ARCO Chemical Europe include solvents, used catalyst, filter cake, product test samples and building materials such as scrap metal, paper and plastics. More efficient monitoring, cleanup and equipment design can lessen some of these waste emissions. Some spent catalyst can be reused where previously it would have entered the waste stream. Foam samples that are used in testing at the Technical Centre are now sold to be used for packing. Materials that cannot be reused or recycled are incinerated on the site or at a company that specializes in incinerating these wastes.

Through the incineration process at the site, 54 per cent of the plant's energy requirements are met. Other non-flammable and non-hazardous solid waste that cannot be recycled is sent to landfill sites. Waste leaving the sites is monitored and registered by employees at the plant and is approved by regulatory officials. The company aims to ensure that the waste is also properly dealt with at its final destination.

The two types of wastewater that ARCO Chemical produces are process water and cooling water. Process water is a result of the manufacturing process and contains by-products of this procedure. At the Fos and Botlek plants, process water is sent through a biological treatment plant. Bacteria are used to consume the organic component of the wastewater. The result is a non-hazardous sludge that is sent to an approved landfill.

The treated water is assessed before being fed into rivers or the sea. The company monitors the pH level, the chemical oxygen demand (COD), the total oxygen content (TOC) and the temperature. The COD level of the water is an international measurement of water pollution: the higher the COD, the more contaminated is the water. If the wastewater from the company's plants were untreated the COD could be as high as 7000 parts per million (ppm). After the water is treated, the level can fall to about 150 ppm, which is a level compatible with aquatic life.

Cooling water is employed to reduce heat produced during chemical reactions in the manufacturing process. The water is drawn from an approved source and filtered before being used. Then it is reused as much as possible before being treated and piped into rivers or the sea. Other water issues on plant sites include rainwater, which is sent through a separate drainage system to prevent contamination from industrial waste. If rainwater is contaminated, it is sent through the bioplant before being sent back into the environment.

The head of SHE monitors environmental programmes in the company's European operations and reports to headquarters in the US. The head chairs two committees; the first is made up of senior managers and formulates the company's environmental policy for Europe, and adapts the company's worldwide policies to the European operations. The second committee is made up of representatives from each of the European sites and deals with coordination and implementation of the policies.

Each of the three plants in Europe and the Technical Centre have a full-time environment health and safety manager who monitors and improves performance in this area. The managers aim to surpass applicable environmental law. They also need to be aware of local public opinion, customer satisfaction and the company's products and technologies. In addition to the SHE plant manager, there is also a SHE office manager at each of the European sites.

The vice-president of operations and supply who reviews SHE as well as other matters also visits each of the European plants monthly. On a daily basis plant managers monitor environmental and safety issues as a normal part of their work. Furthermore, all employees, whether at director or manufacturing level are expected to integrate safety and environmental aspects into their work as an essential part of what they do. The company welcomes employee suggestions to improve SHE performance. SHE training is also continuous and integrated with other SHE matters. Corporate executives feel that they have a responsibility to the surrounding community. ARCO Chemical has been involved in a number of landscaping and environmental improvement projects with community groups. Noise levels were reduced at the Rotterdam plant in response to local concerns. In line with the Seveso Directive, developed because of the Seveso disaster (see endnotes), the company produces information packs and holds community meetings to educate the public about the operations of the plant. They include information on the chemicals manufactured, how they are manufactured and disposed of, and how the manufacturing process is engaged in the process of grounding out safety through continuous improvement (interview with ARCO Chemical Europe public relations staff member, 20 December 1994).

'Grounding out' safety refers to the process of reducing the potential for accidents at the plants. 'Grounding out' safety involves the evaluation of 'near misses', worker training, meetings with workers about their views of the safety of the work that they do, and similar activities linked with continuous improvement and incremental innovation. ARCO Chemical Europe meets the standards of US federal law in Europe by reporting annually to the public the amount of hazardous chemicals that they release into the air, land and water, as well as those that are disposed offsite. The company also reports these data to the national authorities in the European countries in which it operates.

The manufactured products as well as the raw materials that the company uses are flammable. Some of the substances are also corrosive or toxic and others can cause skin or eye injuries. Safety and environmental protection in the majority of cases are interlinked. In the cases where there is a direct threat to human life, safety issues take priority over environmental issues. The company's aim is to prevent rather than solve environmental problems, similar to the 3M Corporation's 3P management philosophy, 'pollution prevention pays'. Equipment is designed with potential risks in mind, and these are 'designed out' wherever possible (interview with ARCO Chemical-Europe public relations staff member, 20 December 1994). Remaining potential risks are dealt with through training.

ARCO Chemical Europe uses hazard operability studies (HAZOPS) to identify safety problems when designing plants. Studies have shown that pipes into and out of holding tanks which are located at the top rather than the bottom are safer, and that earth banks and concrete walls can ensure additional safety in some cases. These have been implemented at the Fos plant. Safety devices are also particularly stringent for loading and unloading chemicals, which is a high risk activity in terms of SHE. There are also plant-wide sprinkler systems and toxic vapour detectors to reduce the potential for accidents.

Plant equipment is inspected and maintained regularly. Older equipment is retrofitted with control technologies as needed. Employees are expected to have a 'total safety' philosophy that aims to prevent any accident, however trivial. Workers must wear protective clothing and equipment and follow the company's safety procedures at all times. Safety training is ongoing. Employees are regularly tested on safety procedures and safety drills take place at least once a week. Meetings take place at least once per month in which supervisors, SHE officers and employees discuss safety issues.

The evaluation of incidents which do not result in damage or injury or potentially dangerous situations, 'near misses', was one area which the personnel staff member at ARCO Chemical Europe saw as being a very important part of the company's SHE management system, again indicative of the importance of incremental innovation at the corporation. Employees are encouraged to fill out report forms when such events occur. These have provided important information for improving safety. Near misses are estimated to be ten times more frequent than actual accidents and their analysis forms an important SHE management tool. Employees at the plants are encouraged to speak freely and are given anonymity in providing feedback, which facilitates this process. Even so, the company's safety record seems extraordinary. Between 1974 and 1979, the Botlek, Netherlands, plant achieved 1.5 million working hours without a lost time accident. In 20 years of the plant's operation, there was an average of only one lost time accident per year (ARCO Chemical Europe, 1992b).

Staff at all plants are trained in fire fighting and first aid, and plants at Fos and Rotterdam have their own fully equipped fire fighting teams. The company also informs local fire departments about the procedures for handling their products. Evacuation plans are in place at all offices, plants and laboratories. Under the Seveso Directive, the company has submitted to local authorities a report on the products that are manufactured, the process, its potential hazards, the risks to the surrounding communities and detailed emergency plans. Reports certify the safety measures in place. Plant locations vary greatly; Rotterdam and Fos are far removed from residential areas, while the Technical Centre at Villers St Paul and the polyols plant at Rieme are closer to local communities. Emergency plans reflect these different situations.

The company transports large amounts of hazardous products by road, rail, water and pipeline; this is undertaken by specialist carriers. Carriers are chosen based on their ability to meet the standards of ARCO Chemical Europe. Within the company, transportation pipelines, valves and couplings are systematically checked on a regular basis for leaks. Plants are designed to minimize the need to move hazardous materials.

ARCO Chemical is involved in producing clean technologies; it is the world's largest producer of methyl tertiary butyl ether (MTBE), a high octane lead replacement in petrol. The high oxygen content of MTBE allows for greater combustion in fuel hydrocarbons, and the oxidization of carbon monoxide to carbon dioxide. The production of reformulated petrol with MTBE, which ARCO invented, has been praised by one author as being 'a reason Los Angeles smog has declined by more than half since the first Earth Day [April 20, 1970] – even as the car population of Los Angeles nearly doubled' (Easterbrook, cited in ARCO, 1996).[8] Medical doctors also use MTBE to dissolve gallstones without surgery.

The company converts most of the propylene oxide that it produces into polyols, which are converted by foam-making companies into household furnishings like mattresses and carpet underlay. ARCO Chemical has worked with the foam-making companies to develop alternatives to CFCs as the main blowing agent to produce the foams. At present, they employ hydrochlorofluorocarbons (HCFCs), an arguably more benign CFC, with the aim of CFC-free foams. In the firm's specialized polyols for automotive products such as bumpers, it has developed a new blowing agent, a combination of air and recycled carbon dioxide. The problem of the removal of CFCs in rigid foams, like refrigerator insulation, has proved more difficult to solve. ARCO Chemical has removed 50 per cent of the CFCs in these foams, but greater reduction causes a loss of efficiency, since these chemicals contribute to the foam's insulating properties. Research continues in this area.

Environmental record

ARCO Chemical's environmental record, although largely accident free, is not perfect. From 1990 to 1994, the parent company, ARCO, paid almost US$8.3 million in fines and penalties to governmental agencies for code violations, emissions and failing to comply with regulations, The major portion of this figure was attributed to the fines and penalties resulting from the Channelview, Texas, explosion in 1991 (ARCO, 1996, p22). At the same time that ARCO Chemical is involved with preventing pollution, perhaps largely due to its Texas accident, it is also involved in funding environmentally dubious organizations. This points again to the unevenness and contradictory nature of the process of ecological modernization, that a corporation, which appears to outperform a number of its competitors in its responses to environmental crises, also funds organizations that seek to roll back the environmental agenda. ARCO Chemical, as well as its parent company, is involved in funding groups listed as 'anti-environmentalist organizations' in Greenpeace's guide on the subject (Deal, 1993; see also Rowell, 1996). ARCO funds four, and ARCO Chemical specifically funds two. The first of the two is the Alliance for a Responsible CFC Policy, which is also supported by Du Pont (once the largest producer of CFCs worldwide), Chemicals Manufacturers Association, Dow Chemical and General Electric. Greenpeace reports that:

> *'despite the "responsible" in its name, the Alliance's real goal is to slow down the timetable for phasing out CFCs. It has also won approval for the continued funding of dangerous alternatives to CFCs like hydrochlorofluoro-carbons (HCFCs) and hydrofluorocarbons (HFCs). HCFCs still cause ozone depletion, they simply do so at a slower rate than CFCs. And while HFCs don't deplete the*

ozone layer, they are potent greenhouse gases that contribute significantly to global warming. "The CFC industry has a track record of stalling in the face of mounting evidence that CFCs destroy the ozone layer," cautions Carolyn Hartmann, a lawyer with US Public Interest Research Group. "For 20 years, Du Pont and the CFC industry have vigorously fought against CFC regulations"' (Deal, 1993, p31).

The Alliance's PR, media and lobbying work continues to attempt to delay a complete CFC phase-out.

The other anti-environmentalist organization that ARCO Chemical funds is the Keep America Beautiful (KAB) campaign, 'the oldest and best known US anti-litter campaign' (Deal, 1993, p62). KAB is funded (US$2 million annually) by 200 companies, which manufacture and distribute aluminium cans, paper products, glass bottles and plastics (which account for around a third of the materials in US landfills), and two major American waste haulers, with environmentally challenged records. In addition to ARCO Chemical, other corporate sponsors include: Coca-Cola, McDonald's, Anheuser Busch, Dow Chemical, Du Pont, Georgia Pacific, RJR Nabisco, US Steel, Browning Ferris and Waste Management. It has been testified in legal proceedings that McDonald's was in the 'top 1 or 2 per cent' of litter producing companies in the UK in 1995 (Singh, 1995).

By encouraging consumers to 'Put Litter in Its Place' (the group's slogan) the group tacitly tells them that:

'they're the ones responsible for this trash and that they must solve the problem of litter by changing their habits. Never does KAB call on industry to produce less, recycle more or set higher pollution standards. In fact, KAB President Roger Powers once assured a group of "grassroots" affiliates that "industry will fund you if you respond to its needs"' (Deal, 1993, pp62–63).

Thus, like other large companies, ARCO Chemical is involved in some subversion of the environmental agenda through its support of anti-environmental groups. As noted above though, the company has a good record compared with other similar large chemical corporations.

SUMMARY: ARCO CHEMICAL COMPANY

The management approach which ARCO Chemical Europe is taking to environmental matters is centrally concerned with 'complying with the law' as evidenced in its environmental statement. The corporation is involved in monitoring, compliance reports, training and emergency response programmes, all the hallmarks of a 'compliance oriented' management strategy. However, it appears to move beyond a compliance oriented management strategy. ARCO Chemical Europe is engaged in internal audits, in preventing pollution and minimizing waste. It is actively involved in areas that are highly regulated in developed countries. This includes air, water and land contamination issues. In addition, 'waste minimization' and recycling, particularly regarding the issue of wastewater, is often the cheapest and most effective way for corporations to deal with environmental issues. Also, a 'top level commitment' to environmental issues usually reflects that a firm has more environmental programmes in place than one which does not (Booz-Allen and Hamilton, 1991), and environmental matters at ARCO Chemical Europe are handled by senior managers. This also relates to the literature on corporate culture, which suggests that top managers create 'strong cultures'. It is clear that a role culture has been developed with an emphasis on safety, since this is essential to the survival of the firm. Concomitant with continuous improvement around safety issues, it is likely that task cultures exist in corporate divisions responsible for improving economic and environmental performance, since flexibly responding to environmental crises, which occur because of unsafe practices, is paramount at ARCO Chemical. The company also appears to have much in common with many of its contemporaries in the extractive-based sector as discussed in the *UN Survey* data. The corporation provides information on plant emissions for the local population around its plants in Europe, complying with the Seveso Directive. It is engaged in energy conservation and accounts for the savings from environmental adjustments to its production process. This would suggest that 'Preventive management' ('light green') (Type II) represents the company's environmental management style.

In fact most of the environmental management which the company is engaged in seems to be geared mainly to complying with the law, but it also focuses on prevention. According to Anthony Cleaver, chair of IBM UK: 'In IBM I believe we make huge savings – I mean multiple millions of pounds – simply from energy efficiency measures' (Charter, 1994, p60). So, pollution prevention 'makes good business sense'. In line with ecological modernization as a technocratic managerial project, Bruno suggests that 'the business vision of this "new" path [of sustainability] still centres around economic growth, with free trade and open markets as prerequisites... business leaders envision linking environmental protection to profitability' (Bruno, 1992, p15). However, the ARCO Chemical's public relations manager, when agreeing to give an interview, said 'I have nothing to be ashamed of in the environmental actions of this company'. Indeed, in 1995, ARCO was among 12 nominees for the Council on Economic Priorities (CEP) 'Corporate Conscience Award' (Will, 1995, p4).[9]

ARCO Chemical's environmental record seems to be the product of institutional learning around environmental matters. This may have been led by the chemical industry's experience of the loss of shareholder value following accidents. Nevertheless, creating a culture around safety, 'designing out waste', the 'evaluation of near misses' and 'continuous improvement' all seem to be part of a process of innovation for preventing environmental crises that is best explained by ecological modernization as institutional learning. The reasons for the innovation may be primarily the need to maintain shareholder value, but the process seems to have beneficial effects on the responses of the company to environmental crises. In the case of ARCO Chemical, it seems to be best explained by ecological modernization as institutional learning, rather than as a technocratic project, or as cultural politics, since it is a process of innovation, for whatever reason, that improves the environmental effects of its operations. There are other corporations that seem to be best explained by ecological modernization as a technocratic project, and those that seem to be best explained by ecological modernization as cultural politics.

ARCO Chemical makes an interesting comparison with Shell, examined next. In 1995, the same year that ARCO was nominated for a Corporate Conscience Award, Shell was cited as one of the year's 'Ten Worst Corporations' by the magazine *Multinational Monitor*. Shell is one of the largest corporations in the world, and concurrently has a corporate culture that is more amorphous. The culture at Shell can be characterized as built around 'environmental action that builds shareholder value'. All Shell businesses should engage in activities that create shareholder value. There is evidence that the aim to build value can at times outweigh environmental and social factors where these conflict. However, largely, the corporation has been at the forefront of corporate environmental initiatives, facilitated by its massive size and related financial and managerial strength.

SHELL

Shell is one of the largest corporations in the world (number 11 in the *Fortune Global 500* for 2000), with 1999 sales of US$105 billion. It is an extremely complex organization, consisting of over 3000 individual companies operating in more than 100 countries. The companies are organized as the Royal Dutch/Shell Group of Companies and are involved in the extractive/energy sector. They extract, process and refine oil, gas, chemicals, coal, metals and other materials. Similar to other large corporations, the Royal Dutch/Shell Group of Companies (hereafter known as 'Shell' or the 'Group') operates with a largely decentralized management structure, with each of Shell's subsidiaries responsible for shaping the corporation's environmental policy to local conditions. Because corporations are increasingly integrating environmental adjustments to their operational procedures to avoid clean-up operations, and since compliance with environmental law is seen as a normal part of operations, it is difficult to calculate the amount of expenditure that is directed towards environmental issues. Environmental clean-up costs at Shell amounted to £370 million in 1992, £564 million in 1993, and £633 million in 1994.

The company's primary aim is to provide a return for its shareholders, and it is extremely efficient at doing this. Particular emphasis is laid on environmental action that builds value for shareholders. Shell's dominant corporate culture is a role culture; however, due to its diversified and complex nature it is likely to have many other cultures as well. One interviewee suggested that even though Shell UK and Shell International 'are only just across the Thames from one another, there is no communication and they operate like two completely separate companies' (interview with ICC Environment Representative, London, 29 November 1994). If the corporate culture in response to environmental crises for such a vast corporation could be defined, it would be based on responses to environmental crises that build value for shareholders. This characterizes the corporate shared values as evidenced in Shell's responses to environmental crises, both in terms of environmental preservation and in terms of environmental destruction.

Shell's environmental literature[10] suggests that it is unhelpful to think of energy as being nothing but environmentally harmful. People need energy to live and indeed cannot survive without it; they need to heat their homes, have lighting and hot water, to get to work and so on. This is balanced against the findings of many scientists who indicate that global warming is probably taking place because of fossil fuel burning. If this is the case, Shell argues, developed countries need to use energy more efficiently (which would have economic benefits for the company) as well as transfer useful technology to developing countries. It maintains that new technology can help with the greater efficiency of energy use. The corporation's position is that this can only occur through the lessening of trade barriers to stimulate economic activity through which new technologies can be developed. The United Nations has found that technology transfer of 'environmentally sound technologies' between corporations and the developing countries is often blocked for a number of reasons.

Some of the 'barriers' cited by corporations are:

- It is not profitable enough to sell environmental technologies in developing countries.
- It is too costly to maintain environmentally sound technologies in developing countries.
- 'It is unreasonable to give away patent protection.'

Some of the 'barriers' cited by developing countries are:

- Corporations set too high a price for the local markets for environmental technologies.
- Corporations refuse to license environmental technologies in developing countries.
- Corporations are not serious about environmental protection outside their home countries (UNCTC, 1991, Annex 7 and 8).

Other barriers cited by developing countries are that 'environmentally sound technologies' from developed countries often ignore much simpler and more appropriate local 'environmentally sound technologies' (UNCTC, 1991, Annex 7 and 8).

Shell is active in all aspects of the oil, gas, petrochemicals and coal industries, it is also involved to a great extent in metals processing, forestry, solar power and other areas. The major part of Shell's operations is the oil business which includes exploring and extracting petroleum, as well as transporting it on roads, sea[11] and pipeline, and refining and marketing the product. The other areas of Shell's operations are similarly complicated. Shell employs about 133,000 people not including contractors and their staff.[12]

Environmental policy

Shell accepts responsibilities to four key groups: shareholders, employees, customers and society. It has had Policy Guidelines on Health,

Safety and the Environment since 1977./Since 1990, Shell has incorporated a policy of continuous improvement, similar to ARCO Chemical, which aims to work towards no emissions of environmentally degrading substances. In 1991, a guideline was brought into place, which is directed towards ensuring that products are not especially harmful to the environment and should be recycled if possible, or disposed of safely./It also has a number of policies that can be described as illustrating a sustainable development management style.

The Group advocates a decentralized 'M-form' management structure with companies having their own national identities, environmental aims and objectives, guided by standards that are applicable across Shell. It can be argued that such a decentralized management form also allows for more flexibility, more innovation and a more 'organic' approach to change. The M-form also allows national companies in some cases to follow local (possibly less stringent) environmental laws, while distancing the parent company from liability if problems occur. It is a line responsibility primarily, supplemented by specialist knowledge from London or The Hague. Companies in the Group review environmental performance annually. The link between the M-form management structure and flexibility at Shell is seen as important for innovation and therefore increased wealth creation by Shell's managers. In support of this one commentator notes:

> '*Significantly ... Shell refuses to set overall objectives for its subsidiaries. Instead, it allows individual companies to decide their own strategy, "reflecting the national and cultural background in which they work". Shell portrays this as a strength, arguing that by putting the responsibility on local managers' shoulders, it encourages a sense of ownership, which in turn provides the most fertile ground for innovation. "Striving for consistency," said one Shell manager, "would be the kiss of death for continuous improvement"'* (Wright, 1995, p15).[13]

As part of the policy of continuous improvement, each Shell company must take account of all emissions, effluents and discharges from each operation and devise ways to reduce and, if possible, to eliminate them over time. At the Moerdijk chemical plant in the Netherlands, a new technology, an anaerobic bioreactor, is used to treat wastewater; the biogas produced is used as an energy source. The Shell Coal Gasification Technology process is another innovation used by power generation companies; it converts coal into 'clean' gas, carbon monoxide and hydrogen in particular, and steam. Elemental sulphur, another by-product, is sold, and the leftover benign slag can be used in civil engineering applications. This is particularly efficient and different types of coal can be used. The process is also more environmentally benign than traditional forms of energy production. Almost 100 per cent of the sulphur is recovered, 50 per cent less cooling water is employed, and carbon dioxide emissions are reduced by between 10 and 25 per cent because less coal is burned in the process (Shell International Petroleum Company, 1992). Goossen, a Greenpeace campaigner, sees a certain contradiction in Shell trumpeting the success of this example of 'environmentalism' since the corporation has only made changes after persistent pressure from environmental organizations. With respect to the corporation's introduction of sulphur emission controls at its Rotterdam factory, Goossen argues:

> '*It used to be the number one source of acid rain in the Netherlands. We had to work very hard to get Shell to improve environmental standards there. Finally, they agreed, and then, of course, they claim all the credit*' (cited in Wright, 1995, p17).[14]

A progressive aspect of the firm's policies and practices is in the area of oil spills; Shell has an oil spill advisory service that has specialist equipment and response teams. This may, in part, have been spurred by the company's experience off the Louisiana coast in the US in December 1971. At that time, a Shell Oil well exploded, spilled oil and sparked a fire. Oil slicks were seen almost 19km away from the accident in which four were killed and 38 injured (*Chemical Week*, 1972). The company had difficulties extinguishing the fire, and the United Nations Centre on Transnational Corporations (UNCTC) commented that:

> '*It is unclear if the firm had a contingency plan to deal with accidents of such a nature. Nor is it clear if there was any collaboration between the firm and the local authorities in responding to the incident. In any case, contingency plans involving the firm and local authorities may be helpful in terms of calling forth a speedy response*' (UNCTC, no date, 'Oil Spills/Blowouts/Tanker Accidents', p27).

In more recent years, the oil spill advisory service did not seem to be in effect in Nigeria. Greenpeace research showed that Shell spilled 7.3

million litres of oil in the Nigerian Delta Region between 1982 and 1992; almost 40 per cent of its spills worldwide in the same period (Vidal, 1995a, p4). David Williams, a company spokesperson, claims that in 1992 alone, 60 per cent of the spills in the Nigerian Delta Region (Ogoniland) were 'caused by deliberate sabotage so that compensation claims could be made'. Shehu Othman, an independent oil analyst based at Oxford University, has said that the Ogoni may have engaged in acts of sabotage at Shell's installations:

> *'It's certainly a very small minority though, and compensation is certainly not the motivation. The idea is absolute nonsense, because compensation for spills is a very small sum paid for the loss of crops, not for the loss of the land itself. Frankly, if there is sabotage it strikes me as a legitimate act of the powerless'* (cited in Kretzmann, 1995, p10).

Regardless of whether or not global warming is occurring Shell believes that there is enough scientific evidence for governments to take initial steps to deal with it. Whatever measures taken should be 'economically viable and practical'; for example, increased energy efficiency would be an appropriate first step. This, therefore, does not necessarily oblige Shell to scale down production. Shell claims to be reducing gas flaring (which releases greenhouse gases into the atmosphere) and increasing its own energy efficiency. However, it seems probable that Shell has had 'double standards', operating relatively 'cleanly' in developed countries, and having environmentally challenged operations in developing countries. A salient case in this regard is Shell's operation in Nigeria[15] where the corporation is involved in extensive gas flaring. Although the company has said that it is not happy with gas flaring in Nigeria, footage shot in Ogoniland for the British Channel 4 documentary *The Drilling Fields* reveals that gas flares are routinely situated near villages. Ken Saro-Wiwa, the executed environmental activist who had championed the social and environmental rights of Ogoni people[16] describes the gas flaring in a 1992 pamphlet as having

> *'destroyed wildlife and plant life, poisoned the atmosphere and therefore the inhabitants of the surrounding areas and made the residents half dead and prone to respiratory diseases. Whenever it rains in Ogoni, all we have is acid rain which further poisons water courses, streams, creeks, and agricultural land'* (cited in Kretzmann, 1995, p10).

In Nigeria 'Many of Shell's practices and equipment would be illegal according to the environmental laws of most countries. Irresponsible flaring of gas, poor pipeline placement, chronic oil spills, and unlined toxic waste pits plague the Nigerian Delta region' (Kretzmann, 1995, p10). The company acknowledges that there are 'problems' in Ogoniland but maintains that activists have inappropriately characterized it as an area of environmental devastation. Pictures of the region show poorly maintained, above ground pipelines that criss-cross villages, some even through people's homes. According to a Shell Briefing Note, if the pipelines through Ogoni were laid end to end, they would stretch from London to New York (cited in Saro-Wiwa, 1995, p163). Shell admits that it did not complete environmental impact surveys when the Ogoniland site was first developed in the late 1950s, and that later impact studies were more 'theoretical' than those done today (Vidal, 1995a, p4).

Shell maintains that overall efficiency at its refineries around the world has doubled in the last 30 years. Some examples of action in this area include Swedish Shell's Gothenburg refinery, which for the last ten years has contributed waste heat to the city's central heating system, and supplies 25 per cent of the city's energy demand. The city's heating plant has saved 513,000 barrels of oil annually because of this project.

Shell has investigated three areas of renewable energy. These include solar energy, liquid biofuels and biomass. It is unclear whether these are being explored primarily as environmentally sound energy options or primarily for new energy markets, or both. Solar energy photovoltaic systems have experienced a 20 per cent rise in global sales between 1989 and 1990, however the main markets are meeting small demand for power far removed from the nearest grid supplies of electricity. Liquid biofuels are four to six times as expensive as fossil fuels, and for the moment do not seem to be considered an option by the company. Biomass could be cost-effective for power generation but is still in the research stages. Shell's investments in renewable energy only represent about 1 per cent of its overall budget, which leads its critics to argue that the pursuit of alternative forms of energy is not high on Shell's agenda at present (Corporate Watch, 2000).

Environmental record

Shell operates under a ten point statement of business principles. Profitability is central to the operation of Shell; its managers claim it allows them to put their principles into practice, and serve the needs of the consumer. Shell controversially maintains that it has 'little' influence in the social, political and economic milieux in which it operates, but that people's needs are best served, in general, by a market economy.

Shell claims to advocate honesty and integrity and asserts that offering or paying bribes is unacceptable.[17] Shell Corporation asserts that it removes itself from party politics but will speak out on matters that affect the interests of its employees, customers and shareholders as well as areas of general information. Shell maintains that it does not pay political parties or their representatives.[18] In 1977, over 400 other corporations admitted to having made 'dubious' payments to government officials and political parties in countries in which they operated (*CTC Reporter*, 1989, p50). Shell has been a significant contributor in 'soft money' to US Political Action Committees (PACs). Although the US government limits the amount of 'hard money' contributions – direct contributions to individual candidates – there is no limit to 'soft money' contributions to general party accounts or political foundations, like the Republican Party GOPAC (Ruskin, 1995). The corporation has also been involved with many oppressive regimes that engage in human rights violations, including Myanmar (Burma) where it has had multimillion dollar contracts since 1989 (O'Rourke, 1992).

The investment by corporations in states with poor human rights records has been argued to provide 'significant economic support, international credibility, and moral legitimacy to the repressive regimes... Foreign investments invariably increase home country financial, and therefore political, commitments to the present structures of racism or martial law' (Gladwin and Walter, 1980, p201). In practice, corporations operating in countries which regularly commit human rights violations can respond in three ways: by withdrawing their operations (divestment), by continuing with 'business as usual', or by using their 'influence' to bring about change. These options have been carried out in the following cases:

- In 1993, Levi Strauss, the US based clothing manufacturer, withdrew its operations from China because of human rights abuses (NC/CEP, 1993, p42).
- A soft drinks company decided to continue to invest in Myanmar, despite the military regime's human rights violations; the reason for the 'business as usual' option was that its decision was 'guided by our firm belief that trade is one of the best ways to build bridges between people...[which will] help open lines of communication, find common ground, stimulate dialogue and thus bring people and their nations closer together' (Allen, 1993, pxii).
- In March 1989, the CEO of Volvo wrote to the President of Colombia encouraging him to stop acts of aggression against

banana workers in plants owned by a Volvo subsidiary (NC/CEP, 1993, p42).

In an unpublished and restricted memo, supplied to me by Greenpeace, Major Okuntima, chairman of the Rivers State Internal Security in Nigeria, states 'Shell operations still impossible unless ruthless military operations are undertaken for smooth economic activities to commence'. The document goes on to recommend that soldiers undertake 'wasting operations', 'wasting' Ogoni leaders who are 'especially vocal individuals'. It finally recommends 'pressure on the oil companies for prompt regular inputs as discussed'. Ken Saro-Wiwa, one of the vocal individuals eventually executed by the military government, argued that:

> 'Shell knows that the military dictatorships which have ruled or misruled Nigeria over the years have depended almost entirely on the revenue which Shell generates and are therefore beholden to the company in a very crucial manner. The company therefore adopts a godlike "we can do no wrong" attitude' (Saro-Wiwa, 1995, p167).

Multinational Monitor reported that after Saro-Wiwa's imprisonment, Shell executives offered to intervene with Nigerian officials on his behalf, in return for an agreement to stop criticizing the company. He refused, and 'was executed shortly thereafter' (*Multinational Monitor*, 1997). Three Ogoni who have emigrated from Nigeria are presently suing the corporation in the US. Their sponsor, the Center for Constitutional Rights in New York, believes that 'there is a basis in US law to hold Shell accountable [for Saro-Wiwa's execution] ' (McGregor, 2000).[19]

The conflictive relationship between host governments in developing countries and corporations has been evaluated by Dunning (1993) who argues that conflict is derived from four different issues:

> 'from the fact that [the corporation] is private *and hence may clash with the social and national goals; that it is* large *and oligopolistic and hence possesses market and bargaining power which may be used against the interests of the host country; that it is* foreign ... *and hence may be serving the interests of a foreign nation; and that it is* western *and hence may transfer appropriate know-how, technology of management practices, or products, designed with characteristics not needed in developing countries'* (emphasis in original, p251).

Shell claims to comply with environmental legislation and carry out its operations in a safe and environmentally sensible manner. As noted above, individual Shell companies may shape their practices to meet local conditions based on corporate policy. In practice, this may mean that individual Shell companies can 'do what they like'. In early 1997, the World Council of Churches (WCC) released a 106 page report after a visit to Nigeria by a senior WCC official which argues that 'It is no wonder why Shell has been the target of international sanctions: its environmental record in Ogoniland and in other minority oil producing areas is distasteful' (*The Guardian*, 1997, p9).

Following the problems in Ogoniland, Shell revised its Business Principles, with the help of 'pressure groups'. The Principles now include the sentence: 'To express support for fundamental human rights in line with the legitimate role of business and to give proper regard to health, safety and the environment, consistent with [our] commitment to contribute to sustainable development' (Cowe, 1997, p19). The corporation's CEO, Cor Herkströter, also said that 'I believe there is now sufficient evidence to support prudent precautionary action' with regard to climate change (Cowe, 1997, p19).

Shell has also been cited as being a contributor to three 'anti-environmental' organizations, along with ARCO. The first is the Foundation for Research on Economics and the Environment (FREE). This think tank advocates 'resource development' in wilderness areas, national parks and other protected areas in the developed countries. The chairperson of FREE, John Baden, argues for private 'environmental groups' and business working together to develop public lands. For example, at the Audubon's Rainey Sanctuary in Louisiana 'Natural gas wells have operated within the preserve for more than 25 years without measurable damage to the surrounding ecosystem' (Deal, 1993, p55). Under FREE's plan federal nature preserves such as the Arctic National Wildlife Refuge (ANWR), which is purported to be sited on huge petroleum deposits, would quickly be 'sold to the highest bidder' (Deal, 1993, p55). ARCO, along with BP and Exxon, are the major producers of oil along the North Slope of Alaska (the state's northern coastal plain along the Arctic Ocean), only 10 per cent of which has been saved as part of the Arctic National Wildlife Refuge.[20] The ANWR is the birthing ground for a herd of 180,000 caribou and is a refuge for polar bears, brown bears, wolves, musk oxen and millions of migratory birds (Deal, 1993, p26). The three corporations are the owners of the 800 mile Trans-Alaska Pipeline System that ships oil from the North Slope to Valdez in the southern part of the state (Knaus, 1993).[21]

The second organization supported by Shell Oil is the National Wetlands Coalition, which similarly lobbies for the opening of wetlands, home to one-third of endangered species, to commercial development (Deal, 1993, p70).

The third anti-environmental organization, that Shell has been involved with is the Global Climate Coalition, which exists 'to convince Congress and the public that global warming is a myth' (Deal, 1993, p56). This group also contributed to 'one of the greatest disappointments of the 1992 Rio Earth Summit' when it successfully lobbied for voluntary carbon dioxide controls rather than the mandatory and timetabled controls which the hundreds of scientists from 40 countries which comprise the Intergovernmental Panel on Climate Change (IPCC) had previously advised to avoid global warming (Deal, 1993, p56; Wright, 1995, p15).

SUMMARY: SHELL

Shell has long operated 'double standards' in Ogoniland in particular and Nigeria generally (see also Onwuka, 1992), and many would argue that the corporation would be prevented by environmental regulations from operating in the same way in the UK and other developed countries. In the UK, conversely, the company is environmentally active. The head of Environmental Affairs at Shell was seen as a corporate environmental leader in 1994 by environmental consultants to corporations interviewed for this research (interviews with corporate environmental consultants, London, 19 January 1993; 31 June 1993). However, when asked what in fact the company was doing in concrete terms to reduce emissions and prevent pollution, no specific information was given. On the other hand, the importance of regulations, the concomitant fact that Shell 'doesn't operate in a vacuum' and an expressed lack of faith in whether 'the public *really understand* the (environmental) issues' was discussed (interview with Shell environment staff, London, 9 February 1994). The company was actually quite alert to those who questioned too deeply the environmental impact of their operations. Both the Shell environmental representative and the Shell consultant interviewed for this project were extremely reticent to discuss concrete aspects of the company's environmental record as well as its future aims (interview with Shell consultant, London, 11 November 1994; interview with Shell environment staff, London, 9 February 1994). The corporation has been praised in developed countries because it 'maintains its plant meticulously, donates large amounts of money to communities and conservation groups and invests heavily in environmental protection' (Vidal, 1995a, p4). The aim of Shell's Better Britain Campaign was described by a company spokesperson: 'to get over to people not normally interested in conservation the message that they could do something' (cited in Elkington and Burke, 1989, p221). WWF and Greenpeace have both acknowledged that Shell has 'made significant, if not dramatic progress in the last few years, notably in technical fixes to reduce polluting emissions involved in production work' (Wright, 1995, p17).

In developed countries, Shell is involved in renewable technologies; it donates waste heat to Gothenburg, Sweden, providing 25 per cent of its heating demand; and it is involved with treating waste and conserving energy. In the UK, it buries pipelines so as not to disturb farmers' fields or 'fragile habitats'. Shell has global policies and auditing, has had an environmental policy statement, and claims to be responding to the sustainable development debate. However, it has also used its considerable economic and managerial strength for less environmentally benevolent aims. The preservation of free trade and undermining of controls on carbon dioxide emissions are two contentious examples of this. Due to the corporation's size it has been both the developer of environmentally useful technologies, and responsible for significant environmental impact. In developed countries, Shell could be placed in Environmental Management Type IV 'Sustainable development management' since it moves 'beyond compliance', is involved in energy conservation, pollution prevention and renewable energy sources, and has global policies, audits and accounting. It follows the advice of scientists on the most 'environmentally sound' disposal of its oil platforms (Dickson and McCulloch, 1996). The corporate managers have benefited from institutional learning regarding environmental issues. The company has attempted to respond to all of the more environmentally problematic examples cited in this chapter. At the same time, it seems that those policies put into place are not always followed in the same ways in its developing country operations. Shell, in essence, is the paradigmatic example of the contradictions of the 'greening of the corporations'.[22]

Shell's dominant corporate culture is based on a role culture, very similar to Weber's ideal type of bureaucracy. Shell is an old, large and profitable corporation with a product with long life cycles and is therefore most likely to favour such a culture. Since its success as a corporation has come from its ability to build value for its shareholders foremost, its corporate culture related to its response to environmental crises is characterized as based on environmental action which builds value for shareholders. Role cultures are known as being slow to change since they are geared to maintaining stability over long periods. Shell has integrated environmental issues into its practices, particularly in developed countries where they have had a greater effect on the profitability of the firm. It is likely that task cultures have developed in certain areas of Shell which have been geared towards responding with creative, innovative, flexible and strategic solutions to environmental crises, such as in certain research and development departments and in certain subsidiaries in which the market is extremely competitive, and where speed of reaction is important, such as those dealing with renewable fuels and other clean technologies.

CONCLUSION

While ARCO has a corporate culture based on safety, Shell has a corporate culture based on 'environmental action that builds shareholder value'. Both have dominant role cultures although it is likely that task cultures exist in some departments and/or subsidiaries. The evidence from this chapter suggests that the integration of economic and environmental aims in both cases is fragmented. In developed countries in particular, Shell's integration is more complete, perhaps due to its size, while some of its developing country operations seem to suffer from a lack of integration of these aims. The degree of ARCO's integration is different. Its main aim is to prevent pollution, to save money and maintain its reputation.

Shell's management style in response to environmental crises can be classified as 'dark green' with the exception of its developing country operations, although research would suggest that some of its operations in developing countries are probably better than comparative local firms (ESCAP/UNCTC, 1990). ARCO's management style can be classified as 'light green' preventive, with some 'green' strategic aspects, notably its work on environmental technologies and products, such as MTBE.

Shell's response to environmental crises is controlled from the highest organizational levels of the corporation, and put into practice through global policies, audits and accounting. Its management of environmental crises is particularly good in developed countries. The main cultural value at Shell is organized around finding ways to build shareholder value, so in some cases where environmental action may affect wealth creation, for example in Nigeria or the Netherlands, the corporation can choose to have shareholder value take precedence over environmental action. If the public finds out 'lessons can be learned', operations can be cleaned up, and environmental crises lessened, in order to preserve the corporate image. When environmental action is a source of potential profits, for example exploring renewable technologies, these new markets are pursued. If sustainable development means increased energy efficiency, Shell can provide the environmental technologies needed for increased energy efficiency.

The cases of Shell and ARCO reveal that the process of ecological modernization is not a homogeneous one. 'Shades' of ecological modernization exist. The best explanation is that it exists within developed countries as a process of determining the financial possibilities of environmental crises. The response to environmental crises in 'traditional corporations' such as Shell and ARCO is institutionalized in the organizations, through policies, programmes and cultures.

Traditional corporations have an incentive to respond to environmental crises in order to build shareholder value. These include increased energy efficiency, fewer costs associated with waste products, markets in environmental technologies, good public relations and the avoidance of legal costs and fines. Through incentives like tradable rights to pollute, which give market incentives to increased efficiency, competition can facilitate greater environmental progress, and further ecological modernization.

The next chapter presents the cases of corporations that have a social-environmental corporate culture. The particular cultural values that exist in Ben & Jerry's Homemade Inc, and The Body Shop International plc, are quite different on some levels from those at ARCO Chemical and Shell and Chapter 5 considers whether these corporations are examples of the hope which ecological modernization can represent (Hajer, 1996).

An Analysis of Two Corporations with a 'Social-environmental' Corporate Culture

INTRODUCTION

This chapter investigates two further cases of corporations and the environment: The Body Shop International plc, and Ben & Jerry's Homemade Inc. Both represent the 'dark green' management style because they are more proactive in responses to environmental challenges than similar corporations of their size and type. 'Dark green' corporations are highly active in social and environmental causes and contribute significant amounts of their pre-tax profits to such causes. They are also involved in what are known as 'fair trade' programmes.[1] More importantly, they also have well-developed environmental management responses and approach environmental problems innovatively. These responses include unique waste treatment processes, use of renewable resources, corporate structures dealing with creative responses to energy use and recycling, and environmental policies and auditing which cover all aspects of their operations.

I define these corporations as 'social-environmental'[2] in character because they present an image of their corporations as embodying the social and environmental idealism commonly thought of as associated with the zeitgeist of the 1960s. The dominant corporate culture which exists at The Body Shop and Ben & Jerry's can be characterized as a power culture. The two companies are at the forefront of what has been labelled the 'ethical business movement'. They operate on the basis of 'cause related' or 'social' marketing, and actively dissociate themselves from corporations with a 'traditional' corporate culture examined in the previous chapter; which they tend to see as socially and environmentally problematic. Whereas Shell and ARCO Chemical are respectively concerned with 'safety' and 'environmental action which builds shareholder value', as central defining features of their corporate cultures, The Body Shop and Ben & Jerry's are respectively concerned with 'profits and principles' and 'linked prosperity', as defining features of their corporate cultures.

Their enigmatic founders have shaped both corporate cultures. The Body Shop culture is greatly defined through the activities of Anita and Gordon Roddick, its founders and managers, and revealed in visits to the company as well as interviews with its staff, and its corporate statements, programmes and other literature. One management writer has defined The Body Shop's corporate culture as based on 'Missionary Greening' because of the vocal pronouncements of The Body Shop founders. The focus here is on the idea of 'profits and principles' which is repeated in the statements of Anita Roddick and employees, as well as observations of corporate life at The Body Shop. The cultural theme of profits and principles is more accurate because of the order in which these are stated relative to their importance. The Roddicks would argue that the foremost aim of The Body Shop is wealth creation; Anita Roddick criticizes employees who come to work thinking that their job 'is about saving the world and not about cashing and wrapping'. She has also said that she 'is not some sort of loony do-gooder but rather a trader looking for trade'. At the same time, Roddick has stated that The Body Shop 'has always been an unashamedly green company'.

Ben & Jerry's has a similar corporate culture defined here as 'linked prosperity'. The concept of 'linked prosperity' alludes to the corporation's tripartite mission statement comprising product, economic and social components, in that order. This was established at the company through the inspiration of Ben Cohen, a Ben & Jerry's co-founder.

Ben & Jerry's founders have always been involved in so-called 'publicity stunts' which raise the profile of the corporation in the media, proclaiming their product as being made with all natural ingredients by 'two Vermont hippies', which implies a social-environmental image. At the same time, the corporation has developed innovative solutions to social aspects of its business, including worker compensation and satisfaction, and environmental aspects of its business including innovative ways of treating their production waste products. Similar to The Body Shop, the corporate culture at Ben & Jerry's is not satisfactory to all its workers who have been uncertain at times whether the expectation is that they are working for a charity or a wealth creating enterprise. Regardless, the company has been voted one of the 100 best corporations to work for in the US because of its many worker benefit programmes.

THE BODY SHOP

The UK based Body Shop has been called the 'socially responsible capitalism' movement's highest profile company (cited in Entine, 1995). Anita Roddick opened the first Body Shop in Brighton, UK, in 1976. The company, a cosmetics corporation with over 1600 stores in 50 countries, over 4000 employees, and based in a small town, Littlehampton, West Sussex, UK, has been an amazingly successful business. It went public in 1984 and profits increased from £1.04 million in 1985 to £33.5 million in 1995, on sales that grew from £4.9 million to just over £500 million in the same period (Jack and Buckley, 1994, p8). By the end of 1999, sales were up to £614 million. It has been identified with environmental issues, and is widely seen as in the vanguard of 'environmentally responsible' companies, having been described as 'one of the world's leading ethically run businesses' (Vidal, 1994, p2). Anita Roddick, its outspoken founder, has campaigned worldwide for the rainforests, whales, the homeless and against acid rain and exploiters of developing countries. The Body Shop is perhaps best known as being 'against animal testing' (Vidal and Brown, 1994, p6).

Environmental policy

The Body Shop has developed environmental management systems that appear to be at the forefront of company environmental action for corporations in the cosmetics industry. The Body Shop's environmental policy is as follows:

> '*Our policy: The Body Shop has always had a clear, top-level commitment to environmental and social excellence. Because of this, we make sure we include environmental issues in every area of our operations. Our goals: This commitment has produced a statement of environmental goals that is realistic for our business and goes well beyond the minimum requirements for environmental protection. Our goals require best practice in the following areas:*

- *assessment of operations;*
- *sustainable resources;*
- *testing and marketing of safe products;*
- *energy efficiency;*
- *waste management & pollution control;*
- *risk reduction;*
- *land use;*
- *communication & information;*
- *education'* (The Body Shop, 1991, p5).

The company has decided to prioritize its efforts and focus especially on those environmental issues that it sees as particularly relevant to its operations. These are energy issues, waste management and product life cycle assessment.[3]

The Body Shop environmental policy reads like a 'sustainable development' management statement. It alludes to being a leader in the area. It is suggested that 'The Body Shop has always had a "clear, top-level commitment" to environmental and social excellence'. Similar to a strategic environmental statement, the environment is included in every area of its operations. It strives for 'best practice', that is the best available management practices in many of the traditional environmental areas, as well as in sustainable resources and education. In terms of implementing its policy, the company has been involved in auditing the environmental aspects of its operations, and publishing auditors' reports.

In 1991, The Body Shop commissioned an independent environmental review of its Watersmead, Littlehampton, site. The scope of the audit covered reduction of energy consumption, environmental impact limitation, reduction of carbon dioxide emissions and renewable energy sources. The findings were that the total energy bill for the company's main manufacturing site and corporate headquarters at Littlehampton was £405,000; 86 per cent of this was electricity expenditure and 14 per cent gas. Savings in a number of areas were identified. These included savings of £23,000, representing 358 tonnes of carbon dioxide per year, through 19 energy efficiency projects in their warehouse, manufacturing production and office building. Additional possible savings of £28,000 per year were also identified.

An analysis of the company's UK carbon dioxide emissions was also carried out. The emissions for the corporate headquarters at Watersmead, Littlehampton, were added to company car emissions, as well as distribution systems and retail shops. This revealed that the retail shops were the main contributors to atmospheric pollution:

they were responsible for 10,450 tonnes per year out of total UK Body Shop emissions of 18,009 tonnes per year.

The review of renewable energy possibilities at Watersmead indicated that options for energy conservation in this area were constrained by various factors. Chief among these was that the site was not designed with renewable energy in mind. Therefore, it was impossible to retrofit[4] wind or solar power generators to the buildings. However, the review was able to identify renewable energy possibilities for the site's visitor centre. The visitor centre is now fitted with solar panels and has a 15kW wind turbine, which produce enough energy for its hot water as well as most of its heating.

The assessment considered the options for creating energy self-sufficiency for the company's operations in the UK. The options considered included renewable energy sources to generate the equivalent amount of energy that the UK operations used; a wind farm for example. Another option was to become part of a joint venture with a company that produced renewable energy.[5] The last option was a contract to purchase only renewable energy from a traditional energy company. The 1991–1992 environmental report indicated that the company 'favoured the joint-venture option'.

As a way of avoiding dependence on nuclear power, the company constructed a wind farm in Wales, which contributes the equivalent amount of electricity that the Watersmead site uses to the local electricity grid. The company acknowledges that it faces problems in whatever actions it takes, owing to the complexity of environmental issues. For example, the company faced local environmental protest in Wales over the visual and noise pollution of a wind farm while attempting to reduce its environmental impact on the land and atmosphere by pursuing non-renewable energy expenditure. This illustrates some of the complexities that the company faces in its decisions.

Interestingly, an environment, health and safety staff member at The Body Shop interviewed for this study, when probed about the Welsh wind farm and the complexity of any environmental decision, stated that The Body Shop's actions, similar to the environmental statement noted above, have always been guided by an environmental vision and that vision has always been 'crystal clear' (interview with The Body Shop environment staff member, Littlehampton, UK, 5 April 1994). When asked what this vision is, and whether it had been articulated in any of the company materials or policies, the response was that it had not always been stated directly but that the vision nevertheless was 'crystal clear'. The vision was to create a values-led business.

The company has a very specific waste policy, which is: 'The Body Shop's approach to waste management is simple: reduce, reuse, recycle (in that order)' (The Body Shop, 1991, p15). The company's primary environmental impact is on water and sea resources. In the area of the south coast of England where the company's main plant is located, most waste is untreated and pumped straight back into the sea. However, the company realizes that as environmental legislation is moving towards greater stringency, taking account of wastewater discharges will help it to stay within environmental regulatory frameworks.

In 1991–1992, the company was producing 115,000 litres of effluent a week that translated into a burden of 20 tonnes COD on water resources. The company installed an ultra-filtration wastewater treatment facility, which removed about 90 per cent of the COD. The filters in the facility extract material with high molecular weights from the effluent, which reduces the amount of effluent in their waste stream.

The material filtered out of the waste stream is loaded into a tanker as sludge to be treated again before disposal. Similar to other corporations and in the spirit of continuous improvement, the company aims to reduce the amount of liquid waste that it produces and make the filtration system more efficient. Another method for reducing waste that the company is developing is an ecologically engineered system of wastewater treatment, broadly similar to the system in operation at Ben & Jerry's, examined below. The system creates microhabitats that help to break down the organic material in the output. The products of the breakdown process are then fed to plants, which are harvested to be used for compost.

The main solid waste by-product of The Body Shop's production process and consumption of its products is waste plastic. The company aims to reduce waste by avoiding excessive packaging. The company sells its products in simple plastic bottles. The second of its tripartite policy on waste is 'reuse'. In this case, The Body Shop operates a refilling service for its products at many of its retail stores. The product containers are also constructed of recyclable materials. Some solid plastic waste is sent to be recycled. Included in this is shrink-wrap used to wrap batches of bottles, which is recycled into the firm's carrier bags. The recycling was a success. In early 1991, the corporation was recycling one tonne of polyethylene a month, and by the end of the year, it was recycling one tonne a week. Post-consumer waste is also recycled in the form of used product containers. The containers are returned to shops, and then collected by delivery trucks. They are delivered to the Watersmead site, sorted by colour and type of material, then shredded, bagged, and sent for reprocessing and recycling.

Some of the main points of The Body Shop's policy on life cycle assessment are as follows:

- *'We are committed to using renewable resources and conserving non-renewable ones.*
- *We strive to obtain raw materials from communities who want to use trade to protect their culture and who practise traditional systems of sustainable land use.*
- *We use only product ingredients that have not been tested on animals in the past five years and suppliers must provide reassurance on this.*
- *Natural ingredients from renewable sources are favoured by the Research and Development Department whenever new product formulations are tested.*
- *Where ingredients and packaging come from non-renewable resources, for example from synthetic chemicals, we make sure we minimize quantities and maximize biodegradability (for ingredients) and recyclability (for packaging)* (The Body Shop, 1991, p16).

The company indicates that in practice the policy is focused on products manufactured 'around natural ingredients' that are beneficial for skin and hair care but unlikely to cause allergic reactions. Increasingly The Body Shop has sourced these ingredients in developing countries under 'non-exploitative trading arrangements' (The Body Shop, 1991, p16).

Examples of this are the aim to develop 'natural preservatives', and to purchase Brazil nut oil from the Kayapo Indians in Brazil. Additionally, the company's suppliers are expected to meet its environmental standards. The company claims to be conducting a systematic review of the ecotoxicology and biodegradability of its ingredients.

Environmental record

In line with a corporate culture based on 'profits and principles', The Body Shop has been extremely active in bringing attention to environmental and social problems. One of The Body Shop's/Roddick's campaigns has been against Shell for its role in Nigeria. Roddick and others protested outside the Shell Centre along with members of Saro-Wiwa's family, Friends of the Earth and Greenpeace (Vidal, 1995b, p4). With these and similar activities, Roddick and The Body Shop have set themselves apart from traditional business and have appealed to a type of consumer with an interest in buying from a business with social and environmental credentials, and this has undoubtedly been linked with the success of the company.[6] In an emotive letter to *The Financial Times* that is illustrative of Roddick's and the company's value system, Anita Roddick admonished Shell for its failure to speak out against Nigeria's trial of Saro-Wiwa and the other protesters:

> *'The death sentences handed down to Ken Saro-Wiwa and other Ogoni leaders by a Nigerian military court this week raised serious questions for those doing business there. Where do we draw the line? What do we as businesses owe to the communities we work in? Sometimes we have to make wholesale changes to how we can do business with vulnerable communities. The only way we can do this is by going, listening, then taking action. It's very clear that Shell has not learned this lesson in Ogoniland... So, will Shell join me and thousands of others in publicly condemning the trial for the sham it is? It is no good whispering advice to General Abacha (the military leader of Nigeria) and hoping he might listen. Only public statements will carry weight. Nothing will save these innocent men except our speaking out'* (Roddick, 1995, p22).

Saro-Wiwa's *Detention Diary* (1995) states one of the occasions when the Nigerian government had confiscated his passport when he was on his way to Vienna to attend the United Nations World Conference on Human Rights in June 1993. Ledum Mittee and other Ogoni activists had been allowed to leave the country. Saro-Wiwa reflected:

> *'The Vienna Conference was useful to the Ogoni because Ledum Mittee met Anita Roddick there, thanks to the UNPO (Unrepresented Nations and Peoples Organization). Anita Roddick and her organization, Body Shop, were later to play a very important role in the Ogoni struggle'* (Saro-Wiwa, 1995, p180).

The role which Roddick and The Body Shop played was never elaborated on further in the diary. But Roddick has continued to be involved in the Ogoni struggle; for example a letter addressed to Anita Roddick was smuggled out of the Port Harcourt jail where activists were being held in appalling conditions (Dynes, 1996).

The corporate culture of 'profits and principles' and its link with environmental values is also evidenced in the company's 1991–1992 environmental statement, which states: 'Concern for environmental and social issues has always been an integral part of The Body Shop' (The Body Shop, 1991, p2). The Body Shop's position at the forefront of environmentally responsible companies was seen as being confirmed in consumer guides published in the late 1980s and early 1990s (see Elkington and Hailes, 1988; Wells and Jetter, 1991) where Anita Roddick was invited to endorse varieties of 'responsible consumerism'. However, The Body Shop, which has set itself apart from corporations with a more 'traditional' corporate culture, often comes under attack over its environmental and social standards. Anita Roddick lamented: 'Why am I always measured against the standard of Mother Theresa – a standard by which even saints will fail – and not against those chairmen of companies who create huge corporate crimes' (Roddick, cited in Jack and Buckley, 1994, p8).[7]

One of the unique features of the company was that it achieved its financial success without the use of advertising (as did Ben & Jerry's, below); the company sees advertising as being unscrupulous. Instead of traditional advertising, the company has relied on Roddick's energetic personality to sell its products. 'Anita Roddick personified the company, and rarely refused interviews. Newspapers and magazines devoted multi-page spreads to Anita's beauty tips, what she ate, how she decorated her home, even her favourite films' (Jack and Buckley, 1994, p8).

The other key selling point of the company was its 'green' image. This is where its 'principles' also linked with its 'profits'. The company used recyclable plastic bottles and entreated its customers to refill their old plastic bottles rather than buy new ones. The company also campaigned against animal testing and covered the interior of its shops (whose predominant colour is green) with placards exhorting its customers to save the whales or the rainforest.

The Body Shop's effort to follow social-environmental principles goes beyond its green policies. The corporate culture of 'profits and principles' is indoctrinated as part of a value system expected on and off the job; the company uniquely permits every employee half a day of paid time off each month to do voluntary work. The company gave £230,000 to launch *The Big Issue*, a magazine sold by the homeless, who retain 60 per cent of the cover price. It has campaigned for employers to provide fair pay, equal opportunities, participative management and childcare. As a way to treat its employees fairly, it opened its own 'workplace child development centre' at its Littlehampton site (Jack and Buckley, 1994, p8). The company backs women's centres and AIDS and drugs initiatives. In 1994, the Roddicks and The Body Shop gave £7 million pounds to charity. In 1996, Anita Roddick started an ethical business school. Her own salary was £140,592; modest for a company with a turnover exceeding £200 million (Jack and Buckley, 1994, p8). Finally, in 1996, the company became the first major British publicly quoted company to publish a social audit of its operations (Baker, 1996).

However, in the 1990s critics began to level a number of criticisms that questioned The Body Shop's social-environmental credentials. The criticisms specifically suggested that there were times when the company's drive for profits outpaced the principles it had professed. The criticisms levelled against the company caused the leading US ethical investment fund, Merlin, to sell its shares (temporarily) in The Body Shop, and caused the company's share price to fall by 5 per cent (Cowe, 1994d, p2). The threat of a fall in share price is an incentive for any corporation to make changes in order to maintain its stock price. The questions raised were originally sparked by an article published by the US television journalist Jon Entine in *Business Ethics* magazine (published 1 September 1994), a Minneapolis, Minnesota, based periodical with limited circulation. The main criticisms by Entine and similar critics at green/ethical consumer 'watch dog' associations,[8] were as follows:

- The Roddicks copied the idea and early products for The Body Shop from a store operating in Berkeley, California, in 1970.
- The ingredients are not as pure as customers are meant to believe.
- The company's animal testing stance is misleading.
- The company's New Jersey plant had three spills of shampoo in 1992–1993 totalling over 280 litres.
- The company's Trade Not Aid policy represents only a small part of its buying practices.
- The company often threatens legal action to silence its critics.

The first criticism is that Anita (presently co-chair of The Body Shop) and her husband Gordon Roddick (presently co-chair of The Body Shop) visited California in 1969/1970, saw the first 'Body Shop', copied it and its products and recreated it in Brighton in 1976. The original Californian company had remarkably similar plastic bottles, recycling philosophy, store and logo design and a product list with catalogue descriptions of its products (all defining features of the 'Roddick-founded' The Body Shop) (Entine, 1995). Once the Roddicks' company began expanding, one informant for this research said that they then made a US$3 million settlement with the original

American owners of the Body Shop (interview with consumer association staff member, Newcastle upon Tyne, UK, 8 August 1994).[9] The
company maintains that Anita Roddick started The Body Shop in
Brighton in 1976.

Critics argue that the company manufactures a green image, its
dominant colour is green, the products are based on 'natural ingredients' like camomile, blue corn and raspberries, but in fact it also uses
many conventional ingredients of the mainstream cosmetics industry
(interview with consumer association staff member, Newcastle upon
Tyne, UK, 8 August 1994). Entine's article states more emphatically
'The company's most basic myth is that it sells "natural products"'
(Entine, cited in Cowe, 1994c, p15).[10] The company alludes to the
purity of its ingredients; for example, the 1991 *Global Consumer*
states: 'As part of The Body Shop's environmental policy, it uses only
renewable ingredients in its products; a measure which coincides with
the need to maintain a market for tropical oils' (Wells and Jetter,
1991, p172). According to the critics and the company's own environmental statement from 1991 (see above), the company does not use
only renewable ingredients (interview with consumer association staff
member, Newcastle upon Tyne, UK, 8 August 1994). This is
confirmed in the booklet that lists the ingredients of the company's
products, available to the public in The Body Shop retail stores, and
identified on their bottle labels. While it is true that the products
contain natural ingredients, such as brazil nut oil, honey and blue
corn, they also contain many of the standard non-renewable chemicals and synthetics used regularly in the cosmetics industry, such as
artificial colours, fragrances and preservatives derived from petrochemicals (Entine, 1995). Their products are also packaged in plastic
bottles. The company does not, in fact, deny that their products are
not wholly natural.

The Body Shop runs tours at the company's Littlehampton
headquarters where the guide concedes that the company needs to
use preservatives due to their system of production and distribution.
The 1991–1992 environmental report indicated that 'In the forth-
coming year a special effort will be made to research "natural
preservatives" – compounds with natural anti-microbial activity
which could reduce the need for synthetic preservatives in some
products' (The Body Shop, 1991, p17). The company has also said
that it 'does not use naturally-based ingredients if that would involve
higher energy use and more packaging' (Cowe, 1994c, p15).

Another highly visible claim of The Body Shop is that the
company is 'Against Animal Testing'. Entine states that despite this
stance, the company regularly uses products that have been tested on

animals at one time. The article cites an internal company memo from 1992 that reported an increase in the number of ingredients that were tested on animals, from 34 per cent to 46 per cent. It also states that the company has used products tested on animals for pharmaceutical purposes, because its corporate policy is restricted to cosmetics testing (cited in Cowe, 1994c, p15). The Body Shop's policy is that it does not use products tested on animals in the last five years, as it would in fact be impossible not to use ingredients that have never been tested on animals (Cowe, 1994a, p14). The company, and other 'bathtub firms', labelled this way because they are said to keep the controversy about animal testing alive, have given an incentive to consumers to pay a higher price for their products by playing on the animal testing issue.[11] Between 1980 and 1986 many 'traditional' cosmetic companies were said to have cut animal testing by up to 95 per cent. In 1990, a lawsuit by the German Society for the Prevention of Cruelty to Animals and the German government forced The Body Shop franchises to stop claiming that they were operating under a higher ethical standard. At this point, The Body Shop changed its slogan 'not tested on animals' to the now familiar 'against animal testing' (cited in Entine, 1995).

The Body Shop tends to play down any negative information, and is said to come out 'all guns blazing' at the 'slightest hint' of criticism (interview with consumer association staff member, Newcastle upon Tyne, UK, 8 August 1994). Interestingly, this behaviour is typical of corporate power cultures. Handy notes that power cultures are 'often seen as tough or abrasive' (1985, p189). (Later we shall see that Ben & Jerry's has been especially protective of its corporate image.) Before Entine's article was published, it was revealed that one of his allegations was that there had been some 'emissions' from the company's bottling and warehousing plant in New Jersey. Gordon Roddick sent a letter to the editor of *The Financial Times*, writing:

> *'There were no "emissions" from our former New Jersey "factory". Rather, there were two accidental spills of 30 gallons of shampoo at our former bottling plant two years ago. In line with our policy, we immediately notified the authorities. There was no breach of environmental law, no citation, no "emissions". I'm sorry that we spilled some shampoo, but whenever there are human beings around, there will be minor accidents. The reference to "oil-based ingredients" is perplexing: perhaps The Financial Times was referring to mineral oil. If so, then you should be aware that this is the same ingredient*

which has been slapped on babies bums for generations without adverse effect!' (Roddick, 1994, p12).

Roddick's version may be close to, but not wholly the truth. Hanover Sewage Authority, the local body charged with cleaning the water in New Jersey, says that it traced three spills caused by The Body Shop in 1992–1993, totalling at least 280 litres. In each case, the authority detected the leaks and told The Body Shop (Jack and Buckley, 1994, p12).

The Body Shop's corporate culture is concerned with 'profits' first and 'principles' second. This has been confirmed by a Body Shop consultant who said: 'I don't think I'm telling any secrets when I say that some Body Shop employees get upset when Anita's going around headquarters and all she's talking is profits, profits, profits' (interview with The Body Shop consultant, Manchester, UK, 7 November 1994). This is also confirmed by Roddick herself who writes:

> *'every now and then we had someone who got it all about face and thought her primary job was to love the world rather than to trade. (Sometimes people get us entirely wrong and apply for jobs thinking we are an environmental protection organization or a charity; they are quite taken aback to learn that working in a Body Shop means selling and cashing and wrapping)'* (Roddick, 1992, p154).

Linking issues of trade with questions about 'good works' is The Body Shop's best known policy, 'trade not aid'. Critics have also discussed this. The rationale and aim of the policy is stated in a company broadsheet which asserts:

> *'A New Business Ethic: Trade Not Aid: Since 1987 The Body Shop has operated fair trading agreements in developing countries. We've always been fired with curiosity about other cultures and the ways people look after their bodies, so it's no great leap for us to source ingredients and products in other countries. The great challenge is to create successful small-scale trade links that are economically viable without impinging upon local traditions and ways of life'* (The Body Shop, no date).

The Body Shop claims that trade links must be based on fair terms of trade and sustainable use of natural resources. The trade links connect with a variety of social and environmental issues. For example, in Mexico, Nanhu Indian women cultivate and sell maguey cactus to The Body Shop for the company's cactus body scrubs. The Body Shop claims that the market for body scrubs which had been linked with the Mexican tourist trade and brush manufacturers, had collapsed, forcing many of the males to migrate to Mexico City or the US in search of work. The Body Shop has also assisted the Nanhu with afforestation of the cactus by donating 6000 baby cacti (The Body Shop, no date).

In Brazil, the company trades with the Kayapo Indians, which, the company asserts, provides the Indians with a cash income, which allows them self-determination while also preserving the rainforest. The Body Shop also maintains that this has allowed the local people to provide themselves with an educational and medical infrastructure that they could not otherwise afford. The 'rainforest harvest', has come under increased scrutiny by a number of critics (Ben & Jerry's, examined below, has faced similar criticism). However, other examples of the programme include a papermaking project in Bansbari, Nepal. This project supports a local traditional industry using 'sustainable' cloth rags and banana fibre to make the paper, instead of the 'unsustainable' use of the local lokta tree that had caused extreme deforestation. Cash income has provided tuberculosis clinics, as well as cataract operations there. In Tamil Nadu, southern India, The Body Shop purchases 'footsie rollers' made from the 'sustainable' *Acacia niloticca* tree, because it remains alive if harvested at the trunk. Twenty per cent of the income from the project must go towards local welfare, including health care, education and work conditions. There are also several other projects in Zambia, Ghana, and with Native Americans in the US (The Body Shop, no date).

One critic of Trade Not Aid is Stephen Corry of the non-governmental organization Survival International, which supports indigenous peoples. He focuses specifically on the 'rainforest harvest' and maintains that trade not aid is simply another form of a familiar dependent relationship under another name (Corry, 1993). He argues that only a few communities benefit from trade, and some may be successful, but that they will be constrained by the fact that it is, in essence, an unequal trade relationship. If the company can no longer find a market for the product, the business will collapse. In the case of Cultural Survival Enterprises (CSE), also discussed in the Ben & Jerry's case below, the cooperatives can collapse both under the weight of too many orders later rescinded, and from too many orders the volume of which a small cooperative may be unable to meet. The relationship makes the communities more dependent on demand in developed countries, and on the cash economy, rather than on hunting, gathering or growing subsistence crops. Additionally, this leaves consumers in developed countries with the false assumption that they can 'save the rainforest' by buying conditioner or candy rather than by more assertive political action. Gordon Roddick offers the response of The Body Shop to such arguments for this type of delinking in a typically lively fashion as follows:

> *'Consumerism needs to undergo a radical change. And it won't go away, so how do we make it more responsible to everyone? Don't tell me that Stephen Corry or his Survival International staff don't eat candy bars or wash their hair... Indigenous people consistently argue that they often have no option but to be part of the market economy. Why shouldn't they choose partners who respect their cultures and environments?'* (Roddick, 1993, p200)

At the same time, Roddick concludes with the relevant point that these issues are often magnified to gross proportions. For example, The Body Shop's harvest of 4 tonnes of Brazil nut oil in the Kayapo territory is relatively minor compared with the much more devastating environmental and social degradation which people of that area have faced at the hands of (unnamed) logging and mining corporations.[12]

Another criticism of Trade Not Aid, voiced by Richard Adams, is that 'despite the posters and other publicity for its programme – Trade Not Aid represents less than 0.1 per cent of the Body Shop's trade' (Adams, cited in Vidal, 1994, p2). The British organization Ethical Consumer said that Trade Not Aid was more a public relations policy than a serious purchasing departure. The company's response to the criticisms is that it cannot quantify the amount, but that it is 'more than 1 per cent but less than 10 per cent' (cited in Jack and Buckley, 1994, p8).[13]

Gordon Roddick has responded to the questions about Trade Not Aid in a letter to *The Financial Times* about the Entine criticisms specifically:

> *The accusation that I find personally most offensive is the suggestion that we lack "commitment" to our trade-not-aid programme. No one should doubt our commitment. Some of our critics' arguments about trade-not-aid centre around a percentage game that misses the point. They say*

> *that, because our trade-not-aid purchases form only a small percentage of our total, we should not talk about it nor have prominent displays or window posters relating to it. We say that trade-not-aid is a very important part of our business, on which we spend a disproportionate amount of money'* (Roddick, 1994, p12).

The Body Shop is far more adept at supporting, and perhaps marketing, ethical and green causes than most of its competitors. The Body Shop is unique in having provided environmental data on its activities for the last several years. Their 'Green Book' complies with EU guidelines on ecological management and auditing. Critics of The Body Shop in the fair trade movement claim that the company repeatedly refuses them access to the detailed information needed to examine the company's claims. If it gets the 'slightest whiff' of criticism, it begins to engage its legal team (interview with consumer association staff member, Newcastle upon Tyne, UK, 8 August 1994).[14] According to Adams, 'people have taken a lot on trust, the crux is to have independently verifiable information' (Adams, cited in Jack and Buckley, 1994, p8). To receive reliable information, to tour plants and to engage in dialogue with corporations is a standard expectation within the consumer movement (interviews with consumer association staff members, London, 24 February 1994 and New York, 29 March 1995). The extent to which this information is actually shared with outsiders is another matter. Consumer groups that produce reports on corporations charge a great deal for the information, and they are not always agreeable to helping outside, non-paying researchers (interview with consumer association staff member, New York, 29 March 1995).

The company says that it is involved in social-environmental continuous improvement. It hired the former head of Oxfam's fair trading division in Canada to help develop its initiatives. It incorporated its values into its official company memorandum of association.

When The Body Shop controversy broke out in August 1994, the former leaders of the British Green Party, Jonathon Porritt and Sara Parkin, wrote to *The Financial Times* in support of The Body Shop. They said that it was 'one of the leading companies in the field of social, ethical and environmental policy ... a good example of a successful yet caring company with priorities way beyond the usual profit motive' (cited in Cowe, 1994b, p22).

SUMMARY: THE BODY SHOP

In the *UN Survey*, The Body Shop was cited specifically in the section on the ('dark green') fourth level of the environmental hierarchy, 'sustainable development management'; the 'greenest' style of corporate management in operation now. This is because of the company's developing country programmes (Trade Not Aid), its ethical sales policies (Against Animal Testing), its disclosure practices (product information labelling, policy dissemination) and its worldwide policies (developing country activities). This suggests that The Body Shop is among the most environmentally active corporations. Simultaneously, as one of The Body Shop's retail industry advisers remarked 'The whole problem is with the starting point. The fundamental fact of life is that no business can be environmentally friendly' (Richards, cited in Cowe, 1994d, p2).

Shrivastava sees the company's green image as central to its success. In line with a corporate power culture and with a strategy based on Missionary Greening because of Anita and Gordon Roddick's vocal stance, environmental and social issues have been fundamentally important in 'the Body Shop's phenomenal financial success and rapid growth'. This is because the company has been able to distinguish itself within a very homogeneous and competitive market. And the environmental component essentially created a workable market niche that then expanded into the rest of the cosmetics industry with the increasing popularity of 'natural' products 'not tested on animals'. The Body Shop created the niche and then successfully positioned itself as market leader. This edge also proved fruitful in new markets, 'making the company a global success' (Shrivastava, 1996, p85).

At the same time, many criticisms of The Body Shop seem to provoke something of a 'So what'? response. Concurrently, as The Body Shop's critics were being particularly vociferous in August 1994, several thousand hectares of rainforest in Southeast Asia were offered for clear felling on the London Stock Exchange, and the deal was left unqueried. It is likely that in the same week in August, other corporations were involved in the pollution of water resources, toxic releases, exploiting poor communities, yet The Body Shop was criticized for spilling 280 litres of shampoo years earlier (Vidal and Brown, 1994, p6). The main criticisms of Adams, and others, one of whom stated that they 'wouldn't grace the Body Shop with the name "ethical business"' (interview with consumer association staff member, Newcastle upon Tyne, UK, 8 August 1994), are the issues of honesty and public dialogue, and providing independently verifiable information. Gordon Roddick, responding to the animal testing critique, stated that the company's policy has always been clear and that 'I sometimes think we overdose on providing information' (Roddick, 1994, p12).

The Body Shop is a successful corporation, and at the same time it does more than many similar corporations for the environment and social causes. It is probably impossible to expect 'environmental performance' from any corporation. At the same time as Anita Roddick has promoted her own brand of consumerism, she has also raised the general awareness of important social and environmental issues. Today, The Body Shop is guided by 'some very hard-nosed gentlemen who ... know the mix of money and morality is uneasy'. Or, in more frank terms as one interviewee put it: 'the way Anita [Roddick] has shot her mouth off is just unbelievable and [Body Shop executives] know they just haven't got a hope' (interview with consumer association staff member, Newcastle upon Tyne, UK, 8 August 1994). As Vidal and Brown observe 'A maverick chief doesn't always fit in the bitter capitalist world of contracts, corporate lawyers, and screw-you multinationalism, whatever Anita might say' (Vidal and Brown, 1994, p6). Rather than silencing Roddick, to prevent her from making claims which the company cannot live up to, the corporate managers increasingly encourage her to 'pack up her ideals and toddle off (as she always has done) with anthropologists, adventurers and other mavericks to the ends of the earth (with that gold card) [see endnotes] in search of this herb or that banana skin' (Vidal and Brown, 1994, p6). This may also indicate that The Body Shop is increasingly moving away from a 'founder led' power culture to a more formalized and 'traditional' role culture. The Body Shop is an important case of the problems of trying to develop a corporation with a 'social-environmental' culture; raising some important issues about business, its relationship to society, the environment and sustainability, concurrent with ecological modernization as cultural politics.

Similar to The Body Shop, Ben & Jerry's is especially active in social and environmental causes. Also similar to The Body Shop, it has been criticized for not living up to its 'ethical' pronouncements. As an interesting comparison to The Body Shop, the characteristics of Ben & Jerry's corporate response to environmental crises are rather less specifically environmental, and rather more 'social-environmental' than The Body Shop. A notable example of this is the efforts it has made to support the Vermont community of which it is a part, shipping ice cream throughout the US and the world, when the environmental solution would be to open more plants.[15]

BEN & JERRY'S

Ben & Jerry's is a manufacturer of premium 'all natural' ice cream and frozen yoghurt. This means that the products do not have any artificial ingredients or preservatives. Some of the cookies, candies and chocolate add-ins do have artificial ingredients and preservatives. The only sweeteners that the company uses in its frozen products are pure cane and beet sugar. In response to customer heath concerns, the company, which began with superpremium ice cream with about 15 per cent butterfat and less than 20 per cent air content, developed 'low fat', frozen yoghurt products, which contain 2 per cent or less fat content (Ben & Jerry's, 1993).

The company, based in Waterbury, Vermont, USA, was established in 1978. By 1985 annual sales were US$9 million and by 1993, they were over US$140 million. In 1994, the company was trading in the US, Canada, UK, the Russian Federation and Israel. At the end of 1995 there were 700 employees and sales were US$155 million. By 1996, the company was also trading in Holland, France, and was investigating setting up a production site in Ireland. In 1996, annual sales were up to around US$175 million. At the end of 1999, the company was also trading in Japan and sales were US$237 million. In April 2000, Ben & Jerry's agreed to a unique takeover by Unilever, in which Ben & Jerry's would pursue its social and economic goals with its own board of directors, operating separately from Unilever's North American ice cream business (Ben & Jerry's, 2000).

The company has a commitment to small-scale Vermont family dairy farmers and purchases all of its dairy products from a local cooperative of such farmers, above market prices (Rosin, 1995). As part of its 'local' commitment to the community, the company manufactures all of its products at its home base in Vermont, even when it would be more environmentally sound to have a number of centres of production near its major markets, saving on transport.[16] Ben & Jerry's is a company which has attempted to integrate social and economic aspects of its mission into a type of 'Third Way' which the co-founder Ben Cohen has labelled 'Caring Capitalism'. Its corporate culture is defined here as being marked by 'linked prosperity', since this most accurately delineates the cultural system of shared meanings evident at Ben & Jerry's. 'Linked prosperity' is the company's name for the goals suggested by their three part mission statement, outlined below. Linked prosperity connotes the integration of social aims with economic aims, and of environmental aims with economic aims. These are aims not only of the policies and programmes at Ben & Jerry's but also represent the nature of its workplace. There is a sense of teamwork and common purpose around the company's social mission.

The company has developed numerous policies that aim to define the business by 'linked prosperity'. One of the most notable of these is the donation of 7.5 per cent of its pre-tax earnings to charity (most companies donate less than 1 per cent) (Hollister et al, 1994).[17] In 1994, the company was cited by the CEP as among the top 13 companies in the US for its environmental and social programmes, and was placed on the organization's 'Honour Role' (Hollister et al, 1994).[18] A unique feature of the company has been its policy that until 1990 the highest paid employee could not earn more than five times the lowest paid.[19] However, in that year, the ratio was raised to seven to one. The policy was changed again in 1994, when the company was looking for a new chief executive and claimed it could not hire the calibre of management it needed to 'run a complex and large company without higher salaries to bring in qualified management personnel' (interview with Ben & Jerry's public relations staff member, Vermont, 25 August 1994).[20] The company dropped its salary cap. Bob Holland, the company's CEO hired in 1994, was offered a salary of US$250,000 (Van Grinsven, 1996). His salary including his bonus, in 1995, was US$326,000 or 14.5 times the salary of the lowest paid ice cream scooper (Judge, 1996).

The board of directors has created a three part mission statement, which comprises Ben & Jerry's vision of 'caring capitalism'.[21] Their statement is as follows:

- *Product Mission*: to 'make, distribute and sell the finest quality all-natural ice cream'.
- *Economic Mission*: to 'operate the company on a sound financial basis ... increasing value for our shareholders and creating career opportunities and financial rewards for our employees'.
- *Social Mission*: to 'operate the company ...[to] improve the quality of life of our employees and a broad community: local, national and international' (Ben & Jerry's, 1990).[22]

It can be said that Ben & Jerry's mission focuses more on social aspects of business than environmental aspects per se, with environmental activities tending to come under the rubric of its social concerns. Of course, these issues are often linked within the 'ethical business movement' generally, but whereas some companies might stress particular environmental issues, Ben & Jerry's stresses social issues especially. For example, the company has had a social audit as part of its company report since 1988, but only began a separate environmental audit in the 1994 annual report. This may be partly due to the fact that Ben & Jerry's, being an ice cream company, is not under the strict or pressing environmental constraints of more polluting industries. In Chapter 3, it was argued that many food corporations are not as active in environmental issues, perhaps because their operations are less polluting, and can be described as having compliance-oriented management styles. The main environmental problem faced by its operations are wastewater emissions, due to the milky, high fat discharges of its manufacturing process. This is also the company's main human health problem, since its ice cream products are high in fat, excessive consumption of which causes a number of diseases and debilities.[23] As a result, Ben & Jerry's has developed a number of low fat frozen yoghurts. A spokesperson stated that the company's ice cream should be consumed in moderation 'as part of a balanced diet' (interview with Ben & Jerry's public relations staff member, Vermont, 25 August 1994). In its environmental activities, Ben & Jerry's has focused on transport, energy, biodiversity and biotechnology concerns. As an example of linking the environment with social rather than health concerns, it has protested against the use of bovine growth hormone (BGH), which boosts milk production in dairy cattle, primarily for its negative impact on small family run farms, rather than its potential health or environmental effects (Ben & Jerry's, 1993, p2).[24]

One of the highlights of Ben & Jerry's environmental activities is its signing of the CERES 'Valdez' Principles in 1992, which include a commitment to recycling, conservation and source reduction. Additionally, the CERES Principles provide a means by which the public can assess the environmental activities of business. In 1992, Ben & Jerry's was the largest company to have signed the Principles. The company is also a founding member of Businesses for Social Responsibility (BSR) (Ben & Jerry's, 1993, p1). BSR supports linking profits with environmental and social action. The group also has members of *Fortune 500* companies such as Reebok and Stride-Rite, the footwear corporation. BSR's aim is to be 'a voice for progressive businesses in the media and legislature' (Lager, 1994, p231).[25] Some of the outcomes, which are directly linked to these associations, include Ben & Jerry's packaging, which is constructed from recycled paperboard with a high content of post-consumer material. Its annual reports, brochures and pamphlets are all printed on recycled paper. As its truck leases expire, Ben & Jerry's replaces the freon-based refrigeration systems with cold plating. In the area of the protection of biodiversity, it is engaged in supporting rainforest conservation through purchase and publicity of specially sourced Brazil nuts (cited in Hollister et al, 1994).

'Linked prosperity' in the workplace means that Ben & Jerry's provides health and dental coverage and low cost coverage for families, including same sex partners. Benefits are also provided to part-time employees. The company furthermore provides profit sharing, an employee stock ownership programme, and a 401(k)[26] matching pension programme. Employee advisory groups, which represent all non-management employees, are consulted on major new initiatives. Ben & Jerry's has a free fitness centre for all employees, to help maintain good health and offset the three free pints of ice cream per day available to employees. Finally, Ben & Jerry's has been cited as one of the 100 best companies to work for in the US (Hollister et al, 1994, p80).[27]

Outside the manufacturing plants, 'linked prosperity' is connected with Ben & Jerry's support of a variety of social causes and political stands. These include a protest against the Seabrook nuclear plant, in the US state of New Hampshire, with a billboard stating 'Stop Seabrook, keep our customers alive and licking'. Another protest was about the expansion of the Hydro-Quebec hydropower plant that threatened the Native American community in the James Bay region of Quebec, Canada. The company also supported the Bryant bill in the US congress that advocated more stringent automotive fuel efficiency standards.[28] Ben & Jerry's, similar to The Body Shop (above), did not advertise for many years.[29]

In their retail shops, 'linked prosperity' takes the form of 'partnershops' where non-profit groups and franchises are paired. For example, in Harlem the partnershop employs homeless people and the profits are donated to a homeless shelter, and a shop in Baltimore is staffed by developmentally disabled people and donates profits to related organizations. Young people who are 'at risk' also staff some of its Vermont stores. Ben & Jerry's gives away free ice cream at various events throughout Vermont and the US (Hollister et al, 1994).

The company has a commitment to suppliers; it purchases all of its dairy products from the St Albans Cooperative Creamery to support local Vermont family producers. It purchases these products at a higher than market rate with the understanding that they will be free from chemicals and, since 1994, BGH. The company has bought pecans and peaches from threatened African-American farms in Georgia, blueberries from Native Americans in Maine, brownies from homeless and disadvantaged people in Yonkers, outside New York City, and apple pies baked by recovering drug addicts in New Jersey. Furthermore, the company's ice cream on a stick, called 'Peace Pops', supports the organization One Percent for Peace which aims to redirect 1 per cent of the US defence budget towards the pursuit of peaceful solutions to conflicts.[30]

Environmental policy

This section reviews various elements of the environmental activities of Ben & Jerry's, focusing on specific environmental issues. In 1989, Ben & Jerry's established a position called 'Manager of Environmental Development'. The manager was to assess the corporation's environmental practices and create solutions to problems discovered. In 1991, the company hired a 'Director of Social Mission Development', the only company position of its kind in the country. The 1992 annual report stated that the company had hired a full-time 'Manager of Natural Resource Use' but that year's social assessment indicated that the manager did not report directly to the company president.

While many corporations have officers who disburse funds to charities and do development work, others have dedicated 'foundations'. Ben & Jerry's has a foundation which distributes funds from the company's 7.5 per cent pre-tax charitable donation.[31] The social mission development position was atypical because it was not merely philanthropic, in the traditional corporate sense, but rather was concerned with addressing the company's mission statement (see above), which was unique among corporations in its integration of product, economic and social goals (see also Shrivastava, 1996, p129). The hierarchical position of the post (in the organization) was equal to the company's chief financial officer. The director of social mission development was also the only employee aside from the co-founders to have a seat on the board of directors. The aim of the position holder was to 'get people to own the company's social mission'.

At Ben & Jerry's, while everyone in the company is encouraged to be active, the 'Green Teams' generate support for environmental issues and coordinate the company's participation.[32] Gail Mayville, assistant to the CEO, developed them in 1988. Mayville led the company to initiate recycling programmes and created a consortium of local businesses, including Ben & Jerry's, which developed the use of recycled copier paper, long before this product was ever available to consumers. Mayville led the early environmental activities of the company and brought about the reduction of product packaging, which, similar to the understanding of corporations with a preventive management style, 'not only were an improvement environmentally, but also saved us money' (Lager, 1994, p190).

The creation of the Green Teams at each company site, which 'further increased awareness of environmental issues and identified opportunities for improving our performance throughout the company' (Lager, 1994, p190), is an example of the task culture[33] at Ben & Jerry's. The team's mission statement is as follows: 'Dedicated to motivating and communicating a sense of environmental responsibility throughout Ben & Jerry's community by developing and motivating creative earth-respecting programmes' (cited in Shrivastava, 1996, p124).

The Green Teams meet periodically to review the progress of environmentalism within the company. Shrivastava observed one 40 minute meeting in which the following issues were discussed and decided on:

- methods of reusing and recycling cardboard drums used to store ice cream;
- changing the procedure for picking up recycled paper to improve the recycling rate;
- participating in a fund raiser for a local youth club;
- educating themselves and the company on the use of cornstarch polymers, such as Nuvon, for packaging;
- arranging for the pickup of recycling equipment;
- doing an environmental education skit for the Quality Council (executive committee of the company); and
- improving reuse of paper used on one side by cutting and binding it into notepads' (Shrivastava, 1996, p124).

Each of the above points was discussed, problems and solutions addressed, and members of the team volunteered to take responsibility for each matter. The manager of natural resources was responsible for making financial resources available to implement the actions that were decided. The Green Teams meet monthly to brainstorm environmental issues. More technical issues are passed on to other groups like the 'E-Team', which is in charge of energy programmes as well as the production, maintenance, marketing and design teams (Shrivastava, 1996, p125).[34]

The company sources its dairy products from farmers who have given the company the assurance that they have not treated their cows with BGH. The corporation Monsanto manufactures synthetic BGH.[35] This is part of a huge growth industry, called transgenics, in which farm animals and plants are genetically altered to produce, for example, disease resistant crops. Monsanto, along with other large companies in the transgenics industry, have found that they can genetically alter BGH which, when injected into cows, can boost milk production. However, consumer groups and government officials in North America and Europe have argued that BGH can cause premature growth or breast cancer when passed to humans via the food chain. In cows there is the concern that it can produce mastitis. In the

US, the General Accounting Office and Consumers Union allege that the substance is unsafe. Other groups such as the US National Institutes of Health, the Congressional Office of Technology Assessment, and the European Union's Committee for Veterinary Medicine Products, argue that the substance is safe (Hollister et al, 1994, p346).[36]

In the state of Vermont, dairy farmers produce around 85 per cent of the agricultural output of the state. Ben & Jerry's is worried that the use of BGH will threaten the livelihoods of small-scale, family run farms. In a statement, the company said that BGH, also known as recombinant bovine growth hormone (rBGH), 'poses a threat to the physical health of dairy cows and will seriously undermine the financial health of small, family owned dairy farms, and is simply unnecessary' (cited in Wilson, 1995). The main worry is that the use of BGH by large Mid-Western dairy farmers could increase milk production to such an extent that the small, family run farms in Vermont would be driven out of business. The supervisor of dairy production at Vermont's Department of Agriculture said that:

> 'This product has the potential to change Vermont agriculture as we know it. The issue here is not so much a biotechnology issue, it's the fear that this product could increase the productivity and the economic advantages that the large dairymen [sic] have over the small dairy' (Wilson, 1995).[37]

Ben & Jerry's has a well-established recycling programme. The company recycles about 60 per cent of its office paper. Paper is reused internally, and letterhead is printed on recycled paper. The main part of the company's solid waste comes from packaging materials that are employed to deliver products for manufacturing. Some of the recycling activities in this area include corrugated board, which is baled and sold for recycling. Since 1989 the company has had a recycling programme for large plastic pails in which they received ingredients for manufacturing. In cooperation with Occidental Chemical, a plastics manufacturer, and Vermont Republic Industries, an employer of physically and emotionally disturbed people, equipment was installed to shred the buckets and sell them for recycling. Once this was in operation, the company was able to recycle 1000 pails weekly that would have otherwise gone to the landfill. This led to a 30 per cent reduction of solid waste in 1989 over the previous year. The company's pint container comprises paperboard that is covered with a plastic coating to provide moisture resistance. This is a package that is non-biodegradable and hard to recycle. Alternatives are being tested (Curren, 1994).

Ben & Jerry's experienced a period of rapid growth through the later part of the 1980s and early 1990s. In 1987, the company had more than US$30 million in annual sales and as a normal part of the production process created a high volume of difficult to break down, milky, high butterfat waste at the beginning and end of production runs and from spills. The amount of waste produced was overloading the town of Waterbury's waste treatment system, and as a result the company was assessed a number of costly fines. The company developed a number of innovative solutions to its wastewater problem. The first was to feed the milky waste to pigs, which consumed thousands of litres per week. This is still in operation. Another solution was to use the waste as a fertilizer for local farmers' fields. Yet, Ben & Jerry's was still exceeding its discharge limits, and developed waste pre-treatment lagoons. The company then worked in cooperation with New England ecological engineering firms to create a solar aquatic greenhouse to treat some of the ice cream waste. The greenhouse creates the natural conditions of a wetland in order to break down some of the waste. This system, which had been successful for municipal waste, was not as effective for the company's high volume of fatty waste. Ben & Jerry's then developed an air flotation system which employs carrageenan, a derivative of seaweed, to separate high strength waste from wastewater before this is pumped to the pre-treatment lagoons. This has proved successful and allowed the company to remain within discharge limits. Another environmental innovation is to send packaged frozen ice cream waste to a waste-to-energy incineration plant that generates power for consumer use. Other waste is sent to a local community garden in Burlington, Vermont, to be used as fertilizer (Curren, 1994).

The company also sponsors community projects, campaigns and other events promoting awareness of environmental issues. These include Vermont's Merry Mulching Campaigns that recycle Christmas trees and leftover paint cans. Ben & Jerry's also has a travelling circus, the New Vaudeville Light Circus Bus, which travels the US offering entertainment and ice cream. The vehicle draws attention to renewable (solar) energy by being completely powered by 17 square metres of photovoltaic cells (Shrivastava, 1996).

Ben & Jerry's has a number of responses to the energy dilemmas it faces. Some of these include:

- more energy efficient lighting in offices in plants;
- motion detectors that turn off lights in unoccupied rooms;
- energy efficient compressors, motors and other plant equipment;

- research into energy efficient refrigeration; and
- alternative refrigeration such as the use of winter air.

Beginning in 1992 the company began building an energy efficient engine room at its main Waterbury plant, and installed a pasteurizer that generates 91 per cent of the heat it uses. In its Springfield plant, Ben & Jerry's has replaced old motors with energy efficient ones.

Increasingly, the company's main energy problem is linked to transport. The company's commitment to Vermont products and manufacturing means that it has to ship frozen goods across the US and around the world. Thus, marketing each litre of its product involves a high energy component. Within this transport system, the company is experimenting with cold plate technology instead of freon-based coolants, and rail transport for its products. As noted above, the transport industry has serious environmental effects; a choice has been made at Ben & Jerry's to support the local community over environmental preservation in this case. Of course, there may be other reasons why the more environmental decision, to diversify production sites, is not taken; namely the ice cream's brand recognition and particular market niche.[38]

Environmental record

The social and environmental programmes are impressive, though the constraints of maintaining shareholder value have made the integration of social-environmental and financial objectives difficult, if not impossible in certain cases. To begin with, a major part of the success of the company has probably come from being associated with these various social programmes, as Entine observes above in his discussion of 'social or cause related marketing', and has certainly generated much unpaid publicity. Indeed, Ben & Jerry's is one of the first companies to have made a profit while pursuing extensive non-profit activities (Rosin, 1995). Some critics would argue that the company has a certain interest in maintaining this market image on which its success depends, whatever the 'truth' might be. For example, although the company publishes an annual social assessment in which it reviews aspects of the success or failure of its programmes and policies as well as other issues such as worker safety and environmental concerns, it does not always review more serious questions regarding its business. It has been argued that Ben & Jerry's flagellates itself over minor transgressions (such as an increase in the number of workers who feel, at times, like quitting) but it does not always review more serious questions regarding its business (these questions are reviewed below) (Rosin, 1995).

As with The Body Shop, some investigators have revealed what seem to be inconsistencies between Ben & Jerry's corporate image and its action.[39] The main criticisms of Ben & Jerry's are as follows:

- The company engages in 'publicity stunts' in which it is economical with the truth, most notably its 1994 search for a new CEO.
- Ben & Jerry's pay policy and stance on wealth are misleading.
- The company has mistreated its suppliers.
- Ben & Jerry's rainforest people's initiative actually did more harm than good for those in developing countries.

One of the major 'publicity stunts' occurred in 1994, when Ben & Jerry's opened its CEO search to the general public with great fanfare in a poster which portrayed Ben and Jerry (their faces are on each of their cartons of ice cream) dressed like 'Uncle Sams' pointing their fingers (in a version of the familiar American Second World War armed forces recruitment poster) announcing their 'Yo, I'm your CEO Contest'. Applicants were asked to write an essay and in 100 words or less, state why they would be the best head. The winner was promised the job, and the runner-up ice cream for life. The contest generated over 20,000 applications 'mostly from caged yuppies desperate to escape' (Rosin, 1995). Meanwhile the company hired a headhunting firm to search for a new chairperson, and located Bob Holland, a management consultant with McKinsey & Company and consultant to many corporations with a 'traditional' corporate culture. Holland's poem submitted 'as per direction for Ben & Jerry's "Yo, I'm your CEO" contest' was written after he had been offered the job. The company does not mention this event, but if asked, it does not deny it, which critics find deceptive (Rosin, 1995).

This leads to the second accusation that the company's policy on not paying outrageously large corporate salaries is misleading. Until 1994, the policy was that the highest paid employee earned no more than seven times the lowest paid worker. Ben Cohen in 1988 and head of the company said in the *New Age Journal*: 'It's really interesting what you can do with a business when you don't care about making a lot of money. There is a spiritual aspect to business ... we are all interconnected. As we help others, we cannot but help ourselves' (cited in Rosin, 1995). This is seen as disingenuous because Cohen and Greenfield, in effect, have millions of dollars through their stock ownership.

The third major criticism is that Ben & Jerry's has mistreated its suppliers. One of these suppliers was the Reverend James Carter who ran the LaSoul Bakery in Red Bank, New Jersey. The bakery was unique in that, as part of Carter's ministry, it employed recovering alcohol and drug addicts and utilized counselling as part of the recovery process. LaSoul was a small operation that supplied pies to local grocery stores. In 1992, after seeing Ben Cohen on the American investigative news programme *20/20*, Carter drove up to Vermont with some of the bakery's pies. 'Ben loved both the pies and "Reverend Carter's vision of building a sound business"' (Rosin, 1995).

The company decided to use the pies to make an Apple Pie Frozen Yoghurt. Within three weeks, Carter had a letter of intent to do business with Ben & Jerry's. The minister used this letter to borrow money for equipment to fill the increased volume of orders. Cohen flew to New Jersey to tape a television show of himself and the recovering addicts mixing Apple Pie Frozen Yoghurt. The ice cream went on the market in 1993 (Lager, 1994, p232).

In May 1994, with sales down, Ben & Jerry's reduced its orders drastically leaving Carter with freezers full of pies. Carter had to make all but two of his staff redundant, and called Cohen at the headquarters. The next day, Cohen flew down to New Jersey, and Carter claims that he told him and the remaining staff 'Don't worry, we'll stick with you' (Rosin, 1995).

The orders never revived and in June 1995, Carter received a fax from the company thanking him for 'his good works' and cancelling all remaining orders. In fact, in addition to flagging sales, a Ben & Jerry's staff member interviewed for this research said that the company had been receiving letters of complaint from dissatisfied customers who indicated that 'they did not want drug addicts touching their food and were therefore refusing to buy the frozen yoghurt'; this led those customers to stop buying the company's products (interview with Ben & Jerry's public relations staff member, Vermont, 25 August 1994).[40] At the news of the cancellation, Carter was left bitter and US$500,000 in debt. He reflected 'It's pretty cute, this social mission, but the bottom line is, Ben & Jerry's buried my company'. Ben Cohen claimed that Carter was told to find other orders and was given six months notice. The director of social missions at Ben & Jerry's, Alan Parker, was reminded of a spreadsheet dated 11 November 1994, which projected US$500,000 worth of orders for LaSoul in 1995. Parker replied: 'That spreadsheet was given to [Carter] as a best case scenario for volume expectations. Nothing about that memo could be construed as a firm commitment, and it's really disingenuous for him to cite it'. When asked if the company feels responsible for the bakery's demise, Parker's reply was 'Sure, we feel sad' (Rosin, 1995).

The fourth criticism regards the company's efforts in developing countries. Ben & Jerry's sells Rainforest Crunch ice cream which includes a nut brittle made from nuts harvested by a Brazilian cooperative from the rainforest. The idea is that this promotes use of the forest and therefore prevents it from being cleared. This benefits biodiversity, and fosters long-term use of the rainforest as a resource. Working with anthropologist Jason Clay,[41] Ben Cohen set up CSE, in 1989, to make the main ingredient for Rainforest Crunch, cashew/Brazil nut brittle. CSE also sold the candy in boxes. A note on the package said 'Money from these nuts will help Brazilian Forest Peoples start a nut shelling cooperative that they'll own and operate'. Critics felt that this was somewhat misleading because the cooperative was run by the Xapuri, not Native American, but rather descendants of Portuguese rubber tappers. So while it was technically true that they were 'Brazilian forest peoples', some consumers may have thought they were supporting Amazonian Indians and not people who effectively were Euro-Americans (Entine, 1995; Rosin, 1995).

Ben Cohen and the Roddicks from The Body Shop are also said to be friends.[42] According to Lager:

> 'Anita's belief that a business should be a values led organization in which more than strictly economic considerations were factored into the decision making process was greatly influencing Ben [in 1988] and reinforcing his views on the direction he wanted the company to go in. It had struck a chord with Ben, and had confirmed to him that a consumer product company such as Ben & Jerry's could influence society through its ability to communicate with its customers... "We can't just optimize profits," he reasoned, "we need to optimize the community as well"' (Lager, 1994, pp181–182).

Soon after Cohen launched Rainforest Crunch,[43] the Roddicks brought out the Brazil nut hair conditioner. However, the nut cooperative soon collapsed under the huge demand for orders. Ben & Jerry's ended up changing the wording on its packages, noted above, after it was revealed in one of the company's social assessments that 95 per cent of the nuts were coming in from commercial suppliers and not from the cooperative (Entine, 1995; Rosin, 1995).[44]

Ben & Jerry's has always had to balance social causes with profit in line with its mission statement; this has often been difficult to do in practice, as outlined in the case of CSE above. The company has also experienced a transitional period as it shifts from one dominant corporate culture to another, specifically from a power culture in which Cohen, the co-founder, predominated, to a role culture in which the organization became more specialized, formalized and hierarchical. In line with a power culture, Ben Cohen has been seen as the driving force behind the social-environmental agenda of the company. The corporate management, many of whom come from more 'traditional' corporations with a role corporate culture, tend to see Cohen as, at best, a visionary and, at worst, meddling, out of touch and a jeopardy to the company's success (Lager, 1994). As the company began to experience a slowdown in its growth, Bob Holland, a veteran of the 'traditional' business world was brought in to restore the company's finances in 1994. Holland started work in early 1995 and had announced his resignation by September 1996. This short tenure was said to have been brought about because of the mammoth struggle between Cohen and Holland, typical of a shift from power to role culture. Ben Cohen favoured slower growth that was sensitive to the needs of employees and the Vermont community; since he still controlled a substantial portion of the company's stock, the founder was able to push his socially responsible vision. Bob Holland, and the more 'traditional' set of corporate managers, veterans of companies such as The Limited (a US clothing store chain) and American Express, advocated swifter growth. The company had shifted to compensating top managers with stock options, typical of most traditional role cultures, and the 'traditional' management group, as well as like minded shareholders, were pressuring the 'social-environmental' agenda. Holland argued that Ben & Jerry's needed to expand the brand more aggressively or risk being shut out of key markets. According to one director: 'It's not a fight over whether to grow, but how fast. Some of us think it's necessary for survival' (cited in Judge, 1996).[45]

The link between social commitment and profits continued to be a major sticking point within the company. The launching of the new line of sorbets in March 1996 is an example. Within three months Ben & Jerry's had captured a 25 per cent share of the US$60 million premium sorbet niche. The product was a particularly profitable item, and drove sales growth. Ben & Jerry's, however, had entered this particular market a year behind Häagen-Dazs; the delay was partially due to the absence of a direct link between the new line and the company's social mission. For example, Cohen argued that the product was not particularly helpful to the family dairy farmers that the company has a commitment to support (Pereira, 1996). One solution was to use organic fruit but this was more expensive and therefore affected the product's profit margin.

One way in which Holland argued the company needed to expand was internationally. This, too, proved problematic within the boardroom deliberations. In the winter of 1995, the company planned to enter the French market. Ben Cohen only agreed to go into France if the company took out advertisements against the French government's practice of nuclear testing in the South Pacific. In a typical exchange between the 'traditional' and 'social-environmental', Holland remarked: 'What are we gaining by not being there? If the decision is to punish French consumers because of their government's foreign policy, that doesn't make sense' (cited in Judge, 1996). The 'traditionalists' at Ben & Jerry's won out in the end. The decision was to make the marketing campaign less 'splashy'. But in the end, neither side was happy; to the 'traditionalists' it was 'half-hearted' and to the 'social-environmentalists' it was not the right thing to do (Judge, 1996). Holland acknowledged that the entry into Europe was proceeding apace, but 'not as fast as I would like' (reported in Reuters News Service, 27 September 1996).[46]

On 30 September 1996, it was announced that Bob Holland had tendered his resignation to the company. The reason he stated was the need for a consumer goods specialist. Holland said that 'accelerated succession' was needed because of the 'marketplace challenges' and 'the predictably tough demands associated with succeeding founders', noting the difficulties experienced when a corporation shifts from a power to role culture. Cohen observed that 'Instead of building a brand, it's now more a Coke and Pepsi game, battling it out for shelf space – you know a share point here and a share point there. That's the new skill we need to bring in' (cited in Pereira, 1996). Holland stated that:

> *'We have a high quality reputation that when people talk about what is the best ice cream in the world, about 50% say we're the best and another 30% say we're the second best. That's about 80% of the people saying we're a first class operation. When I look at repeat purchases after trial, I see that we're first rate. So, with a world-class reputation and a high rate of repurchase after initial trial, I ask myself: Why aren't we Number 1? We're not getting trial and we're not getting trial among the right people. That's a tall order. [The new CEO] has to be able to take the organization as it currently functions and inject important market leadership skills'* (Holland cited in Egan, 1996).

He concluded: 'This is a consumer goods company. It will live and die by its effectiveness and whether it can compete in the marketplace.

Staying would shortchange the company with what it needs' (Holland cited in Egan, 1996).

SUMMARY: BEN & JERRY'S

Ben & Jerry's is arguably the most socially and environmentally active company of its size. The company was not part of the sample in the *UN Survey*. It is involved in many of the activities that would distinguish it as a corporation that pursues 'sustainable development management' ('dark green'). Ben & Jerry's has developing country programmes as evidenced in its efforts with CSE. The company has ethical sales policies, it sources ingredients and uses distributors from groups that are 'at risk', or from companies with similar social records to their own. The corporation is actively involved in disclosure, it brings in an independent analyst to complete its annual social and environmental audits. Ben & Jerry's has developed numerous environmental programmes including those which are targeted at global environmental issues. Ben & Jerry's gives its workers decent wages and benefits. It is also active in hiring female managers. It has also developed imaginative and creative solutions to environmental and social obstacles of business, based on a flexible and organic task culture, such as 'Joy Gangs' to enliven the workplace and 'Green Teams' and 'E Teams' to target and solve environmental problems.

The company's social-environmental corporate culture does not mean that there are no problems in its operations. Foremost among these is that the company's main product is extremely unhealthy. It is high in fat, and a high fat content in the diet causes numerous health problems that ultimately contribute to two-thirds of all American deaths (Simons et al, 1992).[47] Its policy of supporting the small dairy farmers of the Vermont community in which it is located also leads to significant environmental impact through the transport of its products by road, rail, sea and air throughout North America and the world. Ben & Jerry's gives decent wages and benefits to its workers, but the tasks involved in ice cream manufacture are repetitive and boring, leading to accidents and injuries. The company could also be more active in involving production line workers in decision making (Shrivastava, 1996, p131).

It is all too apparent that incorporating social and economic priorities has not always been easy or in some cases possible. As the corporation shifts from a power to a role culture, the corporation has had to make the decision that wealth creation or share value would always be the determining factor or, according to the 'traditionalist' managers, Ben & Jerry's would go out of business (Lager, 1994). As the corporation continues to grow, and as it shifts towards a 'role culture', it seems that the friction between the two aims is becoming increasingly difficult to handle. Ben Cohen said that the battle between Ben & Jerry's and Häagen-Dazs is now 'becoming a Coke and Pepsi game', which seems to reveal the frustration between 'social-environmental' and 'traditionalist' approaches. Indeed, the company has been criticized for restricting its competition in the same way it faced being shut out by distributors at the behest of Pillsbury, manufacturers of their rival Häagen Dazs, in 1984 (Shrivastava, 1996). Furthermore, the tenure and ultimate departure of Bob Holland highlighted the increasing difficulty that the company has in 'remaining viable in the marketplace' and following its social programme. It seems evident that this will only become more difficult for Ben & Jerry's to manage. Criticisms of the company's record are also important to keep in mind as they clarify expectations of 'social-environmental' corporations. Ben & Jerry's is still driven by a need to maintain its market share. This means that, as for any business, people are going to be 'buried' along the way.

CONCLUSION

The Body Shop and Ben & Jerry's are two companies which owe a great part of their success to their reputations as 'socially and environmentally aware' companies. Both companies successfully tapped into a 'social-environmental' market that had growth potential. Shrivastava's distinction between The Body Shop's missionary greening and Ben & Jerry's organic greening highlights an important distinction between the two approaches.

While Ben & Jerry's has focused on its suppliers, its workers and its operations, The Body Shop has been involved with external 'campaigns': Ken Saro-Wiwa, the burning of the rainforest and animal testing. The Body Shop has been outspoken in its 'beliefs' and 'stance'. This has in turn brought about the greening of the organization when the company has had to live up to its own reputation (interview with consumer association staff member, Newcastle upon Tyne, UK, 8 August 1994), therefore bringing about change from the outside in. Ben & Jerry's, conversely, has been more characterized by an introspective greening. In this case the greening has been typified by considering the impact of its operations and bringing about change from the inside out.

Both of these 'social-environmental' corporations present a challenge to the operations of more 'traditional' corporations. The Body Shop has been more vocal in protesting against the operations of corporations with a 'traditional' corporate culture, and highlighting important social and environmental issues. Ben & Jerry's has been involved in 'publicity stunts', but these have been more understated and more related to raising awareness of its own products. Through its social and environmental programmes, it may present a challenge to other corporations by its example (Abraham, 1995).

'Social-environmental' corporations raise some important questions about what can be expected from business. Raising awareness of the fact that business does not have to be exploitative has probably helped to make the public more aware of some selected problems of the social and environmental effects of business. Radical critics of the social-environmental corporations and investigative journalists who argue about the inconsistencies between their policies and records provide an example of the cultural politics of ecological modernization as well as its rhetorical aspects (Myerson and Rydin, 1996). What is interesting is the contest over meaning of what constitutes environmental problems and what business should do to solve them. It has been argued that the answer is bound up in the ways that it has been defined, presented and socially constructed (Hannigan, 1995).

In addition, social-environmental corporations that strive to make social and environmental shifts are more progressive than most corporations that may aim to comply with the law or make their operations more 'energy efficient'. Perhaps social-environmental corporations, which trumpet such successes, are guilty of telling 'good little stories' (interview with consumer association staff member, Newcastle upon Tyne, UK, 8 August 1994) as one critic suggested. At the same time, such corporations raise consciousness about environmental issues. In fact, some would argue that the environmental debate is all about 'good little stories' (Hannigan, 1995; Myerson and Rydin, 1996).

The contest over meaning which occurs with environmental issues includes all relevant social actors: corporations, lawyers, scientists, consumer advocates and journalists, who all have an interest in putting forward their particular definition of an environmental problem. All these actors compete within a public forum for their particular version of events to be established as 'the version'. Whether the social-environmental corporation is merely 'manipulating' the, so-called, 'legitimate' environmental agenda for its own market niche objectives is to some extent not the point. What is important is the role the social-environmental management style has in raising questions and debates regarding corporations and environmental issues: the cultural politics of ecological modernization. Whenever a corporation chooses to market itself as 'social-environmental' there will always be examples of it 'not living up to its principles'.

For example, it has been well documented that The Body Shop has had to backtrack on various policies. One of these is the claim that their products were 'not tested on animals' which shifted to 'against animal testing'. Whether this change occurred as a result of a cynical public manipulation which, when revealed, caused the corporation to backtrack, or whether it occurred as a result of a mistake or idealistic enthusiasm, we shall never know, unless we could get inside to hear the discussions of these issues by The Body Shop's managers. Sociological researchers have great difficulty in uncovering this sort of 'truth' because of the problems related to gaining entry into corporate research sites. Furthermore in this case the relevance of the shift in stated policy by The Body Shop does not contribute to an understanding of corporate management responses to environmental crises. What we can do is look at the overall pattern of actual management responses to environmental crises to determine which management style it represents, and what this analysis means for an understanding of the process of social change which has been defined as ecological modernization.

The issue of whether The Body Shop or Ben & Jerry's takes environmental actions primarily for public relations reasons,[48] needs to be balanced against the degree to which raising these issues in the public forum is useful from an environmental standpoint. Some members of the responsible business community feel that this type of eco-opportunism, which The Body Shop incidentally states it 'rejects entirely', does everyone a disservice because the public can no longer trust the claims of the groups that try to highlight businesses that are 'genuinely' environmentally active (interview with consumer association staff member, Newcastle upon Tyne, UK, 8 August 1994). The debate within the 'responsible' business community over the actions of The Body Shop reflects the questions which corporations with 'social environmental' corporate cultures raise about how companies can and should do business. It is important to remember that many public opinion polls indicate that the majority of people do not trust most of the claims of business.[49]

One similarity between 'traditional' and 'social-environmental' responses to environmental crises is that all have difficulty reconciling the problem of the environment with the needs of wealth creation and marketplace competition. This research suggests that whether the corporation's response to environmental crises is based on a 'traditional' or 'social-environmental' corporate culture, the needs of wealth creation can overtake the environmental dimensions of any business. If the findings of this research are correct, then every business will have difficulties with the integration of environmental and economic aims. If ecological modernization is about the integration of economic and environmental aims then this study suggests that some corporate cultures and styles are more effective at this integration than others.

The social-environmental corporate culture is indicative of the process of ecological modernization as cultural politics. It raises questions about the limits of business sustainability and provides the basis for a debate as society begins to understand the links between the environment and economic growth. These are discussed in further detail in the following chapter.

6

Greening the Corporations:
Shades of Green[1]

INTRODUCTION

The argument in this book has been that all corporations have difficulty integrating environmental and economic aims, whether they are
traditional or social-environmental. What is especially interesting is
that many corporations have begun to merge environmental and
economic aims. The evidence further suggests that corporate
responses are not as contradictory as might be expected. This was
discovered in the investigation of corporate management responses to
environmental challenges. The cases reveal that corporate cultures
are linked to management structures and styles that in turn can determine corporate responses to environmental crises. Within these
responses there is variation that can be best understood in terms of
shades of green analysis.

The data have been studied in relation to ecological modernization theory because the three dimensions of the theory provide the
most dynamic understanding of corporate greening as a social change
process. The sections which follow summarize the explanatory value
of each of the three major strands of ecological modernization theory
in order to demonstrate the link between management styles, structures and cultures as they affect corporate views of environmental
responses. Inasmuch as none of the strands of the theory accounts for
variations in responses to environmental crises, the shades of green
analysis adds to an understanding of ecological modernization theory
by addressing this gap in existing analyses of the model.

The concluding sections of the chapter consider the policy implications of the findings and suggest areas for further research.

ECOLOGICAL MODERNIZATION AS INSTITUTIONAL LEARNING

Ecological modernization as institutional learning helps to explain how industries have shifted their attention to include environmental issues. The extractive industries and in particular the chemical industry have learned how to become more environmentally efficient at the same time as pursuing wealth creation.

The chemical industry had enjoyed good public relations following the Second World War until the 1960s. Following well-publicized disasters such as those at Seveso, Basel and Bhopal, public confidence in the chemical industry fell to the point where roughly only 25 per cent of the populations in developed countries 'trusted' the industry. These circumstances led the industry to focus more directly on preventing accidents and pollution. After the Bhopal accident, the Chemical Industries Association set up Responsible Care, in order to facilitate communication and best practice among its members. Because it was perceived that any accident affected the public relations of the whole industry, it also acted as a kind of industry pressure group to maintain standards within the chemical industry.

ARCO Chemical is a good example of an extractive industry that has benefited from institutional learning. ARCO Chemical had suffered its own accident at the Channelview, Texas, plant. As a result there was a strong incentive among the top management to incorporate a culture of safety based on the Du Pont model. This included the incorporation of the evaluation of 'near misses' and the process of 'grounding out' safety, both of which attempted to reduce the possibility of accidents due to human error. Both were based on the notion of continuous improvement. The corporation also began to reduce its hazardous waste, water and other emissions through the Waste Minimization Programme.

In the case of ARCO the process of change may be best explained by ecological modernization as institutional learning because its response to the environmental crises it faced resulted in a process of innovation which improved the environmental effects of its operations. In this case ARCO responded to changing public opinion. Its response was strengthened by the support of industry associations such as Responsible Care. The added benefit was to reduce costs by reducing pollution. This suggests that a learning process can occur, especially after accidents, which can result in environmentally useful practices, responding to public concern at the same time. This creates a win–win situation for the industry by improving public opinion while at the same time maintaining profits.

ECOLOGICAL MODERNIZATION AS TECHNOCRATIC PROJECT

Ecological modernization as technocratic project helps to explain the failure of some corporations to link environmental and economic aims successfully. In this case corporations only take environmental action when they can link it to their economic interests, such as pursuing new markets or increasing profits through pollution prevention. The greater extent to which environmentalism is a business opportunity the more likely the environmental message will be appropriated and remanufactured into 'corporate environmentalism'. This is most evident in the actions of corporate executives,[2] public relations[3] and corporate structures when responding to environmental crises. These are best seen in the key environmental structures within some traditional corporate cultures, which are based on a 'problem solving' approach, developed primarily to ensure compliance with regulations in developed countries. It is rooted in the paradigm of environmental managerialism that aims to define 'environmental problems' and then 'solve them'.

Shell provides a good example of this approach to environmental action in some of its operations in developing countries in particular. Most notably this could include oil development in Ogoniland. The environmental needs of this area had only been considered after developmental objectives had been met. Environmental assessments of the Niger River Delta, site of Ogoniland, were essentially theoretical in nature when completed. Social and environmental concerns were later taken into account but were addressed in a way that was inappropriate to local conditions. For example, Shell cites the building of roads in Ogoniland as something it provided for the community. Local critics suggested that this required farmers to wear shoes, something that they could not afford. Shell pursued its development of oil in Ogoniland first and then compensated Ogonis later after problems had arisen and protests had taken place.

Responding to environmental crises as a technocratic project can be problematic because the full environmental repercussions of many aspects of production are, as yet, unknown. Environmental issues are sometimes ignored in developing countries operations of major corporations because of their diversified management structure. However, the basic corporate infrastructure can ensure that the operations of corporations can meet and exceed developing country regulations, and even guarantee that the environmental aspects of their production surpass those of local firms. This creates a situation where environmental concerns are considered only after corporate economic objectives have been met. In this case the environment sometimes wins and the corporation always wins.

ECOLOGICAL MODERNIZATION AS CULTURAL POLITICS

Ecological modernisation as cultural politics helps to explain how environmental change can occur through a democratic process of informed debate within a corporation. This is exemplified by a cadre of small corporations that can best be described as having a 'social-environmental' corporate culture and an associated 'sustainable development management' style. In addition, key 'social-environmental' corporate actors within these companies tend to see themselves as 'caring or green businesspeople', and to present themselves as having developed a 'new form of business'.

Corporations with a social-environmental corporate culture base their activities on green, 'cause related' or social marketing. Companies like Ben & Jerry's and The Body Shop have a history of not advertising; they have drawn attention to their products through the support of various social and environmental causes, such as The Body Shop's 'Stop the Burning Campaign' or Ben & Jerry's protest against the Seabrook, New Hampshire, nuclear facility. In each of these cases the corporation involved has contributed to the social debate surrounding these issues. Thus, they are equally contributing to the debate on the role of business in society.

Another way they contribute to this debate is through their proactive investigation of green issues and the ways in which their businesses can be made more environmentally sensitive. These corporations are not so closely tied to complying with environmental regulations or reacting to regulatory changes; instead they generate flexible and 'organic' structures through the assessment of the firm's impact on the environment. Ben & Jerry's Green Teams are an example of this response to environmental issues.

There are also networks of 'social-environmental' business leaders such as Businesses for Social Responsibility, which contribute to the debate by sharing ideas about how their operations can be more environmentally sound, how to treat their workers more humanely and how to be more active in benefiting the communities in which they operate. These debates again provide a win–win situation for the companies and the environment.

To conclude this analysis of the usefulness of ecological modernization theory to an understanding of the nature of corporate responses to environmental crises, it could be said that it provides a partial answer by helping to describe the process of corporate environmental responses. However, when coupled with the sociology of management theory a fuller explanation can be provided. The latter is analysed in the following section.

STRUCTURES, STYLES AND CULTURES

Ecological modernization theory helps us to understand the macro social process of corporate greening; the sociology of management helps us to understand the more micro level of management responses to environmental crises. In order to explore this level of sociological analysis, three corollary areas investigated include:

- management structures;
- management styles; and
- corporate cultures.

There are management structures, styles and cultures consistent with corporate greening, although these may be best understood in terms of a 'shades of green' analysis. Each of these elements of corporate management environmental responses can be illustrated through a consideration of the four cases assessed in this book. Table 6.1 summarizes the findings in relation to these elements of corporate greening and uses examples from the cases to demonstrate their relationships to corporate environmental responses. It can be seen from Table 6.1 that the two traditional corporations, ARCO Chemical and Shell, have mechanistic structures largely characterized by formality and rigidity; this is typical of large, mature, extractive-based corporations. Their extensive managerial and financial resources have allowed both to be active in developing solutions to environmental crises. I have classified ARCO Chemical as having a light green/green preventive/strategic management style based on its primary concern with preventing accidents. Shell can be said to have a dark green 'sustainable development management' style. Because of its size and wealth, Shell has been able to develop innovative environmental management policies since the 1960s. However, the corporation has not always applied these standards in practice; the most glaring example of this is Nigeria. Shell managers have responded to environmental crises by making a rational choice based on comprehensive and long-term cost-benefit analyses. Similarly, ARCO Chemical managers have made a rational choice to pursue solutions to environmental crises based on the need to maintain public confidence in their company. In line with ARCO Chemical and

Table 6.1 *Environmental management structures, styles and cultures in four cases*

	Management structures	Management style	Corporate culture
ARCO Chemical	Mechanistic: formal, rigid	Light green/green: preventive/ strategic	Role: 'safety'
Ben & Jerry's	Organic: informal, flexible	Dark green: sustainable	Power: 'linked prosperity'
The Body Shop	Organic: informal, flexible	Dark green: sustainable	Power: 'profits and principles'
Shell	Mechanistic: formal, rigid	Dark green: sustainable	Role: 'environmental action which builds shareholder value'

Shell's structural response to environmental crises, both have role-based corporate cultures in which expectations and tasks are strictly defined. While the corporate culture regarding environmental responses in ARCO Chemical is based on safety, the culture at Shell is based on 'environmental action, which builds shareholder value'.

Ben & Jerry's and The Body Shop, the two social-environmental corporations, can be seen as having organic structures based on informality and flexibility; this is typical of some young, small corporations. Both have dark green 'sustainable development management' styles due to their extensive corporate responses to environmental crises in developed and developing countries. The case studies of social-environmental corporations reveal power corporate cultures that are defined by their founders. In the case of Ben & Jerry's the corporate culture regarding environmental crises is based on 'linked prosperity' and in the case of The Body Shop is based on 'profits and principles'.

Regardless of the difficulties which some social-environmental corporations have had in integrating environmental and economic aims, it does seem that The Body Shop and Ben & Jerry's social-environmental corporate cultures can offer something to their 'traditional' counterparts, ARCO Chemical and Shell.[4] Along the lines of ecological modernization as cultural politics, their most important contribution may be the widespread raising of awareness of the links between big business and environmental action and the diffusion of the idea that corporations 'do not have to be environmentally destructive'.

There are some innovative aspects of the 'social-environmental' corporate culture that can be taken on by the larger, more mature corporations. Due to their industry type and size, one set of corporations could not wholly take on the culture of the other set of corporations, nor would they want to. However, Shell's addition of social and environmental dimensions to its statement of business principles may reflect some institutional learning. This could be due to Anita Roddick's letters to them regarding their practices in Ogoniland, or to the example provided by corporations with a 'social-environmental' corporate culture, or to the questions raised about how to conduct business responsibly following the development of corporations with 'social-environmental' corporate cultures. Corporations like Ben & Jerry's and The Body Shop also have much to learn from the experience of the larger, more mature corporations like ARCO Chemical and Shell. As they grow both Ben & Jerry's and The Body Shop, as the discussions of those case studies indicate, appear to be taking on more of the cultural and structural attributes of the corporations with a traditional corporate culture.

IMPLICATIONS FOR FURTHER STUDY

A key area for follow-up is an investigation of the role of different management styles in sustainable development. Corporations with a social-environmental corporate culture may represent a new type of corporation that has a more positive impact on the environment than corporations with a traditional corporate culture. A question that follows from this is whether 'social-environmental' business practices are ultimately environmentally sustainable. The main strategies of environmental NGOs, such as WWF, the World Conservation Union (IUCN) and global environmental intergovernmental organizations such as the United Nations Environment Programme (UNEP) are to work with business to forge environmental–economic integration. Can these groups, working in conjunction with more progressive businesses, help to create even more sustainable business practices? Other issues related to understanding corporate greening which must be addressed include: the role of industrialized countries in global environmental change, and rising rates of consumerism and its socio-environmental impact.[5] Future research could also focus on more systematic development of policy proposals to facilitate corporate 'greening'.

POLICY IMPLICATIONS

Because corporations respond to environmental crises for a variety of reasons, policy objectives concerned with management styles might provide a useful starting point for encouraging corporate greening. For the most conservative styles, in particular 'compliance-oriented management', dynamic command and control regulation could be focused on in order to engender environmentally useful practice. Environmentally problematic practices could be monitored, and there would be an incentive to integrate environmental aims through increased efficiency and improved competitiveness. For corporations further along the 'green spectrum', such as those with 'preventive and strategic management' styles, market instruments might support their environmental performance through policies such as environmental taxes and tradable rights to pollute. The environmental activities of the most progressive corporations would benefit from academic research to explore the limits of sustainability, as well as debate and dialogue about the role of corporations in society. National policies would probably support a combination of all three of these approaches because each contributes positively to resolving the environmental crises facing society.

Beyond constructing ways to make corporations more environmentally responsible, consideration must be given to the efficacy of the controls that could be put into place and enforced to achieve this end. The main issue regarding the largest corporations based in developed countries is that they have the power to operate in a variety of settings across national boundaries, and it can be difficult to regulate transnationally, or to engender useful practices in the various operations of these corporations. Regulation of corporations in developing countries could potentially be as strict as in some developed countries. However, because developing country governments often want the corporation's 'business', the threat of corporate divestment, or the loss of cash through the alternative of the nationalization of industries, tend to bring about fewer regulations so as to attract industry. A review of guidelines adopted by IGOs regarding global business and the environment indicates that most of the corporate policies in this area at this time are in the form of statements of good practice. This is a useful first step; however, going beyond this will require greater analysis of the socio-economic issues facing developing countries.

CONCLUSION

Corporate management responses to environmental crises have a great deal to tell us about processes of social change. In the past, corporations and their managers, a central institution of late modern societies, have pursued a strategy of corporate expansion coupled with the destruction or marginalization of threats to operations. This occurred in times when threats were mainly military-ideological. Such a contradictory relationship was characteristic of the times, the threats and their resolutions. The present crisis to business and society is different, it is socio-environmental. The global environmental crisis has the potential for a complete and permanent impact on human life. This is a threat the like of which developed societies have yet to encounter. While some corporations have responded to the present crisis in ways similar to crises of the past, other corporations have responded through a more thorough integration of economic and environmental aims. This indicates that there is some institutional learning around environmental crises taking place. Other corporations have shaped their businesses in ways that raise questions about the role which business can play in societies. If corporations can solve the present threat to late modern societies, then this kind of economic–environmental integration will be an important part of the resolution. As others have said, we are witnessing a process of social change unique to late modernity. Because corporations constitute the major institution of late modern societies, the ways in which they struggle to resolve this crisis may forever change our understanding of corporations and indeed society itself.

Endnotes

INTRODUCTION

1 In the text of the book, I refer to this document as the *UN Survey*. Using Harvard referencing, I refer to it throughout as: (*UN Survey*, 1993).

2 Because the *UN Survey* materials were primarily factual reportage, the data are particularly valuable. I have carried out the first independent analysis of the *UN Survey* (Robbins, 1996).

CHAPTER 1

1 Under the Clean Air Act, the Environmental Protection Agency (EPA) is responsible for regulating airborne toxic emissions, many of which are carcinogenic, some of which are lethal. It has been argued that corporations affected by the legislation have resisted EPA enforcement since its enactment. More than 25 years after the original legislation only seven of the original 191 toxins labelled carcinogenic have been regulated against, due to pressure from the automobile, petroleum and other related industries (Hawken, 1994).

2 Greenhouse gases are those produced because of human activities that are believed to contribute to the greenhouse effect and therefore may cause global temperatures to rise. The most important of these gases is carbon dioxide, which although not as potent as other gases in producing global change, contributes half of the effect of greenhouse gases because of the large amounts emitted into the atmosphere.

   Molecule for molecule, one of the CFCs, CFC-12, is 5400 times more active as a greenhouse gas than carbon dioxide, but is produced in small quantities compared with carbon dioxide. Of the other major greenhouse gases, methane is 21 times more powerful than carbon dioxide and nitrous oxide is 290 times more destructive (Crump, 1991, p116).

3 This was largely suspected to have been sparked by the race for the market in CFC substitutes. Du Pont, the largest manufacturer of CFCs

in the world, spearheaded this shift when it announced its intention to stop producing CFCs and began making CFC substitutes (see Buttel et al, 1990 note 27).

4   It should be pointed out that sulphur dioxide and nitrogen oxides at this point are largely emitted by public utilities and only to a lesser degree by private industry (cited in *UN Survey*, 1993).

5   Acid rain, which is caused by the atmospheric fallout of industrial pollutants, was the first widely recognized example of transboundary pollution, pollution that crosses the borders of nation-states. It was created in part when in countries such as the UK and the US, pollution from power stations was evident, and tall smokestacks were used to reduce pollution levels. Such solutions dissipated pollutants by emitting them higher into the atmosphere, where they were blown to other areas or states and precipitated in the form of dry deposits or acidified natural precipitation. As a result, countries suffering from acid rain were not necessarily responsible for having created it (Crump, 1991, p9).

6   The transport industry including car manufacturers, petroleum refiners, chemical corporations, road builders and others have a serious impact on atmospheric and other environmental crises. This chapter focuses on corporate responses to specific environmental crises and those industries most directly linked to those crises. Industries that may have an impact on several crises are considered in Chapter 3.

7   A base is a 'substance capable of combining with an acid to form a salt and water and usually producing hydroxide ions when combining with water' (Hawkins and Allen, 1991, p116).

8   An intermediate is 'a chemical compound formed by one reaction and then used in another, especially during synthesis' (Hawkins and Allen, 1991, p741).

9   Neff (1990) argues for the enactment of a similar law in the US.

10   However, in the case of very hazardous substances such as PCBs and dioxins, there is the problem in a 'compliance-based management approach' of treating hazardous materials as 'local problems' to be covered by a (perhaps nonexistent) national regulatory framework. An area of potential concern to the international community is that many corporations claim not to be aware of issues related to toxic chemicals and hazardous waste in their developing country operations (*UN Survey*, 1993). The export of toxic waste to developing countries is unlikely to be halted: corporations need to get rid of the waste and governments in developing countries need 'the business' (Slaughter, 1990), even if this is at the cost of the lives of some of their own citizens (for the case of Africa, see Mpanya, 1992). In the US, businesses must inform the EPA each time hazardous wastes are exported. Notices of intent to export hazardous waste rose from 12 in 1980 to 626 in 1989 (Worldwatch, 1989). Leonard (1993) argues that more and more of this waste is being exported to poorer countries in Southeast Asia.

11 Wastewater is the liquid by-product of manufacture.
12 Agenda 21 is the policy document that was the outcome of the 1992 UNCED conference. It:

> *'is intended to set out an international programme of action for achieving sustainable development in the 21st century. It seeks to be comprehensive in its scope, and to make recommendations on the measures that should be taken to integrate environment and development concerns. To this end, it provides a broad review of issues pertaining to sustainable development, including statements on the basis for action, objectives, recommended activities, and means of implementation'* (Grubb et al, 1993, p97).

13 The preservation of freshwater resources is an important activity which corporations can be engaged in, particularly in the case of ground and surface water. In developing countries, most drinking water is surface water, and therefore it is of utmost importance that it be uncontaminated. Only a few companies that operate in the developing world tend to have freshwater policies and, as noted above, substantial numbers of companies are unaware of freshwater issues in their developing country operations (*UN Survey*, 1993). It is made slightly more problematic that it would be relatively inexpensive for corporations to be active in the area that is essentially a matter of life and death in poorer countries.
14 Carbon sinks such as vast tracts of tropical forest and other vegetation play an important role in absorbing carbon dioxide from the global atmosphere (Crump, 1991, p42).
15 Biodiversity is a measure of species richness and natural genetic variation that can apply either within or between species of wildlife. Species diversity means the variety of differing wildlife species while genetic diversity refers to the mixture and range of genes. Genetic diversity has had its most noticeable impact in agriculture. Between 1930 and 1975, over half of the yield increases in cereal crops, sugar cane, cotton and groundnuts could be attributed to the contribution of genetic resources. Improved genetics also accounted for 25 per cent of increased milk yields in cows over the same period. Human activities, bringing about loss of habitats, overexploitation of natural resources and competition and predation through introduced species, are rapidly destroying or restricting the range of both wild species and genetic resources. The loss of habitats which show the greatest diversity, such as tropical forests and coral reefs, is depleting the world's pool of genetic material, weakening the ability of the system to evolve and adapt to any changes, and reducing the global genetic pool from which a selection can be made (Crump, 1991, pp32–33).
16 Monoculture is the 'cultivation of large tracts of land to produce a single variety of crop which is harvested all at once, the process being regularly repeated. It is a typical feature of modern large-scale agriculture as it reduces labour costs and maximizes machine use and

marketing efficiency. The alternative is intercropping (or polyculture), the growing of a mixture of crops either together or in sequence. Disadvantages of monocropping are pest problems, vulnerability to drought and other natural phenomena affecting production, and loss of soil productivity, fertility and moisture. Thus, more pesticides, nutrients and water must be added. Most modern large-scale farming methods are based on monoculture (Crump, 1991, p176).

17 The most notorious example of this was Love Canal, which is the location of a landfill chemical disposal site near Niagara Falls in the US. The Hooker Chemicals and Plastics Company used it as a dumping site for its waste. Over 43,000 tonnes of chemical waste, much of it carcinogenic, was dumped there from the early 1940s to 1952. In 1953, the site was sold to the local Board of Education for US$1 on the condition that the company was absolved of any future responsibility that might arise from chemicals at the dump. A school was built followed by a housing estate. In 1977, the dump was found to be leaking. Air, soil and water around the site were all heavily contaminated with carcinogenic and toxic chemicals. In 1978, the New York State Commissioner for Health ordered the evacuation of 240 families; the dump site was fenced off and declared a Federal Disaster Area. People living on the Love Canal site suffered from unusually high incidence of diseases and genetic damage, which could be attributed to exposure to toxic and carcinogenic chemicals (Crump, 1991, pp165–166).

18 Business managers in the forest products trade can also conceptualize their corporations' effect on the environment in terms of a 'technological fix'. One argued that the ecological rationale behind cutting down old growth forests and farming trees was the idea that 'if the forests are the earth's lungs, new lungs are better than old lungs' (interview with Forest Products businessperson, Indiana, 18 August 1993).

19 A safety zone is a cordoned off area of land surrounding a plant. In the event of an accident, if a safety zone is in place, human death and injury are likely to be minimized. Notably, in Union Carbide's Bhopal accident in which thousands of people died, safety zones were minimal or nonexistent (Shrivastava, 1992).

20 This paragraph is based on findings of the *UN Survey*, 1993.

21 The Superfund is the name given to a federally supported fund which is used to finance clean-up operations on sites in the US that have been contaminated by the dumping of hazardous wastes. Potentially dangerous chemical wastes are believed to have been dumped in at least 20,000 uncontrolled sites throughout the country. Properly known as the Comprehensive Environmental Response, Compensation and Liability Act, the legislation, passed in 1980, was the last bill signed by President Carter.

Following the polluter pays principle, the Superfund is financed by the industries that are deemed to have caused the problem. Industry is required to pay 88 per cent of the fund's total capital, which, after much argument, was set at US$1.6 billion. In 1986, the sum was raised to US$8.5 billion but this is nowhere near enough to pay for the clean-up of the 10,000 contaminated sites across the country, which the US government's Office of Technology Assessment has identified. By 1986, the US EPA had designated 842 'priority' sites as being in need of remedial attention, estimating that US$1.6 billion would be needed for the clean-up programme on these sites (Crump, 1991, p235).

22 The London Dumping Convention (LDC) is the common name for the Convention on the Prevention of Marine Pollution by Dumping of Waste and Other Matter. Fifty-eight countries originally signed it in 1972. It is a United Nations body that came into force in 1975 and has been ratified by at least 63 countries. The international treaty covers all of the world's oceans with the main aim of controlling the dumping of waste from ships and aircraft. Under the LDC, a 'black' list of compounds has been drawn up and the dumping of materials on this list is strictly prohibited. The list includes organo-halogen compounds, mercury and related compounds, cadmium and related compounds, persistent plastics, crude oil, fuel oil, high level radioactive waste and materials produced for chemical or biological warfare. The 'grey' lists covers materials that may be dumped, but only with special permission; these include lead, copper, arsenic, fluorides and pesticides or their by-products (Crump, 1991, p165).

23 The application of biological organisms, systems or processes to indus-trial processes is what is entailed by the term biotechnology. Living organisms can be manipulated to produce food, drugs or other products, and have been exploited for centuries. Micro-organisms have been used to make bread, convert milk to cheese and brew alcoholic beverages. Common substances such as vinegar, antibiotics and vitamins are manufactured through manipulation of microbial organisms. Over the past 15 years, genetic engineering has allowed an unprecedented degree of flexibility and control to be exerted in these industrial processes, with the ability now to alter or insert single genes (Crump, 1991, p35).

24 Merck, the world's largest pharmaceutical company, based in the US, received a 1995 America's Corporate Conscience Award from the American corporate 'watch dog' Council on Economic Priorities. Merck rated in the top two categories in each factor examined by the organization including the environment, charitable giving, community outreach, women's advancement, minority advancement, family benefits, workplace issues and disclosure.

The main reason for its award was its 'ground breaking' partnership with the Costa Rica National Institute of Biodiversity (INBio). INBio supplies Merck with plant and insect samples, which could become the basis for new medicines. Merck supports INBio's work in addition to funding conservation efforts to preserve the rainforest. Before this arrangement, company executives had taken samples from developing countries, similar to the rosy periwinkle example. Merck's arrangement represented the first time a developing country could receive royalties if a drug were developed by samples provided by INBio.

The Institute trains people in Costa Rica to be 'parataxonomists', or semi-skilled species taggers who send samples of plants and insects to the INBio research centre for cataloguing. The centre provides 'a certain number' to Merck for analysis. Through the programme, INBio hopes to create support for the conservation of Costa Rican national parks by providing markets for its rainforest products (Will, 1995, p5).

25   Chee Yoke Ling, a Malaysia based environmental activist, has argued that the UNCED biodiversity convention was:

> 'essentially about: access to biodiversity; who will own the germplasm that is collected from countries in the South where most biodiversity lies, who owns the biotechnology; who is going to have the monopoly over profits made from selling the biotechnology products derived from the biodiversity. The ordinary person in the world looks at the Biodiversity Convention as a conservation treaty, but the fight is really over access, patents and profits [which, in the end] was very good for corporations because it allows ownership to be asserted by those who hold the gene banks, thus ensuring access by the corporations and subsequent patenting of the products' (Ling, 1992, pp21–22).

26   Cost-benefit analysis involves assessing all the potential financial and social costs and benefits of a given endeavour within a corporation. The corporate aim would be to maximize benefits and minimize costs. With environmental issues, this can be especially difficult if, for example, an environmental issue is not reducible to monetary value (such as an area of natural beauty). This is made even more complicated when costs conflict and benefits conflict and therefore cannot be reduced to a simple equation of 'pro' versus 'con' (eg see Bennett, 1992). Pearce and Moran (1994, p131) suggest that the 'greener' end of corporate environmental management practice may incorporate 'cost effectiveness analysis' which more positively focuses on the benefits derived from a given monetary budget.

27   An example of a strategic alliance around environmentally relevant issues is the development of the Trans-Alaska Pipeline, owned and developed by ARCO, British Petroleum and Exxon, which allows excavated petroleum to be piped through an ecologically sensitive area of Alaska from the North Slope to Valdez in the southern part of the state (Deal, 1993).

28   Although these concepts are common within the management and sociology of organization literature, this particular classification is derived from Gouldson and Murphy (1998).

29   Innovation can be defined as a process involving: 'the search for and discovery, experimentation, development, imitation and adoption of new products, new processes and new organizational set-ups' (Dosi, 1988, p222).

30 Continuous improvement is a management approach similar to total
quality management (TQM) that is based on the idea that operations
or products could always be perfected, and a system needs to be in
place to ensure that performance 'continues to improve' (Ledgerwood
et al, 1992). Another related perspective is the *Kaizen* or 'small steps'
approach. This encourages organizations to constantly review and
improve small aspects of performance between major changes in
performance standards and goals. It involves everyone in the organization participating in a positive way to improve the business
performance (Richards in Allenby and Richards, 1994, p11).

31 Freeman suggests that:
    *'Most of the productivity gains associated with the diffusion
    of a new technology do not come about as an immediate
    consequence of the first radical innovation. On the contrary,
    they are usually achieved as a result of a fairly prolonged
    process of learning, improving, scaling up and altering new
    products and processes'* (1992, p77).

32 Environmental technologies can be defined as those that reduce 'the
absolute or relative impact of a process or product on the environment'
(Gouldson and Murphy, 1998, p29).

33 This occurs through the engineering 'Design for X' process, where 'X'
represents a product characteristic such as the reliability or
manufacturability that the company wants to maximize in its product
design (Richards, in Allenby and Richards, 1994, p11).

34 One example of this is environmental TQM. The TQM approach
involves what is called the quality loop. This consists of thinking about
what the goals are, the targets to be achieved, the route to be taken and
measurements to track success. Goals set could be zero defects in a
production process, or no billing errors or discharge rates within a
specified limit. The next step in environmental TQM is planning. Who
will have to do what, and by when, to achieve the goal? What resources,
skills and expertise are needed? Is there a requirement for new
resources, training or other steps? Doing is the implementation of the
plan, striving to achieve the goal through simple, repeatable steps in an
effective and efficient manner. Measuring is the key to assessing
effectiveness of the doing stage, it assesses progress and focuses on the
areas for improvement in the process. It leads to further thinking and
refinement of the system. Does the firm need to do anything? What
needs to be modified or changed? What new measurements should be in
place? The aim of environmental TQM is a constant 'honing' of the
process to achieve even higher standards of performance, aiming at 'zero
defects'. At the same time things are not perfect, 'zero defects' is a goal
that can be set, but as milestones are approached along the way, things
can go 'off course'. This is seen as normal. The quality loop allows
changes to take place to redirect towards the target, through taking
corrective action (Gilbert, 1993, p11). Chapter 4 argues that ARCO
Chemical's attempt to 'ground out safety' is an example of this process.

35 The greening of accounting procedures encompasses five main areas:
   - modifying existing accounting systems (as in energy costing);
   - eliminating conflicting elements of accounting systems (as in investment appraisal);
   - planning for financial implications of the environmental agenda (as in capital expenditure projections);
   - introducing environmental performance to external reporting (as in annual reports);
   - Developing new accounting and information systems (as in eco-balance sheets) (Gray et al, 1993, p5).

Accountants have also identified implications of environmental issues and the responses of business. The pressures come under two broad categories, legislative (local, national, regional) and market based. As a result, companies need to invest in pollution protection, in cleaner technologies, change processes and products, review asset values and spend on waste treatment and disposal. For example, UK companies are bound by legislation, especially the Environmental Protection Act 1990, the Water Act 1990 and the register of contaminated land. A wider range of EC legislation came into effect in the mid-1990s including the changing nature of packaging, especially recovery and recycling, rising costs of waste treatment and disposal, the need for companies to make more information known to the public, and the need for heavier industrial processes to adopt environmental management practices.

36 Environmental impact assessment (EIA) stems from the US National Environmental Policy Act 1969 (NEPA) and essentially involves the systematic examination of all significant effects an action is likely to have on the environment before the decision to take action is made (Wood and Gazidellis, 1985, p1). It is the process of predicting and evaluating an action's impacts on the environment: the conclusions to be used as a tool in decision making. It aims to prevent environmental degradation by giving executives better information about the consequences that actions could have on the environment, but it cannot achieve that prevention. Early discussions on EIA suggested that it should be applied to the earlier, more 'strategic' tiers of decision making – policies, plans and programmes – as well as individual projects. To date, EIA has primarily been carried out for projects – like power stations, industrial installations and housing developments.

The emphasis and effectiveness of these symptoms vary greatly. Many countries have official EIA systems established through regulations; others have non-mandatory EIA guidelines; and in others, EIAs are prepared on an ad hoc basis for specific large-scale development projects. In some countries, only government departments perform EIA for public sector projects, in others only private developers perform it; and in others, both the public and private sectors conduct EIAs. EIA has greatly facilitated public participation in the planning process for major projects in many countries but only minimally if at all in others. The objectivity and thoroughness of an

EIA is also influenced by the organization that carries out the assessment, not by the local authority or a neutral government agency (Thérivel et al, 1992, p6).

EIA can be distinguished from strategic environmental assessment (SEA), which is the application of environmental impact assessment to the level of policies, plans and programmes.

'SEA can be defined as the formalized, systematic and comprehensive process of evaluating the environmental impacts of a policy, plan or programme and its alternatives, including the preparation of a written report on the findings of that evaluation, and using the findings in publicly accountable decision-making' (Thérivel et al, 1992, p11).

37   Ecological weakness analysis comes after environmental assessments have been made and involves creating priority lists by product, area, material or location to assist management when making decisions. It is important for companies to identify ecological weakness in order to safeguard their competitive position. It also allows for making environmental problems less complex, more understandable to management and yet still scientifically accurate. It is important that indicators developed are applicable to the different sectors and different types of businesses (Winter, 1995, p221).

CHAPTER 2

1   These specific classifications of ecological modernization are adapted from Hajer (1996).

2   Externalities can be defined as
'consequences for welfare or costs that are not fully accounted for in the price and market system... In a free market economy individuals only attempt to maximize their own private utility or profit, and external costs and benefits will not be reflected in the prices of things. A firm may make perfumes very cheaply, but nevertheless be polluting the atmosphere in the process, affecting non perfume buyers. Unless the cost of this pollution is reflected in the price of the perfume, people will buy more of it than they would choose to if they had to pay for the entire cost to society of its production. In short, it is the full social *costs that are important in determining an efficient resource allocation, and private costs that determine prices'* (Bannock et al, 1987, p152).

3   One way to deal with externalities is to create:
'a structure of taxes and subsidies [that] can be designed to internalize (or "integrate") the externalities and ensure that the full costs or benefits of production are reflected in the prices charged. In this case, even if a factory causes pollution,

> *it can carry on producing as long as it properly compensates*
> *society for the damage caused'* (Bannock et al, 1987, p152).

4   Free goods are 'commodities that have no price because they are not scarce and do not require the use of scarce factors of production to create them, for example, fresh air and sunshine (in certain parts of the world)' (Bannock et al, 1987, p166).

5   Technology is the study or use of the mechanical arts and applied sciences. Technocracy begins with (environmental) problems and attempts to 'manage' them in, what some critics argue is an

> *'ad hoc, piecemeal fashion. The paradigm is a positivist one,*
> *that assumes responsibility for resolving issues with whatever*
> *technical means are at our disposal. Thus the armoury of*
> *environmental [technocracy] consists of different methodolog-*
> *ical techniques, each of which enables the environment to be*
> *better "managed"'* (Redclift, 1994, p127).

6   These insights fostered what is now known as the contingency approach, which establishes relationships among different structures and various contextual factors, especially environment, technology and size. Organizational forms can differ on several dimensions, specialization of tasks, and formal roles and procedures. The contingency approach assumes that different forms of organization are appropriate for different contexts. The approach is descriptive, demonstrating associations among structural and contextual variables rather than explaining causal connections (Reed, 1992).

7   Much of the review of different types of corporate cultures is based on Handy (1985).

8   In Burns and Stalker's (1961) analysis, a task culture is most closely related to their concept of organic management structures.

9   There is also a growing literature in the field of 'green' management studies (Robins and Trisoglio, 1992; Welford, 1993, 1994; Welford and Jones, 1994). Rather than provide an extensive review here, I would direct the reader to Robbins (1996, p237, note 6) where this work is scrutinized at length.

CHAPTER 3

1   Corporate policies are generally public statements of intention.

2   Corporate programmes can be seen as the operationalization and implementation of actions to execute policies at the level of production; they incorporate management and workers.

3   Language that tends to be absent in corporate policies is that which is being used in the international community regarding business and the environment, 'sustainable development', 'environmentally sensitive technologies', 'home/host countries'. Also absent are references to 'green consumerism' (*UN Survey*, 1993, p11).

4   In the comparison of cases in Chapters 4 and 5, this will be explored in greater detail.

5   This chapter is largely based on data from the *UN Survey* (1993) because it provides the most comprehensive data, to date, on corporate management responses to environmental challenges.

6   This compares with European corporations at 41 per cent and Asian corporations at 18 per cent.

7   The tables are divided into responses from corporations based in three geographical regions, North America, Europe and Asia. They are also divided into four industrial sectors: agricultural products (the food processing, forestry and pharmaceutical corporations), 24 per cent of the UN sample; extractive processing (chemical and oil corporations), 31 per cent of the sample; finished products (manufacturing of durables), 36 per cent; and services (tourism, airlines, banks, etc) 9 per cent. Finally, corporations are grouped by annual sales size: the bottom third at US$1–2.3 billion per year, the middle third at US$2.3–4.9 billion per year and the top third at US$4.9–50 billion and above (*UN Survey*, 1993).

8   The Bhopal, India, disaster is one of the world's worst industrial accidents to date. A release of methyl-isocyanate (MIC) gas at a Union Carbide plant killed more than 3150 people and some figures suggest that up to 500,000 have been injured, disabled or mentally and physically damaged as a result of the accident (Crump, 1991, p32).

9   Environment, Health and Safety at Union Carbide's Bhopal plant prior to the 1984 tragedy was reported to be poor. The general secretary of the union at the plant, along with other workers, indicated that plant management had dramatically cut back the numbers of staff at the unit that experienced the leak of MIC gas. The company had cut back on safety training programmes, had lowered the qualifications required for supervisors and had not instilled an ethic of safety. One worker said that 'internal leaks never bothered us'. A 1982 safety audit carried out by the parent company found that it was based on 'rote memorization' without 'a basic understanding of the reasons behind the procedures', that 'there was a high turnover rate in staff, and that personnel were being released for independent operation without having gained sufficient understanding of safe operating procedures'. As a result, the report maintained, 'the plant represented either a higher potential for a serious accident or more serious consequences if an accident should occur' (Gladwin, 1987, p229).

10 Tourism as a growth industry increasingly affects local environments and uses natural resources. Several NGOs are calling for 'sustainable tourism development' (Cater, 1991). One group, Tourism Concern, has developed ten principles for sustainable tourism development which include:
    • using resources sustainably;
    • reducing overconsumption and waste;
    • maintaining diversity.
    Developed country-based airline corporations dominate transport to developing countries. Of the 50 top hotel chains in the world, 30 are headquartered in the US. Some tourism companies cater to 'green' or

'ecotourism'. In the UK, ecotourism companies are endorsed by the 'Green Flag' organization. Notably, the UK airline corporation, British Airways, claims to be environmentally aware (NC/CEP, 1993, p61).

11 Associated through a *zaibatsu* (family run conglomerate) with Mitsui (World Rainforest Report cited in Draffan, 1993). Mitsui is involved in the tropical timber trade. Between 1988 and 1990, it imported 2,239,376 cubic metres of tropical wood to Japan (Draffan, 1993, p61).

12 Between 1988 and 1990, Mitsubishi imported 4.1 million cubic metres of tropical wood to Japan. The Rainforest Action Network called for a boycott of Mitsubishi products, and disseminated the following list of Mitsubishi operations:

- Bolivia: probably the largest logging operation in the country;
- Brazil: extensive logging at the Peruvian–Colombian border as well as having paper mills;
- Canada: a concession of over 7 million hectares of virgin boreal forest in the province of Alberta, and in British Columbia cutting 'native' forests for the 'largest chopstick plant in the world';
- Chile: extensive wood chipping of old growth forests for export to Japan;
- Ecuador: conducting mining exploration in the Andean tropical forest;
- Indonesia: the number one exporter of plywood from Indonesia to Japan;
- Malaysia: extensive logging in the Sarawak region which is opposed by all indigenous groups there;
- Philippines: producing plywood with Agusan Wood Inc (*RAN Action Alert* cited in Draffan, 1993, p60).

13 Oji Paper and Mitsui have a 100,000 hectare concession and sawtimber operation at Selar Panhanjang, Sumatra, Indonesia (Draffan, 1993, p67).

14 Tropical timber is one of the five most valuable exports from developing countries. In excess of 70 per cent of all tropical hardwoods for export are produced by six developing countries: Indonesia, Malaysia, the Philippines, Papua New Guinea, Brazil and Côte d'Ivoire. Notably, Malaysia's tropical forests are disappearing at a rate of 255,000 hectares annually, cleared for rubber and oil palm plantations. Twelve Japanese corporations have been responsible for felling huge tracts of the country's rainforests over the last 20 years (CEP/NC, 1993, p68). Japan is also the largest importer of tropical broadleaf logs and tropical broadleaf sawn wood (Maull, 1992, p363). In particular, Mitsubishi's role in the timber trade in the Philippines, Malaysia, Indonesia, Brazil and Chile made it the prime target of the 1990 World Rainforest Week (*RAN Action Alert*, cited in Draffan, 1993, p60).

15 Perhaps CEOs based in developed countries do not really want to know about what is happening in their developing country operations. One of the major criticisms of corporations' operations in developing

countries is their fostering of consumption practices that are unhelpful to local needs, and even harmful. Through intensive advertising campaigns, corporations can have a radical impact on nutrition, health and the environment. Tobacco corporations mainly feel this in the area of marketing, where there may be few controls in developing countries. Death rates from tobacco smoking are predicted to rise from the current figure of 2.5 million to over 10 million in 2050 (Mackey, 1992). Corporations also market foods and drinks that have limited nutritional value. This is most poignant in baby formula advertising. The campaign has been very successful. In 1954, 95 per cent of all Chilean mothers breastfed their babies after the first year, by 1968 only 6 per cent did so, and only 20 per cent did so for up to 2 months (NC/CEP, 1993, pp37–38). Corporations also market or export to developing countries products that are banned, withdrawn or severely restricted in developed countries including pharmaceuticals, agrochemicals (fungicides, herbicides and pesticides), nuclear waste, industrial chemicals (eg benzene, CFC and other chlorinated compounds) and heavy metals (eg mercury, cadmium, nickel and lead) (NC/CEP, 1993, p64).

16 Sexton argues that at least 100,000 jobs have been closed off to women predominantly in corporations in the auto, chemical, steel, oil, rubber and pharmaceutical industries including: General Motors, BF Goodrich, Allied-Signal, Gulf Oil, Exxon, Firestone, Dow Chemical, Sun Oil, Goodyear, BASF, Union Carbide and Monsanto because of the potentially harmful effects of workplace substances on the fetus. These substances include: lead, vinyl chloride, benzene, carbon tetrachloride, cadmium, coal tar, acrylamide, toluene, carbon disulphide and carbon monoxide. She contends that 'Rather than cleaning up the workplace, these corporations have prevented women from working with ...[these substances] ... because of their adverse effects on the foetus' (Sexton, 1993, p213).

17 It should not be forgotten that many of the victims of the Bhopal disaster still have not been compensated, more than ten years after the disaster (see Cassels, 1993; Urquhart, 1994; Reich, 1994). In the early 1990s, eight years after the disaster, not one of the victims of the gas leak had received final (as opposed to interim) compensation. One of the reasons for this was that Indian government guidelines on compensation for the disaster were vague to the point of being meaningless. Another problem is that many of the victims who had already been processed through the claims documentation process, and who had been classified by injury type, had to re-prove their entitlements in front of claims commissioners. Survivors must establish that their injuries, or the death of a relation, were due to the gas leak and then demonstrate the amount of their entitlement based on the severity of injury, their age, prior income, or degree of dependency on a deceased breadwinner. Proof of causation was the main obstacle to compensation. However, few of the families affected by the leak

obtained necessary documentation in the first place, or retained them in the number of years since the tragedy. As a result, claims tribunals were denying about one out of every two claims because of inadequate proof. 'Social activists allege that the procedures are now so complex, and the burden of proof so high, that the victims will be forced to accept whatever amount they are offered' (Cassels, 1993, p291).

18 One illustration is the OK Tedi gold and copper mine in Papua New Guinea (PNG). Started in mid-1984 by a consortium of corporations, which included AMOCO and a group of German companies under the name MGH, the group was led by the Australian based mining corporation Broken Hill Proprietary (BHP). By late 1984, around 1000 tons of cyanide had spilled into the River Tedi from the mine. Cyanide is a by-product of gold processing and had leaked out through a temporary dam after a massive landslide that struck the mine soon after work began. The contamination became evident after dead crocodiles, turtles and fish were found in the river (UNEP *State of the Environment Report 1985*, 16 April 1985). The PNG government responded by closing the mine until assurances could be given that contamination would not recur.

Before starting operations, the consortium, which had been formed in mid-1976, had undertaken limited environmental fieldwork. The mine was sited in what Pintz (1987) has described as one of the world's most inhospitable regions. Pintz further argued that 'while BHP undoubtedly took its environmental obligations under the OK Tedi agreement seriously, its relegation of environment to a single sentence in a 70 page document shows that establishing OK Tedi's economic and technological viability definitely had priority in the feasibility evaluation' (Pintz cited in UNCTC Consultant's Report, no date, 'Waste Disposal Practices', p1).

The problem was exacerbated when technological uncertainties related to the cyanide were not given adequate attention until after the financial evaluation had taken place. This created an impression among government officials that the consortium was insensitive to environmental concerns, which were a top governmental priority. Further problems occurred when a power struggle within the government prevented it from being able to effectively negotiate with the OK Tedi consortium. While the Office of Environment insisted that all mining projects come under its jurisdiction, the Minerals and Finance Ministries had granted the consortium exemption from environmental legislation.

The UNCTC contends that this affair exemplifies the struggle between development objectives and environmental concerns in developing countries. The government was criticized for leaving environmental monitoring to the consortium. The affair also raises questions about controlling the environmental aspects of corporate operations in developing countries, as well as the difficulty of predicting environmental problems (reported in UNCTC Consultant's

Report, no date, 'Waste Disposal Practices', p1). Pintz (1987) further argues that there were ten major environmental lessons to be learned from the environmental failures of the project. Some of these included the problems associated with the scientific uncertainty over the environmental impact of any development project; the difficulties of developing country governments being committed to environmental aims, as well as needing to pursue economic ones; 'open ended' environmental concerns of developing country governments and local communities which affect the liabilities and associated financial risk assessments of the project funders; and the economic priorities of development funders taking precedence over social and environmental objectives in the locale.

19 A notable example of this is the use and manufacture of chemicals, an industry dominated by large corporations. Of the 3.5 million known chemicals, 65,000 are in commercial use and over 5000 introduced each year. The plastics industry alone uses almost 2500 chemicals or mixtures. The effects of most chemicals on human health, as well as on plant and animal life are unknown. Nothing is known about the toxicity of nearly 80 per cent of chemicals in commercial use in the US (Sexton, 1993, p212).

20 I have argued elsewhere that whether the dominant social-economic system, let alone corporations, can ever be truly 'sustainable', is quite uncertain and even doubtful (Robbins, 1996).

21 This table is a version of Box XIII.1 in the *UN Survey*, 1993, p155. Specifically, the four 'levels' of 'management styles' as well as the corporate activities are versions of what is presented in the survey. I have developed the analysis presented in the third 'reasons for response to environmental challenges' column.

22 The CEP has evaluated Borden as having a 'moderate' or 'mixed' environmental record (Hollister et al, 1994, p63).

23 Unilever plc, the UK food corporation highly involved in tropical cash crops from tea to prawns (*Ecologist*, 1994, 24(4), pp136–137), is also decentralized. Line management ensures that policies are put into practice, while executives at the Unilever headquarters oversee the implementation at the corporate level. A Unilever main board director who is nominated by the board is responsible for the corporation's environmental standards and practices throughout the world. Technical specialists, and committees on which specialists and line managers provide feedback about implementation for the different product groups, advise this person. In 1994, Unilever plc was found to have one of the worst environmental and social records among the 191 corporations rated by the CEP (Hollister et al, 1994). This was due mainly to the poor representation of women and minorities in senior positions in the corporation. The company was rated as having 'above average' performance in the environment since it is working on reducing its packaging (some packaging contains 25 per cent or more recycled paper or plastic content), as well as labelling which easily dissolves in

the recycling process (Hollister et al, 1994, p109). The company's fishing operations in developing countries also source their fish from local communities, which is said to sustain them (Wells and Jetter, 1991, p87). The firm's wages for its workers on tea plantations in developing countries are furthermore assessed as comparing favourably with similar operations, and its environment, health and safety standards for its tea workers in developing countries are also reviewed as being good (Wells and Jetter, 1991, p87).

24 Waste Management International, also known as Waste Management Incorporated, WMI and WMX, is the largest trash hauler and recycler in the world, based in the US. The company has a long, 'environmentally challenged' history, as we shall see below. The WMX corporation produces an annual environmental report with an independent analysis of its compliance with environmental laws and regulations for its worldwide operations. WMX has contracts with thousands of cities in 48 states in the US and 18 countries including Argentina, Venezuela, Kuwait and Saudi Arabia. Sales increased from US$773 million in 1981 to US$6 billion in 1990 (Hoover, 1992).

The Chief Executive of WMX in the UK, Edwin Falkman, who is also interestingly Chair of the International Chamber of Commerce Environment Commission, indicated some of the reasons behind a top level commitment to environmental management:

> '*A recent study conducted at Bradford University has shown a link between strong environmental quality programmes and positive bottom line results. It picked 29 companies that had at least a five year history of environmental quality management, and found that 75 per cent had healthier profit margins than the industry median, and better returns on investment*' (cited in Wyburd, 1994).

WMX has been sued, convicted and fined for numerous environmental, bribery, price fixing and anti-trust violations. The magazine *Everybody* mentions 600 US EPA citations in the 1980s, US$46 million in fines for bribery and illegal waste handling between 1980 and 1988, and 18 grand jury investigations from 1983 to 1988. At the same time WMX Chair in the US, Dean Buntrock, was elected to the board of directors of the National Wildlife Federation (NWF). NWF's president Jay Hair wrote 'we feel Waste Management is conducting its business in a responsible manner' (cited in Draffan, 1993, p97). WMX has the largest toxic waste dump in the US located in Emelle, Alabama. Greenpeace dubbed this site 'America's Pay Toilet'. Waste Management, Inc has also been heavily criticized in the US by representatives from African-American and Latino communities. They accuse the company of numerous environmental injustices:

> '*WMX has located a disproportionate number of its most hazardous activities in minority areas. [Representatives from these neighbourhoods] have sued the company for civil rights violations ("environmental racism"), accusing it of poisoning*

> *people and their natural surroundings, of blatantly disregarding the concerns of local communities, of destroying opportunities for other, healthier forms of economic development and of riding roughshod over democratic decision making processes'* (Karliner, 1994, p60).

The company also supports many 'anti-environmentalist organizations' whose aim is to discredit the environmental movement, weaken environmental regulations and facilitate 'free trade' (see Deal, 1993). WMX's environmental, social and corruption problems have led one activist to rename the corporation 'Criminal Waste Management' (Kiker cited in Karliner, 1994, p60).

25   Yet, as noted earlier, in countries like Nigeria, where environmental regulations are much less stringent, Chevron and other oil corporations have been accused of operating 'double standards' (Saro-Wiwa, 1995).

26   As noted earlier, the company has been seen as an environmental leader in developed countries, yet has been associated via a *zaibatsu* (Japanese family conglomerate) with felling trees in the rainforests of Southeast Asia.

27   No other industry has been more successful at creating market niches than the tobacco industry, which markets a product that most governments around the world acknowledge has serious health risks. A few corporations dominate the industry globally, including American Brands Inc, Hanson plc, Rothmans, Philip Morris, British American Tobacco (BAT) and RJ Reynolds. All spend around £1.5 billion a year on advertising globally. In developing countries, where there tends to be minimal or nonexistent advertising controls, the impact of tobacco is even more problematic (Wells and Jetter, 1991, pp175–183). Notably, companies are allowed to advertise on television, encourage cigarette smoking without warning labels and sell cigarettes with a high tar content. Most cigarette smokers in the world have tended to be adult men, and as a result of aggressive tobacco campaigns in developing countries, young people and women have taken up smoking, which has led to a 'smoking epidemic' (Stebbins cited in NC/CEP, 1993, p37). People in poorer countries are often unaware of the consequences of smoking. They also have limited disposable income, which means that money spent on smoking depletes the amount that can be spent on necessities. Since access to health care can be limited in developing countries, the effect of smoking on the poor or those with restricted access to medical provision can be especially harmful (NC/CEP, 1993, p37). The fact that BAT has developed a 'green reputation' among corporate environmental consultants interviewed for this research speaks to the success of the tobacco corporations in creating a benevolent image (interview with corporate environmental consultant, London, 19 January 1993). BAT has recently been criticized for its subsidiary's aggressive advertising campaigns in Uzbekistan. Uzbek students wrote to the company in April 1996 asking: 'Are you aware that you are poisoning our life and our generation with your tobacco business?' (Balfour, 1997, p5).

28 3M developed 3P in 1975. Allen Jacobsen, CEO and a BCSD member, was not satisfied with the 'success' of 3P and started the 3P Plus Program in 1986. Jacobsen, and his staff vice president for environmental engineering and pollution control, Dr Robert Bringer 'believed that 3M must do more to prevent pollution' (Schmidheiny, 1992, p190). Even though 3M is widely viewed as a 'green corporation' (Hajer, 1995), it has been widely criticized for its environmentally challenged record even after its development of innovative management policies.

Donahue notes that in 1988 (two years after 3P Plus) 3M was the 13th leading toxics producer in the US. In 1989, 3M received the largest fine ever assessed by the state of Minnesota (US$1.5 million), at its Chemolite facility. This was assessed for zinc, cadmium and lead releases. In 1989, the company was also fined US$1.4 million for importing hazardous chemicals without notifying the EPA. Through the litigation process the fine was later negotiated down to US$112,000. The nuclear regulatory commission also fined the company in that year (Donahue, 1991, pp29–31). The US Occupational Safety and Health Administration (OSHA) cited 3M 154 times between 1980 and 1990, even though John Pendergrass, a former 3M manager, headed OSHA between 1987 and 1989 (Draffan, 1993, p59). An offer to complete a case study project on 3M for this book was rejected by the company in August 1993.

29 This may be true for 'environmental performance' in developed countries but not in developing countries. ICI, along with Dow Chemical and Solvay, are the world's leading manufacturers of chlorine. The chlorine industry 'which is at the root of much of the industrialized North's hazardous waste crisis, is stagnating in the US and Western Europe ...[these manufacturers] are expanding into developing countries, investing in chlorine production in countries such as Brazil, Mexico, Saudi Arabia, Egypt, Thailand, India, Taiwan and China' (Karliner, 1994, p61). By and large, however, ICI is seen as an environmental leader by environmental consultants to corporations interviewed for this research (interview with corporate environmental consultant, London, 19 January 1993; Florida, 15 August 1993). Dow Chemical, one of the other leading manufacturers of chlorine, has also been praised for its corporate environmental management within the international business community (interview with corporate environmental consultant, London, 19 August 1993).

30 In 1994, the CEP gave Chevron's environmental rating an 'F' (Hollister et al, 1994, p64), which indicates 'poor performance or little evidence of a good record' (Hollister et al, 1994, p7). This may be largely due to Chevron's activities in developing countries. In developing countries, Chevron is exploring the Iagifu-Hedinia and Juha oil fields in PNG. The company has built a 270km pipeline that runs from the southern highlands rainforest on the Kikori and Nakari Rivers and across the Aird River Delta to the southeast coast of PNG (Draffan, 1993,

pp19–20). The pipeline also runs along the bed of the Kikori River and crosses mangroves at the coast (*RAN Action Alert* vol 71, April 1992 cited in Draffan, 1993, p19). A company refinery is located at Lake Kutubu. In April 1991, local people blockaded the road at the Aio River near the refinery, commandeered a Chevron vehicle and called for talks to resolve the corporation's failure to deliver the infrastructure Chevron executives had promised such as water tanks, schools and clinics. Police later reopened the road (*RAN Action Alert* vols 71 and 73, April and June 1992 cited in Draffan, 1993, p19). The company has also been involved in oil production in Ogoniland in Nigeria since the 1970s. Ken Saro-Wiwa, the Ogoni activist, had criticized Chevron as well as Shell for the environmental destruction in his region and for having 'double standards' in Nigeria (Saro-Wiwa, 1995).

31 Corporations that use a strategic environmental management style are essentially successful businesses, which does not always mean they are 'environmentally sound'. Some companies anticipate and pre-empt future regulations; they have effectively built 'green' reputations; they lobby regulators and politicians; and influence legislation and industrial guidelines through business associations. Avery and others (1993) discuss the case of the Codex Alimentarius Commission that sets world food standards, run by the FAO and World Health Organization (WHO). An analysis of the Codex reveals that corporate agribusiness and their developed country representatives largely control the committees, while developing country representatives were largely absent. An organization that should be advocating healthy eating supports the interests of corporations, many of whom are involved in producing nutritionally questionable processed foods and beverages. For example, in the 1989–1991 session, around half of the US delegation and 60 per cent of the Swiss delegation actually represented industry (see also Sklair, 1995b, p126).

32 However, as noted above, Amoco's operations in developing countries have had different standards. The corporation has been involved in the OK Tedi Mine in PNG, which has caused serious environmental degradation there (Pintz, 1987).

33 Toyota manufactured the first catalyst equipped car available in the UK, the 1988 *Celica GT-4*. Catalysts can reduce the amount of carbon monoxide, hydrocarbons and nitrogen oxide in motor vehicle emissions (Elkington and Hailes, 1988, p122). The company was rated by CEP in 1994 and received ratings in the top two categories except for the environment and disclosure (where they were rated in the third category) (Hollister et al, 1994, p137). One of the reasons for their lower rating in the environment was that their Toxic Release Inventory rating (an EPA reported figure of annual toxic emissions of US plants adjusted for sales size) between 1988 and 1990 increased when the rating for the vast majority of companies operating in the US decreased (Hollister et al, 1994, p24). The status of Toyota's environmental reporting was evaluated as being at stage two out of five, five being the

highest. Although the CEO in the annual report mentioned the environment, its environmental report was not particularly comprehensive, nor was it externally verified or any mention made of the ICC's environmental charter even though the company is a member of the ICC (UNEPIE and SustainAbility, 1994, p80).

34 Volvo has developed a reputation for producing safer and 'cleaner' cars. Volvo was the first automobile manufacturer in Europe to use the 'Aquabase' system of low-solvent car painting. Painting a single car by traditional methods can release between 12 and 15 litres of solvent into the atmosphere. This amount is cut by around 60 per cent with the Aquabase system. Volvo only uses this method on about 15 per cent of its total output. Volvo, along with only a few other European car manufacturers, offers catalysts on its vehicles in the UK at no extra cost. Seventy per cent of the cars Volvo sold around the world in 1988 had catalysts. The company has also met emission standards without having to install catalysts in some models. In the 200/700 series, exhaust gas recirculation reduces the amounts of nitrogen oxide emissions. Volvo has also been involved in switching its manufacturing facilities from oil to natural gas, which cuts sulphur dioxide emissions by 80 per cent (Elkington and Hailes, 1988, pp122–125). The company has also been involved in life cycle assessment; this is the overall process of assessing the complete environmental impacts (manufacturing, marketing, distribution, use and disposal) of 'a system, function, product or service' (SustainAbility et al, 1993, p111).

35 See Chapter 4 in which the case of Shell is examined in detail.

36 Companies that follow the precautionary principle in environmental management may be at the limits of what can be expected in terms of environmentally relevant corporate behaviour. The precautionary principle is based on thoughtful action in advance of scientific proof. In most developed countries, the regulator has to justify the level of protection being sought. A challenge by a discharger can result in a costly and time-consuming appeal. It is therefore likely that in certain cases, the regulator will determine the environmental standard or permitted level of discharge based on evidence that can be supported in court. This will rely on the standard scientific method, which can then become a political weapon in the legal culture of appeal and ministerial determination of environmental quality.

The practice of science may therefore reinforce a non-sustainable economic and social culture. Because the margins of sustainability are unknown, the scientific approach may provide a justification for pushing alteration of the planet beyond the limits of its tolerance. Even by being careful, the scientific approach may create a false sense of security over the natural limits of the Earth (O'Riordan, 1995, p1).

There are four basic points to the precautionary principle as they relate to environmental management systems in corporations. They are as follows:

- thoughtful action in advance of scientific proof;
- leaving ecological space as room for ignorance;
- care in management;
- shifting the burden of proof from the victim to the developer.

The first point relates to the use of wise management and cost effectiveness before there is a direct cause and effect relationship of some forms of degradation and industrial activity. This involves investing a small amount of resources to prevent eventual huge costs. The second point relates to not extracting resources, even when they are available, realizing that the longer-term consequences of virtually total removal are unknown. It also relates to developed countries allowing developing countries to grow unsustainably for a period so they can eventually make an easier transition to a more sustainable economy. The third point relates to creative participation in the process of management since it is not possible to be aware of all the possible consequences of altering a habitat, manipulating an ecosystem or cleaning up a waste dump. This activity is especially important for control of hazardous activities like nuclear stations, incinerators and the release of genetically modified organisms. The fourth point is perhaps the most difficult to achieve. Many advances in the past came out of risk taking; environmental assessments and compensation were funded out of the proceeds of growth. Environmental impact assessments were designed to list the likely consequences of a proposed course of action in a formal and public manner, which was seen as sufficient to sanction a project. Thus, it did not entail comprehensive analysis of all possible environmental effects (O'Riordan, 1995, p8).

Precaution should be distinguished from prevention in that the latter is applied to eliminating known hazards, such as toxic substances, or at least reducing hazardous materials at the point of their production or use. Prevention is a regulatory measure aimed at an established threat. Precaution seeks to reduce uncertainty by requiring wise management, public information and participation, and 'best technology' (O'Riordan, 1995, p9). Chapter 4 argues that because of the public relations problems associated with the chemical industry, ARCO Chemical and other similar chemical companies employ the precautionary principle to some extent because the threat of accidents damaging chemical companies' reputations is so great.

The use of environmental science for prevention has proved to be useful to industry, governmental, non-governmental organizations and the area of environmental science itself. Industry is beginning to create alliances with environmental scientists across a wide variety of themes, such as cost-benefit analysis, environmental impact assessment, risk management, eco auditing and life cycle analysis, as well as conceptualizing new regulations, especially those dealing with the use of new products and the responsibility for cleaning up waste. Environmental pressure groups also hire scientists and liaise with research institutions: Greenpeace, Friends of the Earth and WWF all have a science group responsible for reviewing scientific information and finding gaps or flaws. The use of science therefore becomes important to politics, commerce and social change (O'Riordan, 1995, p11).

37   Turner may argue that there would be a level of environmental management practices beyond the precautionary principle, based on bioethics and consistent with 'very strong sustainability' (Turner, 1993, p60).

38   Evidence of industrial relocation to developing country 'pollution havens' exists in certain industries including asbestos, heavy metals and leather tanning. In developing countries, problems have also come about when there have been no equivalent domestic activities to the relocated corporate operations, or where the host government is uninformed about the environmental effects of certain practices. This has been notable with regard to deforestation, inappropriate mining practices, health and safety problems in factories (especially with regard to work with asbestos and chemical wastes) and the export of hazardous and toxic products to developing countries (including pesticides and herbicides) (NC/CEP, 1993, pp58 and 64; see Castleman, 1985 for other examples).

Chapter 4

1   The discussion in this paragraph is based on this interview with the ARCO Chemical executive public relations staff member (20 December 1994).

2   The Seveso Disaster occurred when an explosion and chemical leak at a factory owned by Icmesa, an affiliate of the Swiss pharmaceutical corporation Hoffmann-La Roche, on 10 July1976, emitted highly poisonous dioxin that killed farm animals and caused skin diseases among residents of Seveso, north of Milan, Italy. Greenpeace has been back to visit the site and found that soil tests revealed similar levels of dioxin to those in 1982. Greenpeace said that 'despite strong concerns raised by the publication of the 1982 figures, nothing has been done to solve the problem of dioxin contamination in the area of the accident' and that dioxin levels there were ten times higher than the level Italy's agricultural committee considers safe for food production (Reuter, 1996, p12).

3   See Chapter 1 for a discussion of the Basel, Switzerland, accident.

4   See Chapter 3 for a discussion of the Bhopal, India, tragedy.

5   The company has already captured 50 per cent of the Chinese market for polyols and propylene glycol. Within 20 years, China is expected to be the corporation's largest PO consumer in Asia, surpassing Japan.

6   Most of the following sections on ARCO Chemical Europe's environmental activities are drawn from their Annual Environmental Statement (ARCO Chemical Europe, 1994a) and Annual Reports (ARCO Chemical Europe, 1991, 1992a, 1993, 1994b), unless otherwise noted.

7   ARCO Chemical as a whole reduced its global volatile organic
    compound (VOC) airborne emissions by 50 percent between 1987 and
    1994. At the same time, total production volume nearly doubled. Most
    of this reduction is due to the company's control of fugitive emissions
    (ARCO, 1996, p10).
8   Interestingly, ARCO's 1995 Environment, Health and Safety Report
    states that 'the number of days pollutants in L.A. exceeded federal
    requirements dropped 90 percent between 1970 and 1994' (ARCO,
    1996, p8).
9   However, in 1994 ARCO received a 'D' in its environment rating (A–F
    scale), in particular for its policies regarding animal testing, from the
    CEP. The company also received a 'C' in 'workplace issues'. By 1995,
    CEP felt ARCO had improved and nominated it along with 12 others
    for a 'Corporate Conscience Award' (Hollister et al, 1994).
10 Most of the corporate information on Shell's environmental activities
    and policy is drawn from annual reports (Royal Dutch/Shell, 1991,
    1992, 1993, 1994) and the Shell International Petroleum Company
    (1992), unless otherwise noted. The environmental policy is expanded
    on in Jennings (1994) and Moody-Stuart (1994).
11 In August 1974, an oil tanker belonging to Shell was shipwrecked in
    the Strait of Magellan, off the coast of Chile. The oil spill was reported
    to have caused the deaths of over 4000 birds as well as killing other
    animal, plant and marine life. A Shell expert as well as a representative
    from the International Tanker Owners Pollution Federation went to
    Chile to advise government ministers on minimizing environmental
    damage from the spill. The company also compensated the Chilean
    government for the clean-up. The government then asked Tovalop,
    another organization in the tanker industry, to prepare contingency
    plans for the country in the event of another spill. This event caused
    the International Maritime Organization to begin to address the
    question of tanker safety (UNCTC, no date, 'Royal Dutch Shell Oil
    Spill (Strait of Magellan, Chile)', p19).
12 Between 1961 and 1977, workers in two plants manufacturing the
    pesticide DBCP (dibromochloropropane), in a Shell subsidiary in the
    US, became sterile. A study carried out by Shell Chemical found that
    16 out of 21 workers exposed to the pesticide at the Denver, Colorado,
    and Mobile, Alabama, plants had sperm counts below 40 million,
    which is considered to be low by medical experts. Of this group, two
    men had no sperm at all, and the counts of the others were between 20
    million and 35 million. Once this was disclosed, the firm 'voluntarily'
    stopped manufacturing the pesticide. The company knew in 1961 that
    the chemical damaged the sperm cells of laboratory animals. Shell
    Chemical had assumed at the time that the product was safe at low
    levels. After the company stopped production of the pesticide, it
    recalled distributed DBCP from distributors and told them to inform
    customers and employees of its dangers. The US OSHA then issued a
    temporary emergency exposure limit, and EPA officials ordered a ban

on further sales of the pesticide (UNCTC, no date, 'Shell Chemical: Worker Exposure to DBCP (California, USA)', p9).

13 Ken Saro-Wiwa, the Nigerian environmental activist, would have disagreed:

> 'In Ogoni, Shell locations lie pat in the middle of villages, in front and back gardens – that should lay a particular responsibility on Shell to be absolutely cautious in its operations. The company remains negligent and wilful… The double standards which the company operated could be easily shown up. There were enough films, magazines and books to show how environmentally conscious Shell was in Europe and America. The story in Nigeria was entirely different' (Saro-Wiwa, 1995, p166).

14 Shell claims to be aiming to reduce waste over time. Procedures are being developed for better handling of toxic waste, with additional provision for processing the waste on site. Other waste is increasingly being used as fuel or recycled; this is particularly the case for plastics. Plants are also designed to be more efficient by producing less waste.

15 Shell's most environmentally challenged operation in Nigeria is in Ogoniland on the Niger Delta in Southern Nigeria. Oil production in Ogoniland began in 1958. Today, Shell's operations include almost 100 wells, two refineries and a fertilizer complex. However, the Ogoni people, a disenfranchised Nigerian ethnic minority, appear not to have benefited much from this economic activity. Nigeria accounts for 14 per cent of Shell's worldwide oil production, and oil is the basis of the Nigerian economy (much of it based on the production in Ogoni). The area is $1046km^2$ and has only one hospital in an unfinished building and schools that are rarely open. Although Shell admits that conditions are 'not ideal', the company blames the Nigerian government for not 'distributing money properly'. A company spokesman claims that the company spends US$21 million a year on Nigerian schools and scholarships (Kretzmann, 1995, p10). A local Catholic missionary, named Sister Majella, says that the company 'spends a lot of time planning and very little time effecting' community assistance programmes.

16 On 4 January 1993, Ken Saro-Wiwa, one of the founders of the Movement for the Survival of the Ogoni People (MOSOP) led 300,000 Ogonis in a peaceful protest against what they said was the devastation of their air, water and soil primarily by Shell. In the Ogoni Bill of Rights dated 1990, it was also stated that since 1958 the value of the oil extracted from Ogoniland was over US$30 million for which the Ogoni were uncompensated. Additionally, the Ogoni, comprising 500,000 people, had no representation in any institution of the Federal government of Nigeria, no pipe borne water, no electricity, no job opportunities for the people in Federal, state, public sector or private sector companies (Ogoni Bill of Rights, 1990, cited in Saro-Wiwa, 1995, p68). Saro-Wiwa has also said of this first mass protest that: 'On January 4 the alarm bells rang in the ears of Shell. I was to know no

peace from then. I became a regular guest of the security agencies. I was stopped and arrested at airports, seized from my office and questioned repeatedly' (Saro-Wiwa, cited in Vidal, 1995a, p3).

17 However, there have been a number of examples where executives at other corporations have been caught bribing officials. One of the best-known cases of bribery occurred when an agricultural corporation paid US$1.25 million to a Honduran finance minister at a time when corporations were being charged a high export tax on bananas. The export tax was cut in half for the company, which saved between US$6 and 7 billion. When the scandal broke, this brought down the government in power (Harrison, 1984).

18 Wright, commenting on Shell's role in Nigeria, examined below, asks 'But is this possible in a case like Nigeria, where a repressive military regime, heavily dependent on oil, is clamping down on demands for land rights and a greater share of oil revenue from a community with articulate, politically able leaders?' (Wright, 1995, p16).

19 Four days after the memo written by Okuntima, four Ogoni leaders were killed and although Saro-Wiwa was in the custody of the military at the time, he, and others, were charged with their murder. Michael Birnbaum QC attended the trial on behalf of Article 19 (a British group which advocates fair trials). He stated that 'the fundamental breaches of human rights I have identified are so serious as to arouse grave concern that any trial before this tribunal will be fundamentally flawed and unfair' (cited in Olojede, 1995, p7). Pressure for Shell to intervene on Saro-Wiwa's behalf was met with Shell's insistence that its policy is not to intervene in the activities of the states of the countries in which they operate. 'A subsequent Shell release urging Nigeria to grant clemency to the nine men headed for the gallows [seemed an effort characterized by being] too little too late' (Mokhiber and Wheat, 1995, p10). Saro-Wiwa was executed on 10 November 1995. In an ironic twist to the end of the story, four months after the executions, Shell was ready to begin work on a major gas project in the region. The company took out full page ads in major developed country newspapers responding to criticisms arguing that cancelling the project 'would certainly hurt the thousands of Nigerians working [there] ' (cited in Mokhiber and Wheat, 1995, p10).

20 The US government estimates that if oil were found in ANWR, it would probably represent only 200 days' worth at the present rate of US consumption (Deal, 1993, p26).

21 A 1993 article reports that:
    'an obscure accounting gimmick in the... shipping charges is pouring millions of dollars of hidden profits into the pockets of pipeline owners (ARCO, BP and Exxon) each year (to an estimated total of US$22 billion by 2015) at the expense of pipeline shippers including the state of Alaska' (Knaus, 1993).

22 In an interesting epilogue to this case study, Shell has admitted that the fiascos of Nigeria have highlighted the corporation's problems with

being 'too introverted and too concerned with government relations' (Cowe, 1997, p19). At the same time, *Multinational Monitor* (1997) points out that Shell has never apologized for the destruction of Ogoniland.

CHAPTER 5

1   Fair trade programmes aim to provide developing country producers with a 'fair' price for their products, usually higher than they could earn from the world market.

2   'Social-environmental' companies and investment groups have their vociferous advocates and their vociferous critics, some of whom will be examined in this chapter. Mark Campanale, an ethical fund analyst has said that ethical investment funds which invest only in 'ethically responsible' companies are 'mere marketing gimmicks... a sop to the conscience of naive investors'. Surveys suggest that British consumers spend many billion pounds a year with companies seen as progressive (cited in Entine, 1995).

3   The next sections on The Body Shop's environmental programmes are based primarily on their environmental reports (The Body Shop, 1991, 1992, 1993).

4   As noted in Chapter 1, retrofitting involves upgrading equipment or facilities with environmental or control technologies.

5   See Chapter 3 for a discussion of the benefits of joint ventures for corporations making environmental investments.

6   Gordon Roddick, chairman of The Body Shop, has said 'we will continue to develop our business with the highest of ethical principles' (Roddick, 1994, p12). In the words of one commentator:
    'Body Shop has grown because it has been different.
    Customers have been prepared to buy its products – often at
    higher prices than equivalents in conventional shops – because
    of the company's values. And investors have been prepared to
    buy the shares at prices usually much higher than other retail-
    ers', because of the magic of the Roddick formula which has
    maintained success against the odds' (Cowe, 1994a, p14).
    Shrivastava (1996, p83) notes that The Body Shop products are priced 20–40 per cent above equivalent brand name products in some categories.

7   Roddick has been known to attack competitors in the mainstream cosmetics industry as 'monsters' who 'lie and exploit women' and her financial backers who are 'traditional' rather than 'social-environmen-tal' as 'pin striped dinosaurs' and 'wankers' (cited in Entine, 1995).

8   These included Ethical Consumer and Richard Adams at New Consumer (examined below), both based in the UK.

9   The Body Shop retains the law firm Lovell, White, Durrant. It is said to be one of the largest law firms in Europe (Vidal, 1994, p2).

10 Entine accepts that what is 'natural' can be difficult to define (cited in Cowe, 1994c, p15).

11 Corporations with a 'traditional' corporate culture like Gillette and Proctor & Gamble have developed alternatives to animal testing. Gillette also publishes a rationale for each of its tests (Entine, 1995).

12 Anita Roddick made a television commercial for American Express in which she was seen looking for natural ingredients for The Body Shop products in developing countries, and extolling the benefits of using the American Express Card. Many saw this as revealing the true self from behind the 'cynical mask' (see below). An example of this was that Roddick says in the commercial: 'I'd rather work for justice, human rights and fair trade than ever sell a bubble bath'. The Body Shop sells more than a dozen kinds of bubble bath. Another is that the commercial shows Roddick looking for ingredients for her products in developing countries, while it was revealed that some of these stories have been fabricated for marketing purposes. Roddick ultimately gave her £35,000 fee to a health clinic (Entine, 1995).

13 The company also faced criticism when it came out against trade with China. The slogan which Anita Roddick used was based on Nancy Reagan's drugs slogan from the 1980s, 'Just say no'. Roddick also praised another company with a 'green' reputation, Levi Strauss, for pulling out of China because of human rights and labour abuses. Even with this outspoken stance, Body Shop sourced baskets from China (Entine, 1995).

14 The company, as well as the Roddicks, won a libel suit against Channel 4 in 1993 when a *Dispatches* programme alleged that the couple's stance on environmental and social issues was a 'cynical mask' (cited in Vidal, 1994, p2).

15 The transport industry, including the petroleum exploration and refining, vehicle manufacture, use and disposal, and road building, all have a particularly degrading effect on the environment. See endnotes in Chapter 3, and case studies in Chapter 4 in which the degrading effects of aspects of the transport industry are examined in more detail.

16 A message on a carton of Ben & Jerry's ice cream bought in 1995 states:

> 'We Support Family Farms: We buy our milk from the St. Albans Cooperative Creamery, owned and operated by 500 Vermont family farmers. We support family farmers because we believe they are central to the heritage and quality of life in Vermont and across America'.

17 In 1988, Ben & Jerry's won an America's Corporate Conscience Award for its uncommonly high volume of charitable giving (Hollister et al, 1994, p390).

18 Ben & Jerry's received an 'A' (A–F grading scale) in all areas except minority advancement in which it received a 'B' (the company claimed that Vermont has a low percentage of minority residents). Ben & Jerry's hired Bob Holland, an African-American, to be its chief executive, in

1995. Compare Ben & Jerry's with The Body Shop which was rated substantially lower in the same year. The Body Shop received 'B's in minority advancement and family issues in 1994, and a 'C' in workplace issues. It received 'A's in environment, community outreach, women's issues, and disclosure and a question mark (unknown) in charitable giving (Hollister et al, 1994, p63).

19 Compare this with The Body Shop, where in 1991, the salary of the lowest paid was £11,600, while the salary of the highest was £116,000, ten times higher (Shrivastava, 1996, p77).

20 Interviews with employees, as part of the company's social audit, revealed that some felt that there was a corporate culture at Ben & Jerry's where people were expected to work long hours. At the same time, management personnel felt that they were being paid wages as if they worked for a charity when, in fact, they were working for a large company. As one incoming manager said to Ben Cohen when the salary ratio of highest paid to lowest was five to one: 'Five to one is fine with you and Jerry. You've already got your millions' (Lager, 1994, p172). Production line workers on the other hand have responded that they are worried about losing their jobs through injury because equivalent jobs at other companies would not have as many different kinds of support for workers as Ben & Jerry's (Ben & Jerry's, 1995).

21 The philosophy of linked prosperity was created, perhaps ironically, through the success of Cohen and Greenfield's business, which started modestly as a small one-shop establishment in Burlington, Vermont. Greenfield tells the story of the idea's genesis:

>   'We looked at ourselves and realized that we were suddenly no longer ice cream men but we'd become businessmen. We were, you know, writing memos and correspondence. It was a shocking revelation – we had a very negative reaction to it – because we felt like businessmen were, you know, bad people; that companies exploited their workers and exploited the community. So our first thought was to put the business up for sale. Then Ben [Cohen] ran into this eccentric old restaurateur in Southern Vermont, and this old guy said: "Ben why are you going to do that?" And Ben said: "Maurice, you know what businesses do? They take advantage of the community and their workers." And Maurice said: "Ben, if there's something you don't like about your business, why don't you just change it?" And Ben said it had never really occurred to him' (cited in Coles, 1996, p3; see also Lager, 1994).

22 In the words of one board member, the mission statement was 'a great conciliation that captured what had come through the board's ideological and practical debate. We're here to make money, we want to have an impact on the global community, and we have a pride and craft as ice cream makers' (cited in Lager, 1994, p184).

23 An enormous amount of research has accumulated to suggest that a diet high in fat is linked with an increase in cancer and cardiovascular

disease, which together account for around two-thirds of deaths in the US. In the US, nutrition experts have said that Americans eat six to eight tablespoons of fat every day, much more than the body needs. Furthermore, most of the fat comes from red meat and dairy products. Both of these types of food are high in cholesterol and saturated fat, a particularly dangerous form of fat. A diet high in fat and cholesterol leads to arteriosclerosis, or hardening of the arteries. In arteriosclerosis, the arteries become narrowed by cholesterol-rich deposits on their walls (plaques) which results in elevated blood pressure and an increased risk of heart attack and stroke. Dietary fat is also strongly linked with many types of cancer including breast, colorectal, pancreatic, prostatic and uterine. It also contributes to obesity which is strongly associated with stroke, diabetes, heart disease, back problems, kidney and gallbladder disorders, and other complications (Simons et al, 1992, p11).

24 See discussion of biotechnology in Chapter 1.

25 Following the end of the Cold War, BSR was reorganized in 1993. At that time it absorbed other business social programmes which the company was involved with such as the Business Partnership for Peace, and ACT NOW, a fuel efficiency advocacy campaign which also campaigned for reduced dependence on foreign oil (Lager, 1994).

26 A 401(k) matching pension programme is based on section 401(k) of the US Internal Revenue Code. This allows the employer to invest employee pension contributions tax free. Employers also match employee contributions, and employees can continue to invest in their pensions as they move from job to job. For these and other reasons, the 401(k) is very popular with workers.

27 In line with the culture of 'linked prosperity' the company's social initiatives include supporting women, who represent about 50 per cent of workers and top management. For example, the chief financial officer is a woman. Vermont has a low population of minority groups and the company has made special efforts to attract minorities. An African-American, Bob Holland, was hired as the company's chief executive in 1994 and another African-American was hired as the company's human resources director. The company has established six weeks of paid leave to new mothers, which includes adoptive mothers, as well as two weeks of paid leave and up to ten weeks unpaid leave for new fathers. Childcare is provided at headquarters as well as flexitime and phased return to work for new mothers. The company is one of the highest paying employers in New England, and was listed as one of the best companies for new mothers by *Working Mother* (cited in Hollister et al, 1994).

28 Critics see these 'protests' as well as the lore of the company's 'good works' as producing a type of delirious 'fawning' within the media over the company (hundreds of articles have been written about the company and its 'two Vermont hippie' founders). This media interest produced the brand name recognition of a company ten times its size while saving millions on advertising (Rosin, 1995).

29 The company has begun to use advertising.

30 Its customers do not always support the company's social programmes. Some wrote letters disagreeing with the company's pacifist stance (interview with Ben & Jerry's public relations staff member, Vermont, 25 August 1994). There was also conflict within the corporate management about whether the donation was too much of a political statement (Lager, 1994).

31 Since the Ben & Jerry's Foundation was created in 1985, it has given away millions of dollars. Beneficiaries include:

- INFACT (formerly known as the Infant Formula Action Coalition), a Boston based campaign group currently staging a boycott against General Electric because of its role in the production of nuclear weapons;
- Farmworker Power Project, a programme based in Denver, Colorado, which trains farm workers to more effectively negotiate labour agreements with growers;
- Teamster Rank and File Education and Legal Defense, a Detroit, Michigan based programme designed to promoted democracy in the Teamster's Union;
- The Devastators, an all children African-American percussion band whose music is aimed at battling AIDS and homelessness and promoting world peace and environmentalism;
- The Heifer Project, which provides farm animals to poor communities;
- Worker-Owned Network, which mobilizes community resources for worker cooperatives;
- The Women's Institute for Housing and Development (Hollister et al, 1994).

32 Another company programme, worker 'Joy Gangs', exist as 'an ad hoc volunteer committee who try to figure out ways to bring more joy to the workplace' (Greenfield cited in Coles, 1996, p3).

33 It has been noted that while there is often one dominant corporate culture within any one corporation, at least one culture also coexists within the corporation. In addition to a power culture, Ben & Jerry's also has evidence of a 'task culture'. A task culture is job or product oriented, which can be best described as a 'team culture'; the focus is on a particular task and 'getting the job done'. The task culture is extremely adaptable, groups or project teams can be formed or reformed as needed. The task culture works well where flexibility and sensitivity to changes and improvement are necessary (Handy, 1985).

34 The company's environmental programmes aim to deal with all the environmental aspects of the company's operations. These include minimizing and eliminating wastes, conservation, exploring renewable energy sources, creating links between the company's products and environmental action, and establishing environmental awareness programmes (Shrivastava, 1996).

35 Monsanto manufactures pesticides, herbicides and other toxics, in
    addition to synthetic bovine growth hormone, bovine somatotropin
    (BST). It is widely seen as a 'green' corporation because, among other
    things, it has made pledges to cut its emissions eventually to zero
    (Hawken, 1994).

36 In November 1993, the Commissioner of the US Food and Drug
    Administration (FDA) approved the hormone (4BST), saying that after
    review, he was satisfied that both 'milk and meat from BST treated
    cows is safe to eat'. Earlier, the US Pure Food Campaign, which
    boycotts genetically engineered products internationally, asked
    consumers to request that local stores and restaurants provide written
    statements on their policy about BGH, and not to buy from companies
    selling these products. After FDA approval, the organizers of the
    boycott stated that they would continue to refuse to purchase any
    products from BGH treated herds, and press the FDA for a product
    label stating BGH use (Hollister et al, 1994). The product remains
    banned in the European Union. Europe, Canada, Australia and New
    Zealand have all produced moratoria on the use of BGH. In the words
    of one farmer: 'Europe and Canada subsidize [dairy] farmers, unlike in
    the United States. So for them to allow technology that would produce
    more milk doesn't make sense' (cited in Wilson, 1995).

37 The BGH case is a good example of a corporation supporting local
    people against the globalizing tendencies of big (dairy) business and big
    science, though for highly luxury consumerist principles; pointing to
    even more contradictions of corporations with a social-environmental
    corporate culture (Sklair, 1995a). Globalization questions like this one
    are fascinating, but would take another book altogether to explore.

38 Identifying the ice cream as an exclusively Vermont product has specific
    brand advantages, in terms of presenting it as a 'pure and all-natural
    product', distinct from other brands which are not 'pure' or 'all-natural'.
    In the US, Vermont is seen as an idyllic rural state. It is known as 'the
    Green Mountain State'. Most Americans picture its mountains and
    verdant rolling hills as an example of a pristine and wholesome rural
    New England environment. The dairy products from the state are seen
    to be especially pure. The strength of the dairy industry in the state is
    such that motorists driving into the state at one time were greeted at the
    state welcome centre on the motorway with a free glass of Vermont
    milk. It is likely that if Ben & Jerry's were to market its product as an
    ice cream from small dairy producers throughout the US and the rest of
    the world, they would significantly change the brand image of the
    product, therefore its market niche, and possibly affect its sales.

39 Although most of these writers – including Entine, Adams and Rosin –
    agree that the worst these companies, The Body Shop and Ben &
    Jerry's in particular, can be accused of, in most cases, are slight
    exaggerations or greenwashings.

40 In interviews, company representatives were quite sensitive to respond-
    ing to negative letters they received and aimed to 'educate' people on

'what they are really doing' (interview with Ben & Jerry's public relations staff member, Vermont, 25 August 1994). An original stockholder of Ben & Jerry's said:

> 'What's the difference between Ben & Jerry's and Häagen-Dazs? They're both in the superpremium market niche, but the Ben & Jerry's name is "environmental" and "ethical" and this is the reason people buy it. They have to protect that, and this is why they have to spend so much time responding to people's letters, because they don't want people to be upset with them. They want to protect their name' (interview with Ben & Jerry's original stockholder, Vermont, 26 August 1994).

41 Who was to critics 'an anthropologist promoting capitalism in the Amazon' (Corry, 1993; Entine, 1995), or, as the company history states 'the Director of Cultural Survival, a nonprofit organization working as an advocate for the world's native peoples' (Lager, 1994, p205).

42 However, in interviews with both companies, corporate representatives were quick to dispel comparisons between their two companies (interview with The Body Shop environment staff member, Littlehampton, UK, 5 April 1994; public relations staff member, 1 June 1994; Ben & Jerry's public relations staff member, 25 August 1994).

43 Lager notes:

> 'The timing of the product couldn't have been better; it was released just in time for the twentieth anniversary of Earth Day, when the country's environmental consciousness was at a peak. Instead of using the standard container for the flavour, a rainforest-themed package was designed that told customers how they could support the efforts of those who were working to stop worldwide deforestation' (Lager, 1994, p217).

44 Ben & Jerry's said it was incensed by the criticisms of its Brazilian project and indicated it had received a long rebuttal of the criticisms from Jason Clay, who claims that Jon Entine never contacted him when researching the article (Ben & Jerry's public relations staff member, Vermont, 25 August 1994).

45 When Holland was hired, the company's growth had been stagnating. Throughout most of the 1980s and into the early 1990s the company had enjoyed double digit earnings growth. Sales plateaued at around US$150 million in 1994; in that year the company lost almost US$2 million; its stock price fell from a high of US$33 per share to US$10. Holland's management style was more 'buttoned down' and more systematic. The company's sales manager said that people began for the first time to 'have numbers they were accountable for', and a research and development lab was created whereas before there was none. In June 1996, the company broke its weekly sales record by 20 per cent, driven by a new line of no-fat sorbets, the company having entered this market for the first time in March 1996. At the end of 1995, sales had recovered to US$155 million, and earnings recovered to US$5.9

million. The share price settled at US$17 per share. Holland as a manager is described as more 'traditional' and distant. One director argued that Holland 'brought adults to the company' (Judge, 1996). This is clearly having an effect on the corporate culture. One manager said that the atmosphere is 'less family like', and workers questioned the company's commitment to its values as it grows.

46   The Japanese market was a similar struggle. Since the company's financial problems stemmed in part from the fact that the American market was saturated, it seemed imperative to the company's financial advisers that it expand into new markets and new regions. In 1995, Ben & Jerry's competitor Häagen-Dazs, had earned US$300 million in sales there. A large Japanese distributor called Ben & Jerry's and offered distribution. However, after much debate, the company declined the offer. The reason was that the Japanese company had no reputation for supporting social causes and that 'The only clear reason to take the opportunity, was to make money' (Judge, 1996). In this case, the 'social-environmental' perspective won out.

47   Of all the representatives interviewed at Ben & Jerry's, none of them actually ate ice cream (interviews with Ben & Jerry's public relations staff members, Vermont, 25 August 1994).

48   Or, in Anita Roddick's terms, 'A true key to success is knowing what sets you apart from the competition: you must emphasize [the unique aspects], constantly restate them, and never be seduced into watering them down' (Roddick, 1992, p101).

49   Neither do they trust the claims of government, but interestingly they do tend to trust the claims of environmental groups (Rootes, 1997).

CHAPTER 6

1   Part of this chapter is based on an earlier paper (Robbins, 1996).

2   For some corporations, key actors in the 'greening' of these firms are 'corporate environmentalists'. Workers tend to be ignored in the greening process of corporations, but are relied on to carry out the firms' environmental objectives in the production process. Corporate environmentalists then are powerful corporate actors who present themselves as 'green' and extol the virtues of greening to the public and to other corporate elites. Notably these would include actors like Edgar Woolard from Du Pont who draws attention to Du Pont as an 'environmentally aware' corporation by claiming that he is both the company's chief executive officer and its chief environmental officer (CEO). Another example is Rodney Chase, the managing director of BP Amoco, a corporate executive who has supported BP's interests in preventing the environmental agenda from affecting 'free trade' by heading the World Business Council for Sustainable Development (WBCSD) and other 'corporate environmentalist' organizations. Corporate environmentalists are supported by and active in national

business associations, which present themselves as 'greening', such as Japan's Keidanren, governmental groups such as the UK's Advisory Council on Business and the Environment (ACBE), and in global associations like the ICC, BCSD and WBCSD.

Outside the corporation, corporate environmentalist actors are supported by like-minded representatives in government like James Watt, Anne Gorsuch and Al Gore in the US; all of whom have backed corporate interests. Other supportive actors are those from public relations firms, notably Burson-Marsteller (B-M), the biggest PR firm in the world. B-M helped to establish the BCSD, and front groups like the Canadian BC Forest Alliance, which is controlled by 30 CEOs from major lumber corporations, and the Tobacco Institute established by B-M for Phillip Morris. At an ideological level, corporate environmentalists are supported by actors from right-wing think tanks, such as Julian Simon, a University of Maryland business professor, associated with the Cato Institute, who argues against the environmental movement's jeremiad 'gloom and doom' prophesies (cited in Deal, 1993, p40). Free market environmentalist foundation actors, funded by private industry, can play a key role in deciding which causes to support. Notably, in 1995-1996, Joshua Reichert from the Pew Charitable Trust along with his associates 'bought off' defenders of the US Endangered Species Act for US$1.5 million (Cockburn and Silverstein, 1996, p210). Pro-corporate environmental groups also play an important role in promoting industry; this is exemplified by the aforementioned example of the NWF's Jay Hair who praised the environmental work of Waste Management, Inc (cited in Draffan, 1993).

3   Some of the main reasons why some corporations respond to environmental crises are to save or increase profit margins by adhering to and anticipating changes in environmental regulations, minimizing and preventing waste, and pursuing the green market. Corporations are also actively involved in undermining the environmental challenge to their operations through the process of greenwashing. Greenwashing processes may be the most important part of understanding corporate 'greening'. Inside the firm these include developing public relations strategies which highlight corporate green issues to the public, such as waste minimization, pollution prevention and the support of nature preserves. Corporate greening is supported outside the individual firm by major public relations agencies which greenwash corporate images. Waste Management Inc, for example, was a client of the E Bruce Harrison Company, which has a successful track record of 'greening' corporate polluters. In 1990, Bruce Harrison won an award from the public relations industry magazine *Inside PR* for its effective 'environmental communication' (Deal, 1993, p16). Greenwashing can also include membership in corporate front groups created by the PR firms; groups which sound like legitimate environmental groups but lobby for increased corporate control of natural resources. The 'whitewashing' of environmental problems by corporate funded think tanks

helps to reinforce the uncertainty issue about whether there are 'environmental crises'. Legal foundations can create legal precedents that benefit private industry and make it more difficult to curb development of sites of natural importance. Conservative foundations which redirect corporate 'philanthropy' to right-wing anti-environmentalist causes fund research and groups that undermine the environmentalist message. Wise Use 'environmental' groups roll back environmental regulations, backed by private interests. (See also Sklair, 2001.)

4   However, as Ritzer argues in an analysis of Ben & Jerry's: 'At the minimum, to represent a viable alternative, Ben & Jerry's must continue to be vigilant to traces of McDonaldization (ie rationalization) and demonstrate that it can both be successful and ward off McDonaldization in the long haul' (Ritzer, 1993, pp176–177).

5   See Wells and Jetter (1991) and Durning (1992).
One reader of an earlier paper on which this chapter is based has also suggested three other areas for follow-up which include: the ramifications of different *styles* of capitalism for global environmental change; whether it would be possible for capitalism to incorporate the 'sustainable production and consumption patterns agenda' as well as the related debate regarding 'basic needs' versus 'induced wants'; and the question of implications for key NGOs, and the 'double' strategy that many now take. See, for example, Frankel (1995).

References

Abercrombie, N, Hill, S and Turner, B (1994) *The Penguin Dictionary of Sociology*, Penguin, London

Abraham, D (1995) 'Weekend letter: Ice cream wars', *The Guardian*, 11 November, p6

Adams, J (1994) *Risk*, UCL Press, London

Albrow, M (1996) *The Global Age*, Polity, Cambridge

Allen, M (1993) 'Worldly Wisdom', *New Statesman and Society*, vol 6, 21 May, ppR12–R13

Allen, R (1992) *Waste Not, Want Not: The Production and Dumping of Toxic Waste*, Earthscan, London

Allenby, B and Richards, D (eds) (1994) *The Greening of Industrial Ecosystems*, National Academy of Engineering, National Academy Press, Washington, DC

Anderson, K and Blackhurst, R (eds) (1992) *The Greening of World Trade Issues*, Harvester, London

ARCO Chemical Europe (1991) *Annual Report 1990*, ARCO Chemical Europe, Maidenhead

ARCO Chemical Europe (1992a) *Annual Report 1991*, ARCO Chemical Europe, Maidenhead

ARCO Chemical Europe (1992b) *Botlek Plant Community Annual Environmental Report*, ARCO Chemical Europe, Maidenhead

ARCO Chemical Europe (1993) *Annual Report 1992*, ARCO Chemical Europe, Maidenhead

ARCO Chemical Europe (1994a) *Annual Environmental Statement 1993*, ARCO Chemical Europe, Maidenhead

ARCO Chemical Europe (1994b) *Annual Report 1993*, ARCO Chemical Europe, Maidenhead

ARCO (1996) *Environment, Health and Safety Report 1995*, ARCO, Los Angeles, CA

Ashford, N (1993) 'Understanding the Technical Response of Industrial Firms to Environmental Problems: Implications for government policy', in K Fischer and J Schot (eds) *Environmental Strategies for Industry: International Perspectives on Research Needs and Policy Implications*, Island Press, Washington, DC

Athanasiou, T (1996) 'The Age of Greenwashing', *Capitalism, Nature, Socialism*, vol 7, pp1–36

Avery, N, Drake, M and Lang, T (1993) 'Codex Alimentarius: Who is allowed in? Who is left out?', *The Ecologist*, vol 23, pp110–112

Badiane, O (1994) *Trade Pessimism and Regionalism in African Countries: The Case of Groundnut Exporters*, International Food Policy Research Institute, Washington, DC

Baker, S (1996) 'Corporate Britain Set to Embrace "Social Auditing"', *Reuters News Agency*, 23 February

Balfour, J (1997) 'Smoking Trophy: Uzbekistan cigarette market opens for business', *The New Internationalist*, vol 288, March, p5

Bannock, G, Baxter, R and Davis, E (1987) *The Penguin Dictionary of Economics*, Penguin, London

Beck, U (1992) *Risk Society: Towards a New Modernity*, Sage, London

Beck, U (1994) 'The Reinvention of Politics: Towards a theory of reflexive modernization' in U Beck, A Giddens and S Lash (eds) *Reflexive Modernization: Politics, Tradition and Aesthetics in the Modern Social Order*, Polity, Cambridge

Beck, U (1995) *Ecological Politics in an Age of Risk*, Polity, Cambridge

Beck, U, Giddens, A and Lash, S (eds) (1994) *Reflexive Modernization: Politics Tradition and Aesthetics in the Modern Social Order*, Polity, Cambridge

Ben & Jerry's (1990) *Ben & Jerry's 1989 Annual Report*, Ben & Jerry's, Waterbury, VT

Ben & Jerry's (1993) *Ben & Jerry's 1993 IRS 10-K Form*, Internal Revenue Service, Washington, DC

Ben & Jerry's (1995) *Ben & Jerry's 1994 Annual Report*, Ben & Jerry's, Waterbury, VT

Ben & Jerry's (2000) 'Ben & Jerry's & Unilever to Join Forces', Ben & Jerry's Press Releases, http://lib/benjerry.com/pressrel/join-forces.html

Bennett (1992) *Dilemmas: Coping with Environmental Problems*, Earthscan, London

Blaikie, P (1984) *The Political Economy of Soil Erosion in Developing Countries*, Longman, London

Block, W (ed) (1990) *Economics and the Environment: A Reconciliation*, The Fraser Institute, Vancouver

The Body Shop (no date) *Trade Not Aid Broadsheet*, The Body Shop, Littlehampton

The Body Shop (1991) *The Green Book 1991–1992*, The Body Shop, Littlehampton

The Body Shop (1992) *The Green Book 2: 1992–1993*, The Body Shop, Littlehampton

The Body Shop (1993) *The Green Book 3: 1993–1994*, The Body Shop, Littlehampton

Booz-Allen & Hamilton (1991) *Corporate Environmental Management: An Executive Survey*, Booz-Allen & Hamilton, New York

Brown, H, White, A and Himmelberger, J (1991) 'Survey of Transnational Corporations: Analysis of Qualitative Responses', UNCTC Consultant Paper, United Nations, New York

Brown, L, Durning, A, Flavin, C, French, H, Jacobson, J, Lenssen, N, Lowe, M, Postel, S, Renner, M, Starke, L, Weber, P and Young, J (1993) *State of the World 1993: A Worldwatch Institute Report on Progress toward a Sustainable Society*, Earthscan, London

Brown, M (1993) *Fair Trade: Reform and Realities in the International Trading System*, Zed Books, London

Brown, P and Mikkelsen, E (1990) *Toxic Waste, Leukemia, and Community Action*, University of California Press, Berkeley, CA

Brown, P and Nuttal, C (1996) 'Shell "Polluted Water Supply"', *The Guardian*, 27 March, p2

Bruno, K (1992) 'The Corporate Capture of the Earth Summit', *Multinational Monitor*, July/August, pp15–24

Bryant, B (1995) *Environmental Justice: Issues Policies and solutions*, Island Press, Washington, DC

Bryant, B and Mohai, P (eds) (1992) *Race and the Incidence of Environmental Hazards: A Time for Discourse*, Westview Press, Boulder, CO

Bullard, R (1990) *Dumping in Dixie: Race, Class and Environmental Quality*, Westview Press, Boulder, CO

Bullard, R (ed) (1993) *Confronting Environmental Racism: Voices from the Grassroots*, South End Press, Boston, MA

Bullard, R (ed) (1994) *Unequal Protection: Environmental Justice and Communities of Color*, Sierra Club Books, San Francisco, CA

Burns, T and Stalker, G (1961) *The Management of Innovation*, Tavistock, London

Business Week (1983) 'A Big Clean Up Bill for Shell Oil', *Business Week*, 17 October p54

Buttel, F and Taylor, P (1994) 'Environmental Sociology and Global Environmental Change: A critical assessment', in T Benton and M Redclift (eds) *Social Theory and the Global Environment*, Routledge, London, Chapter 11, pp228–255

Buttel, F, Hawkins, A and Power, A (1990) 'From Limits to Growth to Global Change: Constraints and contradictions in the evolution of environmental science and technology', *Global Environmental Change*, December, pp57–66

Cairncross, F (1990) 'An Enemy, and Yet a Friend', *The Economist*, 8 September, p3

Cairncross, F (1995) *Green, Inc: Guide to Business and the Environment*, Earthscan, London

Carey, J (1996) 'McDonald's Unmasked', *Red Pepper*, June, pp11–13

Carley, M and Christie, I (1992) *Managing Sustainable Development*, Earthscan, London

Carson, R (1962) *Silent Spring*, Houghton Mifflin, Boston, MA

Cassels, J (1993) *The Uncertain Promise of Law: Lessons from Bhopal*, University of Toronto Press, Toronto

Castleman, B (1983) 'The Double Standard in Industrial Hazards', *International Journal of Health Services*, vol 13, pp5–14

Castleman, B (1985) 'The Double Standard in Industrial Hazards', in J Ives (ed) *The Export of Hazard*, Routledge & Keegan Paul, London

Cater, E (1991) *Sustainable Tourism in the Third World: Problems and Prospects*, University of Reading, Reading, UK

Catton, W (1980) *Overshoot: The Ecological Basis of Revolutionary Change*, University of Illinois Press, Urbana, IL

Charter, M (1994) 'IBM and Corporate Environmentalism: An interview with Sir Anthony Cleaver', *Greener Management International*, vol 5, January, pp54–60

Chemical Week (1972) 'Black Pall Off Louisiana Coast', *Chemical Week*, vol 13, January, p71

Cockburn, A and Silverstein, K (1996) *Washington Babylon*, Verso, London

Coleman, D (1994) *Ecopolitics: Building a Green Society*, Rutgers University Press, New Brunswick, NJ

Coleman, J and Fararo, T (eds) (1992) *Rational Choice Theory*, Sage, Newbury Park, CA

Coles, J (1996) 'Tubs Who is Cream of the Crop', *The Guardian*, 28 December, p3

Corporate Watch (2000) 'Greenwash Award: Royal Dutch Shell', Corporate Watch Earth Day 2000 Greenwash Sweepstakes, www.igc.org/trac/climate/gwshell.html

Corry, S (1993) 'The Rainforest Harvest: Who reaps the benefit?', *The Ecologist*, vol 23, pp148–153

Cowe, R (1994a) 'Accepted Wisdom Takes Body Blow', *The Guardian*, 26 August, p14

Cowe, R (1994b) 'Body Shop Brands US Article "Recycled Rubbish"', *The Guardian*, 2 September, p22

Cowe, R (1994c) 'Body Shop Rides Out Assault on Integrity', *The Guardian*, 2 September, p15

Cowe, R (1994d) 'Shares Fall Back But Fund Managers Take Accusations in the Stride as Ethical Investors Await Clarification of Issues', *The Guardian*, 23 August, p2

Cowe, R (1997) 'Shell Supports "Fundamental Human Rights" As It Battles to Rebuild Image', *The Guardian*, 18 March, p19

Crump, A (1991) *Dictionary of Environment and Development: People, Places, Ideas and Organizations*, Earthscan, London

CTC Reporter (1989) 'International Cooperation', *CTC Reporter*, No 27, Spring

Curren, M (1994) 'Ben & Jerry's Scoop on Environmentalism', *Forum for Applied Research and Public Policy*, Summer, pp33–37

Cutter, S (1993) *Living with Risk: The Geography of Technological Hazards*, Edward Arnold, London

Cutter, S (1995) 'Race, Class and Environmental Justice', *Progress in Human Geography*, vol 19, pp107–118

Daly, H (1991) *Steady State Economics*, Island Press, Washington, DC

Daly, H (1993) 'Introduction to *Essays Toward a Steady-State Economy*' in H Daly and K Townsend (eds) *Valuing the Earth: Economics, Ecology, Ethics*, MIT Press, London

Daly, H and Cobb, J (1994) *For the Common Good: Redirecting the Economy towards Community*, 2nd revised edn, Beacon Press, Boston, MA

Daly, H and Goodland, R (1992) 'An Ecological-Economic Assessment of Deregulation of International Commerce Under GATT', World Bank Environment Department Discussion Paper, Washington, DC

Daly, H and Townsend, K (eds) (1993) *Valuing the Earth: Economics, Ecology, Ethics*, MIT Press, London

David, R (ed) (1991) *The Greening of Business*, Business People Publications, Aldershot

De La Court, T (1990) *Beyond Brundtland: Green Development in the 1990s*, Zed Books, London

Deal, C (1993) *The Greenpeace Guide to Anti-Environmental Organizations*, Odonian, Berkeley, CA

DESD/TCMD (1993) *International Environmental Law: Emerging Trends and Implications for Transnational Corporations*, United Nations, New York

Dickson, L and McCulloch, A (1996) 'Shell, the Brent Spar and Greenpeace: A doomed tryst?' *Environmental Politics*, vol 5, pp122–129

Donahue, J (1991) 'Mischief, Misdeeds and Mendacity: The real 3M', *Multinational Monitor*, May, pp29–31

Dosi, G (1988) 'The Nature of the Innovative Process', in G Dosi, C Freeman, R Nelson, G Silverberg and L Soete (eds) *Technical Change and Economic Theory*, Pinter, London

Draffan, G (1993) *Wasting the Earth: A Directory of Multinational Corporate Activities*, Institute on Trade Policy Task Force on Multinational Corporations, Seattle, WA

Dunning, J (1993) *Multinational Enterprises and the Global Economy*, Addison-Wesley, Wokingham, UK

Durkeim, E (1960) *The Division of Labour in Society* (originally published in 1893), Free Press, Glencoe, NY

Durning, A (1992) *How Much Is Enough? The Consumer Society and the Future of the Earth*, Earthscan, London

Dynes, M (1996) 'Ogoni Activists in Plea to West over Nigeria "Frame Up"', *The Times*, 15 May, Overseas News Section

Eckersley, R (1992) *Environmentalism and Political Theory: Toward an Ecocentric Approach*, University College Press, London

The Ecologist (1993) 'The Ecologist Campaigns', *The Ecologist*, March/April, p2

Egan, C (1996) 'Ben and Jerry's to Look for a CEO with Marketing Experience', *Wall Street Journal*, 27 September

Ekins, P (1992) *Wealth Beyond Measure*, Gaia Books, London

Elkington, J and Burke, T (1989) *The Green Capitalists: How Industry Can Make Money and Protect the Environment*, Gollancz, London

Elkington, J and Hailes, J (1988) *The Green Consumer Guide*, Victor Gollancz, London

Engel, R (1990) 'The Ethics of Sustainable Development', in R Engel and J Engel (eds) *Ethics of Environment and Development: Global Challenge, International Response*, Belhaven Press, London

Engel, R and Engel, J (eds) (1990) *Ethics of Environment and Development: Global Challenge, International Response*, Belhaven Press, London

Entine, J (1995) 'Caring Capitalism?: Against animal testing: Business focus', *Sunday Times Magazine*, 31 December, Business Section

ESCAP/UNCTC (1988) *Transnational Corporations and Environmental Management in Selected Asian and Pacific Developing Countries*, Publication Series B, No 13, United Nations, Bangkok

ESCAP/UNCTC (1990) *Environmental Aspects of Transnational Corporation Activities in Pollution-Intensive Industries in Selected Asian and Pacific Developing Countries*, Publication Series B, No 15, United Nations, New York

Flaherty, M and Rappaport, A (1991) *Multinational Corporations and the Environment: A Survey of Global Practices*, The Tufts University Center for Environmental Management, Medford, MA

FoE (1992) *Know More Toxics: Will Companies Give Citizens around the World the Right-to-Know'*, Friends of the Earth, Washington, DC

Foster, J (1994) *The Vulnerable Planet: A Short Economic History of the Environment*, Monthly Review Press, New York

Frankel, C (1995) 'Greenpeace Chooses Double', *Tomorrow: Global Environment Business*, vol 5, pp2–23

Frederick, R (1990) 'Introduction' in W Hoffman, R Frederick and E Petry (eds) *Business, Ethics and the Environment: The Public Policy Debate*, Quorum Books, Westport, CT

Freeman, C (1992) *The Economics of Hope: Essays on Technical Change, Economic Growth and the Environment*, Pinter, London

Frey, R (1996) 'The Globalization of Risk: The export of hazardous industries to the peripheral zones of the world economy', revised version of paper presented at the American Sociological Annual Meeting, New York, unpublished manuscript

Giddens, A (1979) *Central Problems in Social Theory*, Macmillan, London

Giddens, A (1990) *The Consequences of Modernity*, Polity, Cambridge

Giddens, A (1994) 'Living in a Post-Traditional Society', in U Beck, A Giddens and S Lash (eds) *Reflexive Modernization: Politics, Tradition and Aesthetics in the Modern Social Order*, Polity, Cambridge, Chapter 2, pp56–109

Giddens, A (1997) *Sociology*, Polity, Cambridge

Gilbert, M (1993) *Achieving Environmental Management: A Step-by-step Guide to BS7750*, Pitman, London

Gladwin, T (1987) 'A Case Study of the Bhopal Tragedy', in C Pearson (ed) *Multinational Corporations, Environment and the Third World: Business Matters*, Duke University Press, Durham, NC, Chapter 10, pp223–239

Gladwin, T and Walter I (1980) *Multinationals Under Fire: Lessons in the Management of Conflict*, John Wiley & Sons, New York

Gleckman, H (1995) 'Transnational Corporations' Strategic Responses to "Sustainable Development"', in H Bergesen and G Parmann (eds) *Green Globe Yearbook 1995*, Oxford University Press, Oxford

Goldblatt, D (1996) *Social Theory and the Environment*, Polity, Cambridge

Goldsmith, E and Hildyard, N (1988) *The Earth Report: The Essential Guide to Global Ecological Issues*, Price Stern Sloan, Inc, Los Angeles

Goldthorpe, J (1980) *Social Mobility and Class Structure in Britain*, Clarendon, Oxford

Gorz, A (1980) *Ecology As Politics* (trans P Vigderman and J Cloud), Pluto, London

Gorz, A (1994) *Capitalism, Socialism, Ecology* (trans C Turner), Verso, London

Gould, K, Weinberg, A and Schnaiberg, A (1993) 'Legitimating Impatience: Pyrrhic Victories of the Modern Environmental Movement', *Qualitative Sociology*, vol 16, pp207–246

Gouldson, A and Murphy, J (1998) *Regulatory Realities: The Implementation and Impact of Industrial Environmental Regulation*, Earthscan, London

Gray, R, Bebbington, J and Walters, D (1993) *Accounting for the Environment: The Greening of Accountancy Part II*, Paul Chapman, London

Grubb, M, Koch, M, Munson, A, Sullivan, F and Thomson, K (1993) *The Earth Summit Agreements: A Guide and Assessment*, Earthscan and The Royal Institute of International Affairs, London

The Guardian (1997) 'Churches Slate Shell', *The Guardian,* 7 January, p9

Habermas, J (1981) *The Theory of Communicative Action*, Beacon Press, Boston, MA

Hajer, M (1995) *The Politics of Environmental Discourse: Ecological Modernization and the Policy Process*, Clarendon Press, Oxford

Hajer, M (1996) 'Ecological Modernization as Cultural Politics', in S Lash, B Szerszynski and B Wynne (eds) *Risk, Environment and Modernity: Towards a New Ecology*, Sage, London

Handy, C (1985) *Understanding Organizations*, Penguin Books, Harmondsworth

Hannigan, J (1995) *Environmental Sociology: A Social Constructionist Perspective*, Routledge, London

Harrison, P (1984) *Inside the Third World*, Penguin Books, Harmondsworth

Hawken, P (1994) *The Ecology of Commerce: A Declaration of Sustainability*, Harper Business, New York

Hawkens, J and Allen, R (1991) *The Oxford Encyclopedic English Dictionary*, Clarendon Press, Oxford

Hennart, J (1988) 'A Transactions Cost Theory of Equity Joint Ventures', *Strategic Management Journal*, vol 9, pp361–374

Hill, S (1981) *Competition and Control at Work*, Heinemann Educational Books, London

Hoffman, W, Frederick, R and Petry, E (eds) (1990) *Business, Ethics and the Environment: The Public Policy Debate*, Quorum Books, Westport, CT

Hofrichter, R (ed) (1993) *Toxic Struggles: The Theory and Practice of Environmental Justice*, New Society, Philadelphia

Hollister, B, Will, R, Tepper Marlin, A, Dyott, S, Kovacs, S and Richardson, L (1994) *Shopping for a Better World: The Quick and Easy Guide to all your Socially Responsible Shopping*, Sierra Club Books, San Francisco, CA

Hoover, G (ed) (1992) *Hoover's Handbook of American Business*, The Reference Press, Austin, TX

IUCN/UNEP/WWF (1991) *Caring for the Earth: A Strategy for Sustainable Living*, Earthscan, London

Jack, A and Buckley, N (1994) 'Halo Slips on the Raspberry Bubbles', *The Financial Times*, 27/28 August, p8

Jennings, J (1994) *The Role of Business in Environmental Protection*, Shell, London

Judge, P (1996) 'Is It Rainforest Crunch Time?' *Business Week*, 15 July, p70

Karliner, J (1994) 'The Environment Industry: Profiting from pollution', *The Ecologist*, vol 24, pp59–63

Kloppenberg, J (1990) *First the Seed: The Political Economy of Plant Biotechnology:1490–2000*, Cambridge University Press, Cambridge

Knaus, H (1993) 'Cash in the Pipeline', *Multinational Monitor*, March, www.essential.org/monitor/hyper/issues/1993/03/mm0393_05.html

Kneen, B (1995) *Invisible Giant: Cargill and its Transnational Strategies*, Pluto Press, London

Knight, P (1993) 'Poised for the Big Leap Forward', *The Financial Times*, 7 July, p14

Knight, P (1995) 'What Price Natural Disasters', *Tomorrow: Global Environment Business*, vol 5, pp48–50

Kogut, B (1988) 'Joint Ventures: Theoretical and empirical perspectives', *Strategic Management Journal*, vol 9, pp319–332

Kretzmann, S (1995) 'Nigeria's "Drilling Fields"', *Multinational Monitor*, January/February, pp8–11, 25

Krimsky, S and Golding, D (1992) *Social Theories of Risk*, Praeger, Westport, CT

Lager, F (1994) *Ben & Jerry's: The Inside Scoop: How Two Guys Built a Business with a Social Conscience and a Sense of Humor*, Crown, New York

Lascelles, D (1993) 'Big Guns to Fire Green Shells', *The Financial Times*, 6 October, p18

Ledgerwood, G, Street, E and Thérivel, R (1992) *The Environmental Audit and Business Strategy: A Total Quality Approach*, Pitman Publishing, London

Leonard, A (1993) 'South Asia: The new target of international waste traders', *Multinational Monitor*, December, pp21–24

Leonard, H (1988) *Pollution and the Struggle for the World Product*, Cambridge University Press, Cambridge

Lerner, D (1958) *The Passing of Traditional Society*, Free Press, Glencoe

Lewis, S (1992) 'Banana Bonanza: Multinational fruit companies in Costa Rica', *The Ecologist*, vol 22, pp289–290

Ling, C (1992) 'A View from the South: An interview with Chee Yoke Ling', *Multinational Monitor*, July/August, www.essential.org/monitor/hyper/issues/1992/07/mm0792_08.html

Luhmann, N (1993) *Risk: A Sociological Theory*, A de Gruyter, New York

Lund, L (1974) *Corporate Organization for Environmental Policy Making*, The Conference Board, New York

McCormick, J (1989) *The Global Environmental Movement: Reclaiming Paradise*, Belhaven, London

McGregor, K (2000) 'USA: Shell to Face Lawsuit for Saro-Wiwa Execution', News, Corporate Watch, www.corpwatch.org/trac/headlines/2000/322.html

Mackey, J (1992) *US Tobacco Exports to the Third World: Third World War*, Monograph, National Cancer Institute, Washington, DC

McKinsey & Company (1991) *The Corporate Response to the Environmental Challenge*, McKinsey & Company, Amsterdam

Manes, C (1990) *Green Rage: Radical Environmentalism and the Unmaking of Civilization*, Little, Brown and Co, London

March, J and Simon, H (1958) *Organizations*, Wiley, New York

Maull, H (1992) 'Japan's Global Environmental Policies', in A Hurrel and B Kingsbury (eds) *The International Politics of the Environment: Actors, Interests and Institutions*, Clarendon Press, Oxford, Chapter 13, pp354–372

Meadows, D H, Meadows, D L and Randers, J (1972) *The Limits to Growth*, Basic Books, New York

Meadows, D H, Meadows, D L and Randers, J (1992) *Beyond the Limits: Global Collapse or a Sustainable Future*, Earthscan, London

Meek, V (1992) 'Organizational Culture: Origins and Weaknesses', in G Salaman (ed) *Human Resource Strategies*, Sage, London

Merchant, C (1992) *Radical Ecology: The Search for a Livable World*, Routledge, London

Mills, C (1956) *The Power Elite*, Oxford University Press, New York

Mokhiber, R and Wheat, A (1995) 'Shameless: 1995's 10 Worst Corporations', *Multinational Monitor*, December, www.essential.org/monitor/hyper/mm1295.04.html

Mol, A (1995) *The Refinement of Production: Ecological Modernization Theory and the Chemical Industry*, Van Arkel, Utrecht, The Netherlands

Moody-Stuart, M (1994) *Environmental Action: A Shared Responsibility*, Shell, London

Mpanya, M (1992) 'The Dumping of Toxic Waste in African Countries: A case of poverty and racism', in B Bryant and P Mohai (eds) *Race and the*

Incidence of Environmental Hazards: A Time for Discourse, Westview Press, Oxford

Multinational Monitor (1997) 'Editorial: Remember Shell, Boycott Shell', *Multinational Monitor*, December, www.essential.org/monitor/hyper/mm1297.02.html

Multinational Strategies, Inc (1990) *The Environmental Finance Corporation: A New Role for TNCs in Developing Country Environmental Management*, Multinational Strategies, Inc, New York

Myerson, G and Rydin, Y (1996) *The Language of Environment: A New Rhetoric*, UCL Press, London

Naimon, J (1995) 'Environment Reports Survey', *Tomorrow: Global Environment Business*, vol 5, pp62–75

Neff, A (1990) 'Not in Their Backyards, Either: A proposal for a foreign environmental practices act', in Hoffman, W M, Frederick, R and Petry, ES (eds) *Business, Ethics, and the Environment: The Public Policy Debate*, Quorum, London

News Direct London (1997) 973FM Broadcast, 13 January, 14:10

NC/CEP (1993) *The Transnational Corporation and Issues for Developing Countries*, New Consumer, Newcastle Upon Tyne

O'Connor, J (1973) *The Fiscal Crisis of the State*, St Martin's Press, New York

O'Connor, J (1988) 'Capitalism, Nature, Socialism: A theoretical introduction', *Capitalism, Nature, Socialism*, vol 1, pp11–38

Olojede, D (1995) 'Licensed to Crush', *The Guardian*, 14 June, p7

Onwuka, R (1992) *A Political Economy of Transnational Corporations in Nigeria*, International Universities Press, Owerri, Nigeria

O'Riordan, T (1995) *Environmental Science for Environmental Management*, Longman, London

O'Rourke, D (1992) 'Oil in Burma: Fuelling oppression', *Multinational Monitor*, 13(10), pp7–11

Ouchi, W (1982) *Theory Z: How American Business Can Meet the Japanese Challenge*, Avon Books, New York

Pearce, D (ed) (1991) *Blueprint 2: Greening the World Economy*, Earthscan, London

Pearce, D (1992) 'Economics and the Global Economic Challenge', in A Markandya and J Richardson (eds) *The Earthscan Reader in Environmental Economics*, Earthscan, London

Pearce, D and Moran, D (1994) *The Economic Value of Biodiversity*, Earthscan, London

Pearce, D, Barbier, E and Markandya, A (1990) *Sustainable Development: Economics and Environment in the Third World*, Earthscan, London

Pereira, J (1996) 'Ben & Jerry's Chief Executive R Holland Resigns', *The Wall Street Journal*, 30 September

Peters, T and Waterman, R (1982) *In Search of Excellence: Lessons from America's Best Run Companies*, Harper & Row, New York

Pintz, W (1987) 'Environmental Negotiations in the Ok Tedi Mine in Papua New Guinea', in C Pearson (ed) *Multinational Corporations,*

Environment and the Third World: Business Matters, Duke University Press, Durham, NC, Chapter 2, pp35–63

Plant, C and Albert, D (1991) 'Green Business in a Grey World: Can it be done? An Introduction', in C Plant and J Plant (eds) *Green Business: Hope or Hoax?*, Green Books, Bideford, Devon

Plant, C and Plant, J (eds) (1991) *Green Business: Hope or Hoax?*, Green Books, Bideford, Devon

Porter, G and Brown, J (1990) *Global Environmental Politics*, Westview, Oxford

Porter, G and Brown, J (1991) 'The Emergence of Global Environmental Politics', in G Porter and J W Brown (eds) *Global Environmental Politics*, Westview Press, Oxford

Postel, S (1993) 'Facing Water Scarcity', in Brown, L, Durning, A, Flavin, C, French, H, Jacobsen, J, Lenssen, N, Lowe, M, Postel, S, Renner, M, Starke, L, Weber, P and Young, J (eds) *State of the World 1993: A Worldwatch Institute Report on Progress Toward a Sustainable Society*, Earthscan, London

Pridham, J (1995) 'Influence of Popular Opinion on Brent Spar Decision', *The Times*, 23 June

Redclift, M (1984) *Development and the Environmental Crisis: Red or Green Alternatives?*, Methuen, London

Redclift, M (1987) *Sustainable Development: Exploring the Contradictions*, Routledge, London

Redclift, M (1994) 'Development and the Environment: Managing the contradictions', in L Sklair (ed) *Capitalism and Development*, Routledge, London

Redclift, M and Benton, T (eds) (1994) *Social Theory and the Global Environment*, Routledge, London

Reed, M (1992) *The Sociology of Organizations*, Harvester Wheatsheaf, London

Reich, C (1970) *The Greening of America*, Random House, New York

Reich, M (1994) 'Toxic Politics and Pollution Victims in the Third World', in S Jasanoff (ed) *Learning From Disaster: Risk Management after Bhopal*, University of Pennsylvania Press, Philadelphia, Chapter 9, pp180–203

Reuter (1996) 'Dioxins at 1976 Italian Disaster Unsafe, Greenpeace Says', *The Guardian*, 253 October, p12

Reuters News Service (1996) 'Ben & Jerry's CEO Resigns', 27 September

Richards, D, Allenby, B and Frosch, R (1994) 'The Greening of Industrial Ecosystems: Overview and perspective', in B Allenby and D Richards (eds) *The Greening of Industrial Ecosystems*, National Academy of Engineering, National Academy Press, Washington, DC

Rifkin, J (1989) *Entropy: Into the Greenhouse World*, revised edn, Bantam, New York

Ritzer, G (1993) *The McDonaldization of Society: An Investigation into the Changing Character of Contemporary Social Life*, Pine Forge Press, Newbury Park, CA

Robbins, P T(1996) 'Transnational Corporations and Global Environmental Change: A review of the UN Benchmark Survey', *Global Environmental Change: Human and Policy Dimensions*, vol 6, pp235–244

Robbins, P (1999)'The Buying and Selling of "Green": Product image analysis and the green consumer movement', in P Faccioli (ed) *Mondi da Vedere*, Franco Angeli Press, Milan, Italy

Robins, N and Trisoglio, A (1992) 'Restructuring Industry for Sustainable Development', in J Holmberg (ed) *Policies for a Small Planet*, Earthscan, London

Roddick, A (1992) *Body and Soul*, Vermillion, London

Roddick, A (1995) 'Letter to the Editor: Shell should speak out to help the Ogoni', *Financial Times*, 1 November, p22

Roddick, G (1993) 'Letter to the Editor: The Body Shop replies', *The Ecologist*, vol 23, pp198–200

Roddick, G (1994) 'Letter to the Editor: Highest ethical principles always upheld', *Financial Times*, 24 August, p12

Rootes, C (1997) 'Environmental Movements: Acting globally, thinking locally', paper prepared for the Workshop on Environmental Movements, ECPR Joint Sessions, Bern, Switzerland, 27 February – 4 March, unpublished manuscript

Rosin, H (1995) 'Ben & Jerry's Problems with Profits', *The Guardian Weekend Magazine*, 4 November, pp48–51

Rowell, A (1996) *Green Backlash: Global Subversion and the Environmental Movement*, Routledge, London

Rowlands, I (1995) *The Politics of Global Atmospheric Change*, Manchester University Press, Manchester

Royal Dutch/Shell (1991) *Annual Report 1990*, Shell, London

Royal Dutch/ Shell (1992) *Annual Report 1991*, Shell, London

Royal Dutch/Shell (1993) *Annual Report 1992*, Shell, London

Royal Dutch/Shell (1994) *Annual Report 1993*, Shell, London

Rüdig, W (ed) (1990) *Green Politics One*, Edinburgh University Press, Edinburgh

Ruskin, G (1995) 'Gingrich's GOPAC Patrons Take Out a Contract on America', *Multinational Monitor*, March, www.essential.org/monitor/hyper/issues/1995/03/mm0395_07.html

Rydin, Y (1993) *The British Planning System: An Introduction*, Macmillan, London

Sachs, W (1992) 'Environment', in W Sachs (ed) *The Development Dictionary: A Guide to Knowledge as Power*, Zed Books, London

Sachs, W (1994) 'The Blue Planet: An ambiguous modern icon', *The Ecologist*, vol 24, pp170–175

Saro-Wiwa, K (1995) *A Month and a Day: A Detention Diary*, Penguin, London

Schein, E (1985) *Organizational Culture and Leadership*, Jossey-Bass, San Francisco

Schmidheiny, S (1992) *Changing Course: A Global Business Perspective on Development and the Environment*, MIT Press, London

Schnaiberg, A and Gould, K (1994) *Environment and Society: The Enduring Conflict*, St Martin's Press, New York

Schumacher, E F (1973) *Small Is Beautiful: Economics as if People Really Mattered*, Abacus, London

Schutz, A (1972) *The Phenomenology of the Social World*, Heinemann Educational Books, London

Sexton, S (1993) 'The Reproductive Hazards of Industrial Chemicals: The politics of protection', *The Ecologist*, vol 23, pp212–218

Sharp, M and Pavitt, K (1993) 'Technology Policy in the 1990s: Old trends and new realities', *Journal of Common Market Studies*, vol 31, pp129–151

Shell International Petroleum Company (1992) *Shell and The Environment*, Shell International Petroleum Company, London

Shrivastava, P (1992) *Bhopal, Anatomy of a Crisis*, 2nd edn, Paul Chapman, London

Shrivastava, P (1996) *Greening Business: Profiting the Corporation and the Environment*, Thompson Executive Press, Cincinnati, OH

Simmons, P and Wynne, B (1992) 'Responsible Care: Trust, credibility, and environmental management', in K Fischer and J Schot (eds) *Environmental Strategies for Industry*, Island Press, Washington, DC

Simon, H (1957) *Administrative Behaviour*, 2nd edn, Free Press, New York

Simons, A, Hasselbring, B and Castleman, M (1992) *Before You Call the Doctor: Safe, Effective Self-care for over 300 Common Medical Problems*, Ballantine Books, Random House, New York

Singh, K (1995) 'The "McLibel Two"', *Multinational Monitor*, September, www.essential.org/monitor/hyper/mm0995.03.html

Sklair, L (1994a) 'Global Sociology and Global Environmental Change', in M Redclift and T Benton (eds) *Social Theory and the Global Environment*, Routledge, London, pp205–227

Sklair, L (1994b) 'Global System, Local Problems: Environmental impacts of TNCs along Mexico's northern border', in H Main and J Williams (eds) *Environment and Housing in Third World Cities*, Wiley, London

Sklair, L (1995a) 'Social Movements and Global Capitalism', *Sociology*, vol 29, pp495–512

Sklair, L (1995b) *Sociology of the Global System*, 2nd revised and updated edn, Harvester, London and Johns Hopkins University Press, Baltimore, MD

Sklair, L (2001) *The Transnational Capitalist Class*, Blackwell, Oxford

Slaughter, T (1990) 'The Improbability of Third World Government Consent in the Coming North-South International Toxic Waste Trade', in Hoffman, W M, Frederik, R and ES Petry (eds) *Business, Ethics and the Environment: The Public Policy Debate*, Quorum Books, Westport, CT

Spaargaren, G and Mol, A (1992) 'Sociology, Environment, and Modernity: Ecological Modernisation as a Theory of Social Change', *Society and Natural Resources*, vol 5, pp323–344

Smith, D (ed) (1993) *Business and the Environment: Implications of the New Environmentalism*, Paul Chapman, London

Souder, W (1987) *Managing New Product Innovations*, Lexington Press, Lexington, MA

Susskind, L (1994) *Environmental Diplomacy: Negotiating More Effective Global Agreements*, Oxford University Press, New York

SustainAbility, SPOLD, Business in the Environment (1993) *The LCA Sourcebook: A European Business Guide to Life-cycle Assessment*, SustainAbility, SPOLD and Business in the Environment, London

SustainAbility and *Tomorrow: Global Environment Business* (1994) 'The Green Keiretsu: An international survey of business alliances and sustainable development', *Tomorrow-Global Environment Business*, vol 4, insert

Szasz, A (1994) *Ecopopulism: Toxic Waste and the Movement for Environmental Justice*, University of Minnesota Press, Minneapolis

Taylor, P and Buttel, F (1992) 'How Do We Know We Have Global Environmental Problems? Science and the globalization of environmental discourse,' *Geoforum*, vol 23, pp405–416

TCMD/DESD (1993) *Environmental Management in Transnational Corporations: Report of the Benchmark Corporate Environmental Survey*, United Nations, New York

Thérival, R, Wilson, E, Thompson, S, Heaney, D and Pritchard, D (1992) *Strategic Environmental Assessment*, Earthscan, London

Toffler, A (1980) *The Third Wave*, William Collins Sons and Co, London

Tokar, B (1991) 'Marketing the Environment', in C Plant and J Plant (eds) *Green Business: Hope or Hoax?*, Green Books, Bideford, Devon, Chapter 6, pp42–51

Tomorrow: Global Environment Business (1995) *Tomorrow: Global Environment Business*, vol 5 whole issue

Toth, F, Hizsnik, E and Clark, W (eds) (1989) *Scenarios of Socioeconomic Development for Studies of Global Environmental Change: A Critical Review*, International Institute for Applied Systems Analysis, Laxenburg, Austria

Tran, M (1994) 'US Franchisees Fear Retaliation', *The Guardian*, 26 August, p14

Turner, R (ed) (1993) *Sustainable Environmental Economics and Management: Principles and Practice*, Belhaven, London

UN Survey (1993) = UNCTC (1993)

UNCTC (1991) *Options to Facilitate Transfer of Environmentally Sound Technologies to Developing Countries on Favourable Terms, Packet 1*, Environment Unit, UNCTC, New York

UNCTC (1992) *Climate Change and Transnational Corporations: Analysis and Trends*, United Nations, New York

UNCTC (1993) *Environmental Management in Transnational Corporations: Report of the Benchmark Corporate Environmental Survey*, United Nations, New York

UNCTC (no date) 'Royal Dutch Shell Oil Spill (Strait of Magellan, Chile)', Consultant's Report, UNCTC, New York

UNCTC (no date) 'Shell Chemical: Worker Exposure to DBCP (California, USA)', Consultant's Report, UNCTC, New York

UNCTC (no date) 'Shell Chemie Dumping of Hazardous Wastes (Gouderak, Netherlands)', Consultant's Report, UNCTC, New York

UNCTC (no date) 'Oil Spills/Blowouts/Tanker Accidents', Consultant's Report, UNCTC, New York

UNCTC (no date) 'Waste Disposal Practices', Consultant's Report, UNCTC, New York

UNEP (1985) 'Cyanide Spill Closes Papua New Guinea Mine', *State of the Environment Report 1985*, 16 April, United Nations, Nairobi

UNEP (1992) *Saving Our Planet: Challenges and Hopes*, United Nations, Nairobi

UNEPIE and SustainAbility Ltd (1994) *Company Environmental Reporting: A Measure of the Progress of Business and Industry towards Sustainable Development*, UNEP/SustainAbility, Paris and London

Urquhart, C (1994) 'Gas Bill to Pay', *The Guardian*, 30 November, pp4–5

Van Grinsven, L (1996) 'Ben & Jerry's Aims to Lick European Rivals', *Reuters News*, 9 July

Vidal, J (1994) 'Integrity Doubt Shocks Body Shop Boss', *The Guardian*, 23 August, p2

Vidal, J (1995a) 'Born of Oil, Buried in Oil', *The Guardian*, 4 January, Society Supplement, pp3–4

Vidal, J (1995b) 'It's So Easy, Shell', *The Guardian*, 6 December, Society Supplement, p4

Vidal, J and Brown, P (1994) 'The Crucifixion of St Ethica', *The Guardian*, 26 August, Society Supplement, pp6–7

Vogel, D (1986) *National Styles of Regulation: Environmental Policy in Great Britain and the United States*, Cornell University Press, London

Wallace, J (1991) 'Rainforest Rx', *Sierra*, July/August

WCED (1987) *Our Common Future*, Oxford University Press, Oxford

Weale, A (1992) *The New Politics of Pollution*, Manchester University Press, Manchester

Weber, M (1947) *The Theory of Social and Economic Organization* (trans A Henderson and T Parsons), Free Press, New York

Weber, M (1979) *Economy and Society: An Outline of Interpretive Sociology*, 2 volumes, University of California Press, Berkeley, CA

Welford, R (1993) *Environmental Management and Business Strategy*, Pitman, London

Welford, R (1994) *Environmental Strategy and Sustainable Development*, Routledge, London

Welford, R and Jones, D (1994) 'Measures of Sustainability in Business: A report of a consultation and networking exercise funded by the ESRC Global Environmental Change Programme', Centre for Corporate Environmental Management, University of Huddersfield School of Business, Huddersfield, UK

Wells, P and Jetter, M (1991) *The Global Consumer: Best Buys to Help the Third World*, Victor Gollancz, London

Will, R (1995) 'Stellar Companies: The 1995 America's corporate conscious awards', *Research Report*, Council on Economic Priorities, New York

Williamson, O (1985) *The Economic Institutions of Capitalism: Firms, Markets, Relational Contracting*, Free Press, New York

Willums, J and Goluke, U (eds) (1991) *WICEM II: Second World Conference on Environmental Management: Conference Report and Background Papers*, International Chamber of Commerce, Paris

Willums, J and Goluke, U (1992) *From Ideas to Action: Business and Sustainable Development*, ICC Publishing, Oslo and Ad Notam Gyldendal, Oslo

Wilson, C (1995) 'To BST or Not to BST?', *Reuters News Agency*, 11 October

Winter, G (1995) *Blueprint for Green Management: Creating your Company's Own Environmental Action Plan*, McGraw Hill International, London

Wood, C and Gazidellis, V (1985) 'A Guide to Training Materials for Environmental Impact Assessment', Occasional Paper 14, University of Manchester, Manchester

Worldwatch (1989) *State of the World 1989*, WW Norton, New York

Worldwatch (1991) *State of the World 1991*, WW Norton, New York

WRI/UNEP/UNDP (1990) *World Resources 1990-91*, Oxford University Press, New York

Wright, M (1995) 'Shell Takes Some Heat', *Tomorrow: Global Environment Business*, vol 5, January–March, pp14–17

Wyburd, G (ed) (1994) 'The Business Charter in Action: Principles for environmental management', summary report of a seminar organised by ICC United Kingdom, 25 May 1994, ICC, London

Wynne, B (1994) 'Scientific Knowledge and the Global Environment', in T Benton and M Redclift (eds) *Social Theory and the Global Environment*, Routledge, London

Yearley, S (1996) *Sociology, Environmentalism, Globalization*, Sage, London

Index